Remembrances of Newark

Top Cover Photo: Raymond Boulevard 1930s, WPA, New Jersey State Archives

Bottom Cover Photo: Mulberry & Market Streets 2021, Miaoli Stoffers

Additional books by author:

Firehouse Fraternity Oral History Series:
Volume I: Becoming a Firefighter
Volume II: Life Between Alarms
Volume III: Equipment
Volume IV: Responding
Volume V: Riots to Renaissance
Volume VI: Changing the NFD

The Newark Riots: A View from the Firehouse

An Eerie Silence: An Oral History of Newark Firefighters at the WTC

Hervey's Boys: New Jersey's First Chinese Community 1870-1886 (And What Happened After That)

Fiction:
The Firebox Stalker
The Hand Life Dealt you
A-zou: A Woman Living in Interesting Times

Children's Fiction:
A Hundred Battles (YA)
A Broken Glass (YA)
Balancing Act (Middle Grade)

Remembrances of Newark

An Oral History of Everyday Life from the 1920s to 2020 as Told by Her Firefighters.

Neal Stoffers

Springfield and Hunterdon Publishing
Copyright 2021
www.newarkfireoralhistory.com

First Printing: 2021

ISBN: 978-1-970034-25-7

Springfield and Hunterdon Publishing
East Brunswick, NJ 08816-5852

To Dr. Ottavio Nepa (Coco the Clown, Coco, or simply Coke) with whom I spent my Newark Childhood in Vailsburg

Contents

Acknowledgements

First, I must acknowledge my long-suffering wife Miaoli who has put up with my obsession to preserve the history of the Newark Fire Department for thirty years. I anticipate another three books will come from the interviews I have already conducted, so her sacrifice has not yet ended. My sister Dorothy took the time to read through the manuscript and point out all the typos, omissions, and repetitions I had inserted while transcribing. And finally, my brother Mark made the cover possible. Of course, in the end I am responsible for the final product.

The credit for much of this book goes to the members of the Newark Fire Department who gave so generously of their time to take part in my oral history project. The hours of recorded conversations they contributed will help preserve the history of Newark's fire department and of Newark itself. A list of those interviewed appears at the end of the book. This is their story. I am honored to tell it.

Foreword

This book is an outgrowth of an oral history project of the Newark Fire Department begun in 1991. The stories recounted here are not focused on the fire department, but are of a more general nature. Anyone interested in stories of what it was like to actually live in the City of Newark will find the remembrances of Newark's bravest interesting. Although parts of some of these stories appear in the book *Becoming a Firefighter,* most are new to print. Originally, I had anticipated this material would be a chapter in a separate upcoming fire department oral history book, *The Best Job in the World*, but it quickly became apparent it should be a standalone book.

The comments of the men and women I interviewed are presented in order of their date of appointment to the fire department. This method is an attempt to give a better picture of the chronology of the dramatic changes which occurred in the city over the last half of the 20th century.

The seeds of this book were unknowingly planted in a small firehouse on Springfield Avenue and Hunterdon Street. It was here as a young firefighter, I sat in the kitchen of Six Engine and listened to conversations between veteran firefighters, captains, and Deputy Chiefs about a city and fire department that existed in another time.

Among the dozens of questions I have asked Newark firefighters over the years are three used to provide a background for understanding their experiences. The first of these is "What was Newark like when you were growing up?" The second is "What was the city like when you were appointed?" The third is "How has the city changed since you were appointed?" An additional question asking whether Newark is a renaissance city was put to those who served during the time period where that question would be pertinent. These are the questions that gave rise to this book. The answers I received range from heartwarming to heart wrenching. One subject not included is the civil disturbance of 1967. Two of my previous books cover that subject. However, I have included a section on the effects of those disturbances on the city.

The men and women I interviewed were appointed between 1940 and 2016. Most were "born and raised" in Newark. They came from every section of the city and were from varying ethnic and racial backgrounds. Some moved into the city as young adults. A few of the childhood memories harken back to the 1920s.

Every rank of the fire department is represented among those interviewed. Two of the interviewees served as Fire Director. Three served as Fire Chief. That being said, this is a story told by the common man. There are no politicians, no great movers of events, no celebrities, and certainly no wealthy elite included. The memories recounted are at street level recalling everyday life in New Jersey's most populous city from the 1920s to the 2020s.

This is the Newark that was their childhood home. It is the city they knew as young adults and the place they worked, where they saw the best and the worst it had to offer.

Setting the Stage

Newark in the 1920s was a humming industrial and commercial center. Its citizens numbered 414,524 in 1920. By 1930 that number had grown to 442,337.

The decade saw the building of Newark Airport which became one of the world's busiest by 1930. The city's skyline was transformed and industry churned out myriad products. The intersection of Broad and Market was said to be one of the busiest in the world. Department stores drew customers to the area from around northern New Jersey.

The city had 63 theaters offering assorted entertainment. A Chinatown was thriving around the intersection of Mulberry and Lafayette Streets. The Morris Canal had been filled in and converted to Raymond Boulevard with the subway running beneath it. The Hudson tubes connected Newark to NYC.

New Jersey's largest city was a thriving metropolis, but the men who added their voices to this book were only boys in their neighborhoods. Over the next 100 years Newark would experience triumph and tragedies unimagined by 14 year old Reggie Fredette when he was avoiding the truant officers up in the "maple woods."[1]

---

[1] Vailsburg was known as the maple woods to Reggie in the '20s. This quick description is based *How Newark Became Newark* by Brad Tuttle

Part One:

A Newark Childhood

Children of the Depression

Conville (appointed 1940): I was in Kearny in Boystown. And then I went to Saint Lucy's and then I went with different families. I was with a family on Parker Street in Newark. The family I was living with were the janitors in the three-story brick apartment. The man worked as a carpenter in the company. But the wife cleaned all the hallways and everything. They were taking care of me, but they needed a babysitter when she went upstairs and cleaned. Next door was where the rectory was on Parker Street. So the priest used to let me come over. They were my babysitter. The church was the Sacred Heart Cathedral on Park Avenue. So, when the lady was cleaning, I would go over there and sit either inside or outside. When the priest got a sick call, he would have to take me on the sick call. He had an open car. He put a blanket around me and I brought in the holy water and the wax and everything. And he blessed the people. But it was a thrill. I rode in a car. I'd get up every morning and say, Dear God, make twelve people sick so I could get twelve rides and tell everybody I've been in a car.

When the family moved, I went to another family that went to Our Lady of Good Council and they didn't like me because I had no name. I lived down Hillsdale Place. Everybody at Our Lady of Good Council was a wealthy family. Lived up on the hill. I lived in the wrong place. The priests up there, they punished me because I came from Saint Michael's. I should have been in Saint Michael's not Our Lady of Good Council. They'd give me the six o'clock mass instead of giving it to one of the rich kids up on the hill. I had to go up there six o'clock every morning. And the priest came down. I did not know he was an alcoholic and he'd give the mass. Then he started to take me up to Branch Brook Park because he ran the baseball team, but he was an alcoholic. I did not know that he drank. I had to get permission because I always had to be home by three o'clock. I had to be in my room and stay in my room until they called me for my supper, so I got permission.

He would take me up to Branch Brook Park and I would put the bags out. You had to pay a dollar and get the bags and get the white chalk. So I sat there with him, but I rode in the car and he brought me a popsicle every day I came up. I had a first baseman mitt and I turned it into a catcher's mitt. I said they don't know how the hell to play. So, he said, "What? Do you think you do?" And I said, "Yeah, I'm better than them." So, I became the catcher on their team. I was in seventh grade. I was the only kid that ever made the team. It was great, but nobody liked me. I don't need anybody to talk to me because I'm a catcher. What the hell do I need? He was the one who told me, "You have to be ten foot tall." So, I told him, "Hey, ten foot tall, nobody, not even in the circus is ten foot tall." So, he said, "I don't mean ten foot tall. You got to think ten foot tall because you're a nothing. You're always going to be a nothing from what you were. But if you are ten foot tall, you're always taller than everybody else." So, from him my whole life style was I have to be a 110% because if I fall down, they throw all this stuff into my teeth.

I went to Saint Benedict's Prep. I paid the first year. But then I made the scholarship. I got a scholarship to Saint Benedict's Prep, playing baseball. I competed against the public high schools. In those days the guys did four years. But then they weren't academically ready to go to college so they had to come to Saint Benedict's. Everybody that came from Central, East Side, West Side, South Side, they were varsity athletes for at least three years. I had to compete against guys that were three years older than me to become varsity.

Fredette (appointed 1942): When I was young Vailsburg was known as the maple woods because of all the trees. This was where we used to play hooky when I went to Alexander Street School. The trees were so dark nobody could spot you. Because you could play hooky all the time and in those days they had truant officers. They could never find you. So, it was what we called the maple wood section. Cameron Field over to where the South Orange Shop-rite is. Say Sanford Avenue all the way up, in fact Parker Avenue there was a peach tree orchard that was Maplewood. There was nothing but peach trees. Then where the car barn is on Springfield Avenue, they called that the Hilton section. That was where Hilton strawberries were discovered. They were discovered by one of these guys who create vegetables and all that and he was the one that made these big strawberries. Previous to that, strawberries were like raspberries, real small. That was the Hilton section and there were peach trees, everything along Parker Avenue on all those side streets. That was all peach trees. They called that the peach tree orchard.

We played baseball, football behind Seton Hall College. They had a baseball field, but at that time, as far as I can remember, there was like a grade coming down from Seton Hall College. We had a lefthanded pitcher. He had a pretty fast ball and with that extra grade that ball seemed to come in a lot faster than on the flat.

The people and the forms of entertainment that we had in those days were great. We had all the parks. You could go down to the park and play football or play baseball. You didn't have to worry about being knocked off. We had Olympic Park where you could go swimming. We had Dreamland Park. You had a lot of recreation. Then you had Newark Bears stadium. We had a lot of YMCAs, the Hebrew Club on High Street, night professional basketball games. Then we had fights at the Laurel Garden. We had the Velodrome. We had fights on Thursday nights. We had the Roller Dome. Years ago, there was a lot of entertainment in Newark.

Vetrini (appointed 1946): Newark was beautiful, beautiful. It had everything there. We had the show houses, the nightclubs, and the restaurants. It was very homey. Your neighborhood, people were out in the street in the evenings. Kids out playing stickball like we used to play, but you can't do that with cars today. It was beautiful.

Kinnear (appointed 1947): I don't think I had any impression of Newark then because I was living there, it was everything. But thinking back it was a great city. It had everything. I lived on Dewey Street. From Dewy Street I could walk half a block for church or for where I went to school. I could walk there and get a bus for downtown Newark or New York. There were neighborhood movies. There was the Hawthorne Theater, the Roosevelt Theater. The Roosevelt was on Clinton Avenue. The Hawthorne was on Hawthorne Avenue. The Park Theater was on Bergen Street. There was a couple up in Irvington I could even walk to without any problems. They built a Shop-rite store on Lyons Avenue and that was in my backyard. So, for shopping you could just walk around the corner and go shopping in a big supermarket. The city was great at that time. Of course, I didn't realize it or even think about it. But looking at the changes that have occurred, it was a great city, really. Downtown they had the Paramount, Proctors, and Bradford Theater, where they had top run films and stage shows. They had Lewy Prima. I don't think Sinatra ever came to Newark. Big bands, Tommy Dorsey, Jimmy Dorsey they played down there. So everything was there and within walking distance or bus ride. I think it was a nickel bus ride.

Redden (appointed 1947): I was born in Newark and lived in Newark until I retired. I lived in the Clinton Hill section, Seymour Avenue, Chadwick Avenue. Went to Blessed Sacrament Grammar School, South Side High School, I guess now known as Shabazz. They were good schools at that time. Newark was a great town, four hundred and ten thousand population, theaters downtown. I used to spend my weekends down in Weequahic Park. They had boat races on the lake, trotting races. They had a regular stadium there with the trotters. I used to like to go through the barns and visit with the horses. They had semi-pro baseball and they would attract three to four thousand people on weekends. So, there was so much to do. The theaters downtown, there were good restaurants in town, transportation was great, the bus system by Public Service. So, it was fine. I enjoyed myself thoroughly in Newark.

Clinton Hill was predominantly Irish and German. It was a great neighborhood. Clean, I lived in a three-story frame. I remember Saturday morning the women washing the front porches off, the front stoop. And of course, at that time hardly anybody had an automobile. There was lots of room at the curb, if you did have an automobile, to park it. But the neighborhoods were great. I went to Bergen Street playground, spent most of my time there playing softball, paddle tennis. In fact, I played with some of the guys who were on the job with me. We all went on at the same time.

You could go anyplace in the city from Clinton Hill. You had theaters downtown where you had first run motion pictures and you also had the big bands coming in to the Adams. Good restaurants. You could walk anyplace in the city when I was growing up. You had no problem what so ever. Weequahic Park was a gathering place on the weekends. Thousands of people would go down there to see boat races on Saturday, trotting races. They had a nice stadium. I'm sure there was betting going on. And the baseball games, again they would have three thousand people, pass the hat around. Westside Park had a big pond with gold fish in it.

Masters (appointed 1947): I was born and raised in Newark on 427 South Tenth Street, the house is gone now. I went to public schools, graduated West Side during the Depression. My dad and all these foreign born, they believed in education. There were no jobs. He said, "You go to vocational school."

So, I went to Irvington vocational school. From Tenth Street, we walked every morning. It was a group of fellows. We would start from Bruce Street, as they came up the group got larger and larger. It was about forty, fifty fellows going there, Irvington vocational and we walked every day. At that time the bus fare was a nickel. Who had the nickel?

I took a general course, machine shop, carpentry, electric, everything. That came in handy later on. I graduated there. When I went looking for a job it was, "Oh, you need experience." How can I get experience if you won't hire me? So, at the time, President Roosevelt signed a bill creating the CC camps. You may have read about it, all over the country. I went down to the Sussex Avenue armory on Sussex Avenue, it's gone now, and I signed up. The guy said, "Where do you want to go?" I said, "I want to go out west." Utah. I spent two years in Utah. You know where Bowab, Utah is? You know where the four states come together? Southeast corner of Utah, I stayed there two years. We were paid well. We were paid thirty dollars a month, but twenty-five dollars went home to your family, your mother and dad and you kept five dollars. Actually, you could use that money, but you're out in the desert. How can you use those five dollars?

It was all good training. When you were in camp, you were under the jurisdiction of the Army. But when you were out in the field working, making roads, or bridges over streams, planting trees, cutting trees down, you were under the jurisdiction of the Department of Agriculture. When you came back into camp, you had to change into Army uniform. Stood at attention while the flag was lowered and they played retreat and all that stuff. There were a lot of fellows in the Depression, especially from the south, they didn't know how to read or write. In fact, some of those southern boys never wore shoes. It was compulsory for them to go to class at night, three times a week. Learn how to write, read, whatever they lacked in. But I took up photography and typing. That was it.

The city of Newark was beautiful when I was a kid. Downtown Newark, they were all beautiful stores, high class stores too. You had Bamberger's. You had Orhbach's. You had all these good men's clothing stores. It was a beautiful city. My father worked downtown. He was with the Street Department.

F. Grehl (appointed 1948): It was a marvelous city, probably one of the best in the nation. You had everything and anything you wanted. It was a clean, nice city. We had our minority section down in Springfield Avenue, South Orange Avenue, Broome and Prince Streets, and Howard and in there. There was poverty and squalor in that area. They just stayed there by themselves and didn't bother anybody. It was safe city. My wife and I used to walk on Sundays right down South Orange Avenue to downtown and go to the movies. Sometimes we'd walk home at night. You had everything you wanted in the city from opera to burlesque, four or five great movies. The Adams Theater was where all the great Big Bands would come in. It was close to Irvington which had Olympic Amusement Park. You had everything, excellent transportation. To me it was one of the finest cities around.

McCormack (appointed 1949): The city was my home. The only place I ever lived. I was born in the city. I grew up in the city. It was home. All my friends lived here. I went to school here. I went to church here.

It was a blue-collar town in my youth. It was a town of factories, industries of all types. There were a lot of blue-collar jobs in this town, huge industries in this town. Bell and Howell telephone and radio was in this town, a major employer. Ronson cigarette lighter was down by Military Park. There were so many of them, Westinghouse, General Electric, huge companies that hired hundreds and hundreds of people. They were blue collar type jobs that were in the shipyard, railroads, the trucking industry, and manufacturing plants. It was an industrial city with jobs all over the place. You had a couple of bastions of wealthy people perhaps or people slightly above the blue-collar class. Like the Forest Hill section was in the early days. In my day it was society hill if you wanted to call it that. There were larger homes up there. You didn't have your crowded three-story frames that you had in other neighborhoods. You had large homes, which, in those days, seemed almost like estates. I mean if you had a hundred feet, a hundred fifty feet lot it seemed like an estate. They had driveways. They had cars, well-manicured lawns. A lot of people had domestic help. They had maids, chauffeurs, butlers, and people of that type. They hired gardeners.

When you go up there now and look at those houses, they probably seem small by today's standards. You might say the middle class has taken over those homes that were once society homes, but in my youth in Newark that was society hill. Those people up there were wealthy people. There were a lot of lawyers and manufacturing people, people from the business community in Newark. There were no blue-collar people in that area. The other area that was probably a little better off was the Weequahic section, which was heavily Jewish in those days. You had a lot of merchants over there. Probably you had a lot of business people and merchants who had various businesses in Newark. They had nice homes up there, better than the three-story frames of the working class.

It was a teeming city in those days. Broad and Market Streets in those days, they used to say it was the busiest corner in the world. Twenty-four hours a day it looked like Times Square. There was a policeman on duty twenty-four hours a day. I remember as a little kid there was a traffic tower, a big tower, right in the middle of the four corners. It was a gothic size structure with the lights on each side and that used to direct traffic. It was right out in the middle of the street. They took that out in the '40s, but that was there in the early days. That was a busy corner.

Masterson (appointed 1949): I was born and raised in Newark. It was beautiful. If Newark was like that today, I never would have left it. When I was growing up, it was beautiful. The neighborhoods were good. The people were good. You could walk anywhere. The streets were safe. It was a really nice city. You had downtown Newark. They used to come from way out, all the suburbs, come shopping downtown Newark. They had about four or five theaters down there. They were all good. They had a few decent restaurants. I wasn't interested in it, but they had the wrestling over there on Eighteenth Avenue, bicycle racing up in Vailsburg, and the boxing arena with outdoor fights up there across from Vailsburg Park. They had the skating rink. They used to have the Newark Bears. We used to get the knot hole tickets to see the Newark games. You'd get them for nothing almost. The only thing you had to worry about, get a sandwich and ten cents, a nickel down a nickel back on the trolley. You'd be all the way Down Neck. We'd spend the second nickel down there and we'd walk home from way Down Neck. I lived up in the Roseville section, up by Saint Rose of Lima's.

Gibson (appointed 1953): I grew up in North Newark, lived there until I went in the service in '43. Adventureland, really, I swam in the Passaic River. My parents told me, "Don't go near the river." Then they found out that I was. I got the shit beat out of me for swimming down there. And then they told me, "Look we know you're going to go there. Prove to us that you can swim across the river and we'll let you go. We won't have to worry about you because we know you can swim." And I did. It took me a couple of weeks. There as a guy down the street, I was only about eight or nine, but Charlie worked for the Prudential. He'd take us down after supper before it got dark and swim, he'd watch me swim and when I swam across the river he came and told my mother and father. Years later, I was in the fire department still and I was driving a truck part time. I turned the corner Down Neck, Main Street and Ferry, and there was Charlie sitting on the sidewalk, lunch hour. So, I got out and talked to him, he was so happy.

There's a big cemetery on Broadway. Down behind there is where we swam in the river. There was a telephone pole that stood along the bank. We tilted it over and put a platform up on top so we could dive off it. Took all the rocks out from underneath where that diving area was, put sand down there. We stole it from the city. Spread it out there, put cobble stones down and made like a beach way, then built a dock. We even had the girls down and launched a boat off the dock. We'd go there five thirty in the morning, go down to the A & P and steal their donuts.

One morning my father came home and he said, "You were out there this morning." I said, "No." He said, "Don't lie to me. They caught your friend." We stole the donuts and milk. I had the milk and Jimmy had the donuts. And the milkman spotted us. He said, "Where'd you get that milk?" "Up there." He said, "Let me see it." I put it down like that and backed up. "You son of a bitch," he said. "You stole that milk." And he came after me. Well, I could run like a deer. He must have called the cops because I went down behind the Florence Kleeger home, down by the river. I'm running up the road and here comes Jimmy Donnelly. He's running. He still got the gold bags under his arms. He's running along the railroad tracks and here's the cop car pacing him. They took him to the precinct and he squealed. My old man said, "You were out this morning. Your friend squealed on you." My old man would say, "You tell me if my son does anything. I'll take care of it." He never hit me, but he had his way about him. I used to get accused of doing things that I never even heard of. "Oh, that's Gibson's son." They called him Hoot too. That was named after a famous old cowboy in the movies, Hoot Gibson.

Alfano (appointed 1953): I was born and raised in Newark. I grew up in the Roseville section really. And my wife did too. My wife's uncle owned the tavern right across from Eleven Engine (Central Avenue and Ninth Street). It was the greatest town in the world. It really was. It was fun. I can remember sleigh riding and of course I played a lot of ball. I made a lot of friends with that. It really was a great town. One of the things I remember is I used to cut school and I'd go to the Adams Theater. They had all the big bands. They had Tommy Dorsey, Jimmy Dorsey, Gene Crupper, Glen Miller, you name it. Louie Primo. We used to cut school, go there, and watch the bands. And then of course you had the Newark Bears, the great baseball team of '37. They could beat most major leaguers. When I was young, they had a knot hole gang. You paid five cents for a ticket and you could go see the Bears. They called it the knot hole, like in the fence. But that was your ticket. They called it the knot hole. We went to the bleachers. They gave us seats. It was on Wilson Avenue and Avenue L. And it was called Rupert Stadium. You know after Colonel Rupert, the beer people.

You had Ballantine's and you had Hensler's and you had Flagstaff. You had quite a few breweries in Newark. You had Pabst, because the water was so good. But anyway, it really was a great town, City Stadium and your football teams and so forth. Then of course you had Olympic Park which was in Irvington. But we used to go there, and different parks. It just was a wonderful town to grow up in. When my sisters and I get together and just say, weren't we lucky. Weren't we lucky to grow up like we did? You didn't see the prejudice that came out later. We grew up with blacks and we grew up with Polacks and we grew up with Irish and German and you name it. You want to know something, it's terrific for you. It's terrific. Cause I didn't grow up prejudice. Of course, my mom and dad help that too probably because they weren't.

R. Griffith (appointed 1953): It was working class. I was born and brought up in the North Ward area, in Roseville area around the city stadium.

In that area most of the people were either teachers or worked for the city. It was a good place to live. North Newark especially was nice. The city itself was nice. I think one of the big things is that most of the people who worked for the fire department lived in Newark. The Police lived in Newark. The teachers lived in Newark. Everybody who worked here lived here. And that made it even nicer. To me it was a super place to be brought up in at that time.

The War Years

Freeman (appointed 1956): Oh, it was great. I was born in the city and lived in the city. At that time, it was good. It was the hub of everything. You had the airport, Penn Station, a railroad, buses, the downtown area. Prince Street you had all the push carts, all the Jewish stores there. You could buy anything you wanted on Springfield Avenue. You could walk there and walk back. It was a real safe city.

I grew up on Somerset Street. My family is from Clinton. That's where my mother was born, Clinton, New Jersey. They came in to Newark. They lived in North Newark, Delavan Avenue and then they moved right off Broad Street. They lived down there until finally they moved into the Prudential Apartments on Somerset Street. I was born there. My grandmother moved to number one, which is on the corner of Montgomery Street. The Prudential apartments were beautiful then. We had tennis courts in the back. They had a playground for the kids. That was between Spruce and Montgomery. The apartments belonged to Prudential, but the grounds belonged to the city and they still belong to the city today. In the summertime they put a sprinkler out in the middle of the area. They had benches, grass, and flowers. It was really, really beautiful. We had no problems there.

Then I moved to Belmont Avenue in the spring of 1942, after the war started because the family started to expand. There were four of us down there in I think it was one bedroom. We had to move. We didn't have any room. We moved to Belmont Avenue, which was over the top of a roofing place called Rothman and Cohen. It was three bedrooms upstairs with a big dining room, a big living room, and a big kitchen, nice place. It was one family on the second floor and the business on the ground floor. We lived there many years. I'd say into the early '60s maybe. Then they moved us to East Orange to my sister's house.

I remember when we first moved there. The place was infested with mice and roaches. The guy had rented out the different rooms. I mean mice all over the place. We put traps down. I remember this paste that used to glow in the dark. Called Jay-o paste, I think that was the name of it. You put it on slices of potatoes. You'd stick it along the walls, under the sink, on top of the counter. You'd go into the kitchen, turn the lights on, and there'd be roaches all over the place. We fought that for a long, long time, the roaches and the mice. But the good thing about it was we were by ourselves. We had nobody else to contend with because it was just a one family house on the second floor. Twenty-one steps up and on Saturdays somebody had to wash those steps down all the way down and do the hallway and the vestibule. The vestibule was tile and tile floor.

There were nine of us: six girls and three boys. My father was the only one who worked. He worked at Singer Sewing Machine Company in Elizabeth, Elizabeth Port. So, we had a pretty good existence. Everything was in walking distance. Prince Street, the Jews owned almost everything in the neighborhood. In fact, the store next to the firehouse across the street, Izzy's we used to call it, we used to go right next door to the firehouse and get meats. Then on the other side of the firehouse was Belmont Liquors, which was Gershenbaum's. If that's not Jewish, his mother's name was Bella and his father's name was Sam.

In most of the stores, even down where I lived on Somerset Street, they had three by five cards. You could get a loaf of bread, a quart of milk, or whatever. If you didn't have the money, he'd write it on a little card and he'd put the amount after it. He'd put it in a little file box. On payday when you came in, you'd ask him, "How much do I owe you?" And you'd give him the money. Everything was above board. Everything was honest.

We had no problems racially that I ever knew of. In the South it was rampant. They were hanging blacks. They called them niggers then, that whole nine yards down South. They tell me it was hidden in the north, but it was there. But in that neighborhood, I don't remember any. Maybe it was because I was young. I didn't know it. You're talking Spruce Street, Somerset, Quitman, Montgomery Street, Kinney Street, Prince Street. All up Spruce Street, all the way up to Belmont Avenue, High Street, Quitman those were all our streets, Quitman, Prince, Charlton, although I didn't go above there because we couldn't. Monmouth Street School was right across the street from where I lived on Somerset Street. We lived at 47, fifth floor walkup.

I went to Monmouth Street School. There was a little candy store right next door to school where everybody would go in the morning. You'd pick up your candy. A loaf of bread was twenty-five cents; a quart of milk was a quarter. You could buy cigarettes for a penny a piece. He broke open a pack of cigarettes if you didn't have the money. Give me two cigarettes. And if you didn't have the money, the guy would put it on a little three by five card and fill it in. You'd pay at the end of the week or whenever payday was. There was never any problem. So, it was a good neighborhood. We played ball there when we were kids, in the back. There was a kid, Holomon Jarmel. He was a little short, fat Jewish kid. We'd all play baseball together. I went to school with a kid named Milton Schilfer and they named a park after his brother, Schilfer Park. There's a little memorial right there in the middle of the park. His brother was one of the guys killed in the war in I think Pearl Harbor.

I don't remember too many fires. Maybe I was too young to realize a lot of things. But it was a great city. You could walk all over the place. We'd walk downtown. You name the way. Usually, we walked over to Springfield Avenue and then walked down to Market Street. Bamberger's was the big store then and it was very busy. Broad and Market Street was a historical business center at that time. It was one of the biggest business centers, I guess in the state at that particular time. If you look at pictures you see trolleys and all kinds of stuff down there. We'd walk all the way down Broad Street, up Spruce Street, up Kinney Street. Those are hills. Or we'd walk across High Street, which was easier, and home.

At night, we'd be out until eight thirty playing kick the can, catch one catch all, hide and go seek. It was a great, great living. There was harmony. You had kid's fights, but nothing beyond that. You had all the Jewish stores in the neighborhood. You could go anywhere and they'd grind the meat up for you. Up on Prince Street, they had live chickens or turkeys. Right on the corner, there was a place right on the corner of Charlton and Spruce. Then there was a good vegetable store between Prince and Charlton called Southern Produce. They had all this stuff. It'd come out half way to the sidewalk. It was all the produce. I mean, you name it and you can get it there, really, really good stuff. Everybody would stop in there.

Shoes, there was a shoe store on the corner of Prince and Spruce. There was Lipschicht's, which was a deli right on the southwest corner of Prince Street. There was sawdust on the floor. I think they had brass rails in there. There was another deli on Prince Street, a lot of delis around. Springfield Avenue right there just below Charlton Street or Beacon Street, there was another deli there. You could get a four or five-inch sandwich, roast beef, corned beef, whatever. Army and Navy store right there on Spruce Street, I used to go in there and buy fatigues. The girl, their daughter, and I became good friends. She worked in a nursery where my daughter used to go. I'd go in that store all the time and buy fatigues because I couldn't afford a suit or shirts or anything like that. You had everything there. Whatever you wanted was within walking distance, a loaf of bread, clothing, whatever. And if you wanted a suit or a hat, Springfield Avenue, you had shops like that on Springfield Avenue, too. It was just a good city. Bamberger's was the big store and Hahne's.

I remember parades in the city, really good parades. Many, many years ago I remember the Thanksgiving Day parade would come down West Market Street and end at Bamberger's. Santa Claus would get off at Bamberger's. They would have that Halsey and Market Bamberger's window there. That would be beautiful. They would have all the mechanized Christmas things in that window, the dolls, the elves, the Santa Clauses, and the trains. If you were meeting somebody down there, "Well, where can we meet?" "Well, maybe under the clock in Bamberger's." That was the place where you would always meet people. The stores downtown were beautiful. You had plenty of places to go, plenty of places to shop. You didn't have crime down there then.

You couldn't do anything wrong with out somebody knowing about it. Your neighbor, your neighbor's kid, your mother's friends and by the time you got home, if you did something wrong, your mother would know. You didn't have to have a telephone. We didn't have a telephone for a long time. My mother didn't work, but if she wasn't home, by the time she got home when you were doing something wrong, you got it. "So and so told me you did so and so. Did you do it? And don't lie. Don't lie." You had respect for your parents. You had respect for adults, no matter who they were or what they were. You know the Bible said, "Don't spare the rod." The rod was not spared in a lot of households there. I would say at that particular period of time at our age, everybody was pretty much on about the same level of discipline. You couldn't stay out beyond say eight thirty because when it got dark, in the house. If you didn't, then your parent would come downstairs with a belt and you'd get whipped up the stairs or spanked up the stairs. I remember my mother spanked me up Spruce Street one day, when we moved and I went down to play. I didn't come home when I should have, right up Spruce Street boy, bang, bang, every block. "And don't you run either. If you run, I'm going to get you." Oh, how embarrassing that was. That was embarrassing. Your mother's walking behind you with a belt. "Come back here."

In the evening, when you came home from school and went out to play, we usually played stickball. They didn't call it stickball then, but it was. You had a little stick and we had a tennis ball. We played baseball that way. The father of this guy Chubby used to come home from work I guess around five o'clock. He'd stick his head out a back window and whistle. Everybody heard that and half the gang would go because your mother told you, "When Chubby's father tells him to come upstairs or whistles you come up stairs, too." That broke the game up. If I didn't come upstairs, my mother would yell out the window, "Come upstairs right now. What's the matter? You can't hear me? You hard of hearing? Wait until you get upstairs?" Now you have to expect a spanking when you got upstairs.

We didn't go across the street. You had to ask to go across the street. A lot of kids went across the street. We had the playground there, Monmouth Street School. The playground was there. In the evening they showed movies in the playground. You'd sit down on the bench and they'd have the little corrugated cover over the roof protecting you if it rained. We'd see movies in the evening and we'd play checkers. Basketball a little bit, it wasn't as prevalent then as it is now. The girls would jump rope, the whole nine yards in the playground there. It was good. Then you would come home after the playground. They had recreation right after school. They would open up. They'd bring out all the checkers and chess and all the games, all kinds of tiddlywinks and all kinds of other things. You had some place to go, something to do. School was good. If you did something wrong in school, you'd get it. You'd better go to school. I think I played hooky from school one time and almost got caught. That's because my cousins were a little less disciplined than I was. My aunt worked, so they more or less did what they wanted to do and they kind of went by the way side. I don't think either one of them finished high school at all. I wish those times would come back.

Griggs (appointed 1956): Oh, great, the city was great. I was born on High Street. My grandmother had a rooming house on Sherman Avenue about a half a jog in from Ten Engine. That's the first place I settled. My father was a police officer and naturally he lived with his mother. We moved in there for a short stay and then my father found an apartment on Astor Street. I went to school at Miller Street, kindergarten. I went to first grade at Saint Columbus. And then I ended up moving Down Neck to the second grade and third grade on Hawkins Street down off of Ferry. In the fourth grade I went to St. Aloysius and I met my bride there in the fourth grade. I was only in there a short time. I got hauled out of there and I was pumped on to Blessed Sacrament on Clinton Avenue. I lived at 499 Clinton Avenue. In the sixth grade I doubled back to St. Aloysius and I stayed there for seventh and eighth grade. I did end up going to St. Benedict's. Thank God I stayed there for four years which was great.

There was a farmers' market on old Mulberry Street. It's gone, over the years. I guess everything is subject to change. I felt years ago that no matter what you wanted to purchase, you didn't have to go out of the city of Newark. And now I don't even think there's an automobile agency in Newark. If you went on Broad Street, there had to be four of them on there. You didn't have to go out of Newark for anything. Bamberger's was a great place. You had Klein's, Kresge's, all big time. How many movie shows did you have there? No matter where you went, you'd go to a movie.

I knew a little bit of Clinton Hill up by Blessed Sacrament. And I knew a little bit over by grandmother's place on Sherman Avenue. We used to walk to Sears and Roebuck when my grandmother was buying things especially for me. The old Cameo Movie over on Elizabeth Avenue, my grandmother used to take me and we used to walk that. She'd walk up to Springfield Avenue to do her shopping up Springfield Avenue to Prince years ago.

The Salvation Army Boys Club on Reed Street by Raymond Boulevard invited everybody in. I was a member of that for years and years. At twenty-five cents a year, how could you go wrong? The Monsignor from St. Aloysius forbade us to go there because I guess he hated the Protestants that were running it. I didn't care what he hated. I went there every night. I had the workshops. There was boxing, basketball, I mean if you played ping pong, pool, they had it all. Yeah, that was my hang out.

McGrory (appointed 1957) It was a workingman's city with quite a bit of diversified industry. The problem with Newark was it was very small. In land area, what's it twenty-one, twenty-three square miles. Twenty-three square miles, that's not much when you talk about a city with four hundred and ten thousand people in it. And then if you look at a map and see how much of that area is devoted to a port area and an airport area, there's not a lot of room for four hundred and ten thousand people to live. It was the mostly densely populated city in the country. The city was a workingman's city, not enough area to expand. My dad, who came to this country from Scotland in 1907, lived on Mount Prospect Avenue. Some of the rich people of the city were living up on Mount Prospect Avenue. They were moving out right after the turn of the century because there was no place for the upper class to live. They were going to South Orange whatever.

I was born in Newark in a hospital, but my family lived in Kearny, in Harrison, East Newark. In January of '42 we moved over to Newark. So I finished up grammar school in Holy Cross, Harrison. Then I went to West Side High School and after that I went to work.

Downtown Newark had great movie theaters, Loews, Proctors, The Paramount, The Bradford. Big names used to come to the Adams Theater on

Bradford Place when I was younger. Big stores, good stores like Bamberger's which everyone seems to think of as a department store, but they had a meat market in there that was tops. And we had great bakeries. Silva's Bakery on Hawthorne Avenue and there was Kiel's. They had Jewish rolls that were like cake. They were delicious. They had restaurants downtown. Kresge's was another good department store. Hahne's was a top-flight department store. You had Military Park there. All the small parks in downtown Newark were beautiful. Some of the nicest statue work you could see is in the parks downtown. The river was always bad because industry lined up on that river. When I was a kid, you could just about walk across.

I liked the city. My memories of Newark in my young teens during World War II are of a really vibrant city. We had quite an influx of people from other states, mainly from Pennsylvania.

Duerr (appointed 1958): I grew up in Newark, yes. I went to Miller Street School and South Side High School. I lived in Newark all my life until after we got married. I lived in the south part of Newark on Vanderpool Street and Sherman Avenue. I was an usher at the Cameo Theater on Elizabeth Avenue and knew everybody that went there because everybody lived in the neighborhood. There were a lot of firemen that lived around the neighborhood. Back then they had the theater detail and one of the firemen who was an elderly gentleman. He was close to retirement. He had the Empire Theater as part of his detail. I think I was about fifteen. He took me down in the back and I watched the show. My first encounter with showgirls.

Newark was a great town. It really was. You got to remember I grew up in the late '30s and early '40s. We had a lot of guys around the neighborhood who used to play sports. We were heavily involved in sports because there wasn't too much to do. We didn't have television or any of the modern conveniences that the kids have today. So we used to play a lot of stick ball and butts up and things like that.

Butts up was like tennis. You would take a square, a sidewalk square, and another kid would have the other square. You had to keep the ball inside the squares. If it went out, you got a point. The guys you played with would determine how many points. If you lost you would put your butt up against the side of a house or a garage and the other members of the team would throw a ball at your behind. We called it butts up. That was pretty popular back then.

I remember growing up, the night before Thanksgiving Macy's used to run their parade in Newark. They used to come down West Market Street down Market past Bamberger's with all the floats and everything. It was a great thing to experience. You didn't have to go over on Thanksgiving because they came to Newark. Actually, I guess what they did is they tried everything out. If it worked in Newark it was going to work in New York.

Belzger (appointed 1959): I was born in the Beth Israel Hospital, 1933. I was a dollar down and a dollar per week type. My father had to pay the clinic costs over years. He used to pay Beth Israel a dollar a month or something like that for years after I was born. He wasn't in the fire department at that time. We lived on Leslie Street, off Hawthorne Avenue. Later on, I grew up on Madison Avenue, right across from Madison Junior High School. And then we lost the house. You could have bought the house for two thousand dollars when I was a kid. Can you image? We lost that and we moved to a cold-water flat on Nineteen Avenue and Twentieth Street. We lived there for quite some time. Then, I got married and we still lived there for a while.

My grandfather used to work in Irvington Varnish. He was a gold seal engineer. Irvington Varnish was the fore runner of the 3M Company. His name was Gorm Clearwater and he used to make the astounding salary of eighteen dollars a week. That's what we all lived on. My father worked for a company called Farm Crest before he went in the fire department. Farm Crest was on Peddie Street in Newark. It used to be a small bakery. He used to run a small bakery truck for them. But it was a part time job. My dad was a baker. He used to bake apple pies down in Five Truck that rose four inches high. Everybody wanted them. He devised the first small pies when he was in the firehouse and he sold it to Drakes for a hundred dollars. Drakes took over Farm Crest and all their stops.

Newark to me was Madison Avenue. The neighborhood was fine. It was I guess mostly Irish and German. I never did well in school. I should have, but I was a wise guy. You could walk on the streets of Newark without any problems. The only gangs were us young kids who used to hang around Madison Avenue School or used to be playing in the yard of Madison. We used to climb the big fence and could play basketball in the wintertime. A lot of people were just hardworking people. They didn't have very much. My biggest meal, because of my grandfather, was a bowl of Wheaties in the morning. Once in a while we'd come into a few dollars and I'd be able to have a sandwich or something like that. It was tough times. I'm not kidding you.

I had the same doctor. His name was Isaac Irwin Miller, for fifty years. He brought me into the world. I can get emotional because he was a wonderful man. I never knew until he died that he was a Medal of Honor holder. He was a major and he was the first doctor into Auschwitz.

I can remember walking to the stores and the people would give you a little piece of candy or anything extra when you bought a loaf of bread. I lived in that neighborhood until I was nine or ten years old and then we went over to Nineteenth Avenue.

Bitter (appointed 1959): What do I remember of Newark? As a kid growing up I lived on Sixteenth Street and Madison Avenue, right across the street from the school. I had paper routes all the time in the area, had one black family for a customer. They lived on Fifteenth Street between Springfield and Avon. Other than that, there were none above Bergen Street. But taking the school bus, 6 crosstown, across town to go to Bloomfield Tech and taking the trolley up Bloomfield Avenue. Other than that, I don't know. It wasn't bad.

Cardillo (appointed 1959): My parents both came from Italy. Poor, very poor, I think my father made twenty-five dollars a week. He worked on the railroad and he owned a house. There was a tenant living on the second floor. You thought he owned the house. He had the car. My father never had a car. He used to play the horses. My father never played the horses. He used to get drunk. My father never got drunk. My father always had to do something for the guy. He'd fix everything. I fix. I fix. He couldn't pay for a carpenter, so he did all the work himself.

That was a good Newark. You can't beat that town. I want to tell you something. Where can you get a town that has an airport? It has a seaport. It has a train center. It has a boat center. It has a minor league baseball team, the Newark Bears. It had horse racing in Weequahic Park. How are you going to get a town like that? It had everything in those days. I don't know why the hell people left there. You didn't have to go to any town. You can get it in Newark. You can get it on Springfield Avenue. I don't care what the hell it is. You could get lumber, meat, everything. So, Newark was a super town, just a super town. With all those things I just told you about. You can get a train. You can get a bus. You can go to the airport. In fact, a lot of planes at that time had to come to Newark to land if it was foggy. They would come to Newark to land.

Denvir (appointed 1959): It was a nice city at the time. I was born and raised in Newark. I was living in Vailsburg on Smith Street when I came on the job. My parents moved to Verona and then they came back to Vermont Avenue about a year later. They were gone about a year. When I was working, I would try to stay at friends' houses around the corner on Kenmore Avenue. Then my parents moved back to Vermont Avenue.

Dunn (appointed 1959): I was born and raised in the East Ward of Newark and I went to a Catholic parochial school. I think the perception I had of the city was limited because at that time you didn't travel out of your community that much.

Basically poor, but we just didn't realize it. That's why we lived on the third floor in a house. I thought we lived on the third floor because you get a better view. That's because that's the way your education went. You were brought up to be optimistic about things. That certainly has changed my outlook on life as I go through it.

There were several movies. I remember at different times going on the bus to downtown Newark to the movies with my family. One of the vivid memories I have is of the Adams Theater, which always had a stage show, of seeing the Three Stooges live as a kid. Then as you grow older, seeing them on TV, they were just as funny then fooling around on the stage in Newark.

We used to, once in a while, take the 31 bus to Maplewood. As you went from downtown to the Maplewood line you would be going past housing that you just didn't see if you were Down Neck. It seemed if you were going to work and be successful the idea would be to live in a one family house with a driveway, which just didn't exist Down Neck. I always thought that's where the rich people lived. I knew a fireman as a kid who was very community oriented. His name was Harp Bacon. He lived on Eleventh Street and South Orange Avenue and he used to bring the kids to his house for Christmas, as we do today, only under different racial things and different ideas. But he did the same thing. He took children out of the three-story frame and brought them up to his house and entertained them over Christmas week. He had a large army of lead soldiers under his Christmas tree. He also had a white Christmas tree which was sprayed with like white wash that I had never seen Down Neck. He was also like our community relations man in the firehouse down there. He would tow cars away and open hydrants for the kids. The quandary that I have, as I grow older, with a man like that was: Why he lived up there and spent his whole social life in a different section of the city. I never knew he had a family and yet his son was a Newark fireman. So, his whole social life revolved around the Ironbound, but his whole family life was in a whole different section of the city of Newark which I wondered about numerous times as I went through.

At that time there was tremendous peer pressure to climb the mountain. We're still doing the same thing, trying to get out of the city environment and "Do you want to live somewhere?" Then you sit down and you sit home at night and you say, "What am I doing here?"

The other growth factor that I've seen in the city that I remember was when I was young, we used to go down to Port Newark all the time. Other guys would take a ride down the shore, whatever you did with your date, we used to take a ride to Port Newark. We would sit on the dock at Port Newark and watch them unload the ships and fantasize about where the ships came from. Because, again very limited experience of getting out of Down Neck at the time. We really were very close to staying in our little two-mile radius of houses. The airport was another favorite stop. You didn't have anything to do, you'd go over to Newark Airport and watch all the rich people get on their airplanes and take a trip. You'd say "Wow that must be great. Imagine going to Pittsburgh on an airplane." So, you looked at that and that's fairly early in life, but all of that has changed. The seaport is now a world-renowned seaport operation. Where there were a few tin huts down there then, now there are a multitude. There are more cars sitting in Port Newark today than probably are in some states in the country; waiting to be shipped out. That stuff didn't exist at that time.

I also remember getting on Route 1 & 9 to go down to Keansburg and Seabright on Sunday for a shore day and sitting in traffic from Route 1 & 9 in Newark. That's changed. The mobility of the city has changed. People can go anywhere, there's more movement through the city. People Down Neck have friends in North Newark. People in the South Ward have friends in the West Ward. Really, when I was growing up that just didn't exist. We really stayed in our own area. Most people didn't have cars either, because I lived in an area where you couldn't park your car.

J. Miller (appointed 1959) I always lived in the city. I was born in Newark. I lived on 12 Cabinet Street right next to the rectory for nineteen years until I got married. I got married at Saint James church Down Neck and I lived Down Neck for about a year. Then I lived in North Newark at 21 Halleck Street, where I was appointed to the job, after that I moved to 501 Hawthorne Avenue.

I started playing baseball in semi-pro because I had had some good tutorage. I was playing with the guy who just was inducted into the Hall of Fame. He was a black baseball player, lived on Boston Street right on the corner from me. I didn't know that in his youth he played in all the black leagues. He played third base. I forget what his name was, but we as a white team used to play them down Newark Bear Stadium. Being with people like that, you learned a lot. You learned how to play baseball properly. No little leagues. We didn't have that. We just had sandlot ball, but I was fortunate enough to get into this with some people who were ex-major leaguers. So at the time I was sixteen years old I was playing with people who had been in the major leagues. Semi-pro ball up in the Essex County League. Maybe they played fifty or sixty games a year plus maybe three or four in other leagues during the week. The old West Side League which was in West Side Park. They had lights. We played night games there. You'd get about four or five hundred people and they'd pass the hat around. That paid for that. But Newark was a good city to live in at the time.

There weren't that many one family homes in the city of Newark where you could own and have a big back yard and traditional family things with the dog. There were some, but there weren't a lot. But if you went out to the rural area like Livingston, West Orange, Sayreville, Perth Amboy, Old Bridge, Holmdel, you have more property. You have that one family home and that's what a lot of wives wanted. In Newark it was more congested. The houses were twelve feet apart, ten feet apart. Even the one families didn't have much backyard. But what you did have was you had the community unit that stuck together. You had the churches that were filled. The schools were filled. The movies were filled.

A. Prachar (appointed 1959): As a child I lived in a mixed-race neighborhood on Sherman Avenue. Never had a problem as far as racial problems or anything. We all grew up together. We played together. We fought together. I went to Miller Street School for a while and then went to Saint Columbus. I graduated from there and went to South Side High School. When I was a senior in high school, I decided that I had enough school. I could have gone to Jersey City State Teachers College on a scholarship, but I was too smart for that. So that was the end of it.

Newark was mostly wood frame buildings, mostly tenement type in the area that I was in. Three family homes, six family duplex type homes, but all wood frames. There was no brick or anything. Homes built close together, possibly three-foot, four-foot alleyways between homes.

I can't honestly remember what the makeup of Newark was. I really had no interest in it at that time so I didn't think about it. We stayed in our area. Every street had their own baseball team. There was a lot of competition between the streets. We played ball in rocky lots that were never cleared out. Everybody had bruises and cuts from playing ball. If you were dumb enough to slide you knew you were going to get hurt. So, I don't know what the makeup was. I really don't know. I didn't know what Down Neck was. I didn't know what Vailsburg was. I just knew my immediate area and you didn't dare leave it. You didn't dare.

I mean, in the area, you could go to the next street and the next street after that because you played ball against these guys. There's some sort of friendship between. A stranger who walked through the area everybody watched because you had to defend your block, your street. It was close knit.

Everybody was the same. Nobody was rich. Everybody lived life day by day. Every store around there had a book where people would go in, get their food or whatever they needed, and sign the book. At the end of the month or whenever they got paid, they'd come in and settle up. Otherwise, there was no food the following week. Just about everybody lived that way in that area. And it was a friendly area. I can recall my mother walking down the street with bags of groceries. I would run and hide so I wouldn't have to carry them. Somebody else's mother would slap them in the back of the head and say go carry Mrs. Prachar's groceries. This was common because it would happen to me too. They would hide and I would end up carrying their mother's groceries. It was a way of life in that neighborhood.

There was an A & P grocery store that was on Elizabeth Avenue right next to Sears. My dad drove a trailer for the A & P, so it was almost an obligation to shop at the A & P because what we brought in the A & P he had to deliver. So, it was just a circle there. Every block had a little. Of course, we all had coal stoves at that time, so you would go buy bags of charcoal to start the coal fire. Three blocks away we had the railroad. Part of my job growing up was to go down to the railroad and throw stones at the trains as they were going by. The guys on the train would throw coal back at you and this was how we got our coal. And that's how we kept warm in the winter. But they knew on the trains what we were doing. We never threw to hit the engineer or whatever his occupation was in there. They'd throw handfuls of coal back at us and we'd pick up the coal and this heated the house. It was a game we played with the guys on the railroad. This was just before World War II when we started that.

During World War II things would be in short supply. My dad had several jobs, one of them working in the slaughterhouse. He used to wield a sledge hammer and hit the horses over the head and then part of his pay at the end of the week was he would get one slice of horse meat. We never knew we got horse meat during the Second World War, but we ate a lot of it. And it was steak to us. Nobody ever got sick from it. My dad logged a lot of hours. He drove the trailer. He worked there. And in between he worked as an auxiliary fireman, so he was a dedicated man too.

That's why we all had a job around the house. And in addition to all that, nobody had refrigerators. You had better empty the ice water out of the ice box in the morning. Because if your dad got up and walked in cold water you were in big trouble.

We were two blocks from Sears Roebuck so I got a job outside Sears selling the newspapers for a penny each. From there I would go to the A & P warehouse on Peddy Street which was maybe ten blocks. There it would be the same deal selling newspapers for a penny a piece and bringing the money home. It was expected of you in that neighborhood. Nobody was rich, but it was a good family life. It was a good upbringing.

We lived in a three-story, six-family house, and all the neighbors got along. We grew up together. We fought together. We went to school together.

It was like six families living in one house that were one family. It gave me an education that I think I passed onto my children.

Schoemer (appointed 1959): I spent most of my life in Newark, but I'm born in Elizabeth. My father is from Elizabeth. I lived on Dayton Street. When I was on Dayton Street there was no Dayton Street School. Used to be Dreamland Park on Dayton Street. It was a big amusement park with a monstrous swimming pool. Then they cut the swimming pool in half and they left the lot. Then they put those two-story garden apartments in down there. That's where I've never seen such big cucarachas in my life. They must have been that big in the basements down there. But I lived there and I moved out of there in 1948. That year they started Dayton Street School. I went to Miller Street School when I was a kid. That was at Frelinghuysen and Miller Street, two blocks away from Ten Engine. We moved out of there up to Vailsburg on Chapman Street. It was an altogether different life. Most of the neighborhood was civil service. Fellow who lived diagonally across the street was Archie Armstrong. He ran Newark Airport. Next door to me was Frank Barns. He was a Deputy Chief.

The Rock and Roll Years

Harris (appointed 1961): Well, I moved to Newark when I was eight years old. I came from East Rutherford, New Jersey. I came to Newark after my father died. My mom couldn't keep the house and we moved to Newark. Newark when I was growing up, you went to the same schools. The schools weren't segregated. I went to Summer Avenue School then to Webster Junior High School, from Webster Junior High School to Central High School. How I was put to Central High School living in North Newark, I still don't know. It should have been Barringer. But Joe Denardo and Emile Nardone were both a grade ahead of me in Central High School.

I believe schools were better then, because you went to school and there were "x" blacks in the class and the teachers taught. They were 90% white teachers in the schools. You as a student learned as well as the white students did because they taught you. Over the years, you can see how it's changed. I would say the school system now is about 70% minority teachers and they're out of the schools before the kids are out. The system and the kids' grades are down. But when I was going to school it wasn't like that.

If I came home with a bad grade, forget about it. I got my butt whipped and you better sit down. You better study. You're on punishment. You don't do this. You had to do your lessons. There were no ifs, ands, or buts. You did it. You couldn't stay home from school because at that time they had truant officers. Today they would send letters home. You get home. You intercept them before your mom sees them. But the truant officer came to the door and knocked on the door and told your mother, "He ain't been to school." That's how it was.

Back then you had movie theaters. We had the Regent down on Bloomfield Avenue at Bloomfield and Broad. There was the Embassy at the top of Bloomfield Avenue. There was the Elwood movie up in North Newark on Elwood Avenue and Broad. And then you had the five movies downtown. But growing up in the city of Newark, you as a minority or black sat in certain sections of the movies in the city of Newark. Then slowly it changed.

Haran (appointed 1961): I grew up in the Roseville section on Seventh Avenue. It runs parallel with Orange Street, which was a main street at that particular time. I can remember the tracks in the street going back then. They used to have trolley cars. The downtown area had all the electrical wires strung across Broad Street. That's the way it was back then. I had two brothers and two sisters. We all attended the same school, which was Saint Rose of Lima School on Orange Street and Humboldt Street.

That part of life circled around Saint Rose of Lima's. We were all in the choir. We were all altar boys. We all attended mass there. My two sisters and both my brothers were married in Saint Rose of Lima's. I was married in the Sacred Heart Cathedral down on Clifton Avenue and Sixth Avenue because my wife was from that area down there. My whole life revolved around the school at that particular time. My sisters graduated. They went on to other schools and I came to the Down Neck area. I went to Saint James High School. Then out of high school, I went to the phone company and then from the phone company I came to the fire department. So, I grew up in the Roseville section, which was a nice section at the time.

There wasn't much to do. We didn't have much. Everybody was in the same boat. We all thought this was the way life was, but everybody was just hardworking families there. Our weekends when I was a kid were spent down at Branch Brook Park. That's where we used to go all the time.

Up until my mid-teens, until I started driving at seventeen, most of my time was spent in that particular area. You didn't go too far out of your area. You had no means of getting out unless you walked. But mostly my friends and everything we needed to do or wanted to do was in that area. There were movie theaters. I think today there are only two movie theaters in the city of Newark, but back then I think there were as many as fifty. On Saturdays everybody went to the movie. Sundays we went to church. Friday night was CYO when I was a teenager. That was basically it. We didn't move too far out. I didn't know too much of the city. I used to take a bus to high school, so I traveled from the Roseville section, which was considered the North Ward then, down to Saint James High School, which was in the Ironbound section. Today the Roseville section isn't considered the North Ward anymore. It's in the Central Ward section now. They broke it up years ago.

Elward (appointed 1962): I lived right around Saint Rose of Lima my whole life. Went to a Catholic grammar school, public high school, Barringer. A Catholic grammar school where the nuns beat the shit out of you. Then you walked into the public school, you look like a scholar. You could read better than everybody else. Then in senior year, everybody signed up for the draft. In no more than nine months I was gone. I was drafted. I went to Korea. I came home worked at a lot of all the Irish jobs, Hugh Haggerty all construction trucks.

My whole neighborhood was consumed with athletics. Consumed, I mean there was nothing else that you could do. Well, I hustled a paper route, walking all over. You don't see that anymore. Everybody walked to the A & P. I always remember the neighborhood, old Irish, they didn't die of a heart attack because they couldn't. They walked all over the world. I mean in my neighborhood it actually was rare to see a car.

Down Neck you saw a lot of factories in the neighborhood, Newark with its industry was sending, at that time, money to Trenton to help out the state. That was when I went to high school and I think Carlin was the mayor. That's how powerful Newark was. They were sending money to support the state, to help out the rest of the state. That's how independent Newark was. It was a cross section for workers.

My mother wouldn't think twice of sending me and my brother over to New York. We used to go over to 109th Street. We had relatives over there in the city. Take us down, put us on the bus. We knew how to use the IRT subway in eighth grade. And she never thought anything of it. Me and my brother used to jump on the IRT, go up to about 79th Street and walk up into the hundreds. Everything was different.

Our grandmother walked to church. The Catholic Church was just at the height of its power. I guess they reached their height like the mid-50s. And then you could see. You could see the first time when you see the Catholic church building with the paint peeling. Not a lot of guys in the neighborhood going up there to volunteer services. That's a sure indication that things are gone. That's only one. There are a million other things. Like in my case, I'm Catholic, it was like breaking a tradition. My sister and my brother, he went to Benedict's and she went to Good Counsel and the nuns said I was dumber than camel shit, so I went to Barringer, but that was a misconception about public schools. You could get a first-rate education. The Catholics didn't realize that. It was free. It was there. They had more to offer.

Dalton (appointed 1963): Newark was nice. None of our fathers had cars. Everything was on the bus, but you'd get on the bus, ride downtown. Get a ride downtown, anywhere. Go around the stores, play in the penny arcades, the games, on Market Street. Then after I graduated from grammar school, I went to St. Benedict's. In St. Benedict's I got a job in a stationary store. The man's name was Jack Singer, a Jewish guy, on Bradford Place. I got to really know all the different offices and everything else even into the Prudential, walking around downtown. Got to know the area really well. And met a lot of people. A few kids I went to grammar school with were working down there. But in the neighborhood I grew up in, you could get jumped. You don't go into those neighborhoods by yourself. As a kid I could handle myself pretty well. I wasn't afraid of them. That's the big thing.

Schofield (appointed 1963): I lived on Avon Avenue between Bergen and Hunterdon. I was in an orphanage in Kearny, Sacred Heart Orphanage and then I ended up in a foster home on North Seventh Street by Saint Francis Xavier. That's where I went to grammar school, right next to Abington Avenue School. My parents weren't dead or anything, but I guess they just couldn't handle everything. It was six of us, six children. So, we ended up in an orphanage, in a foster home, and I eventually got back with my parents. They lived in the Walsh Homes down on McCarter Highway which back then they weren't too bad. That was '53.

Highsmith (appointed 1963): At that time the city was nice. I liked it. Everybody was friendly. There were no big problems around. We had quite a few fires because we had quite a few frame houses, but the city was in good condition. The joke was everybody was happy. Not a lot of crime, no problem with the kids in school. Nothing like it is today.

Cody (appointed 1964): I'm from Newark. I grew up in the First Ward on High Street, High Street and Seventh Avenue. We lived there and then we moved up to Sussex Avenue and then we moved over to Fourth Street right near Orange Street. That's where we lived when I came on the job. I went to Saint Michael's over here. I graduated from Saint Michael's.

That area was really great. It had all the feasts and it had just so many people. They were just always out of their homes. They knocked it all down for the projects. It all centered around Saint Lucy's. We used to walk downtown all the time. This is when I was a kid. It was still nice.

Wargo (appointed 1964): I wasn't born in Newark, but I spent most of my life in Newark in the Ironbound. It was made up of the Dutch neck and the Irish neck. It was sort of chopped up into ethnic areas, but in my area over near St. Casper's there were a lot of Polish people, with a lot of Italian mixed in, and some Irish. There weren't many blacks. The black families who lived Down Neck had been there for a long, long time. So, they were really natives of the area. They had lived there for generations. It was a good makeup. It was a good mix. I went to Catholic grammar school, which at the time was all white because of the neighborhood.

Gaynor (appointed 1965): Well, you look at it from a kid's perspective. Boylan Street, the street that I lived on had one of the four swimming polls that the city operated. So, summers were busy because many, many people walked down your street. During the summer months that was a beehive of activity. All the families on the block had at least a couple of kids. There were tons of children around. We lived in a six-family house of which there were three on Boylan Street. Summer nights were really hot. Everybody would sit outside until midnight with all their kids because you just couldn't go to sleep. There was no air conditioning. I can remember when we went from no television to television. That was the big deal. We got the General Electric sixteen-inch television, I guess it was in the early '50s. It might have been '55.

Right around the corner from where I lived was Alexander Street School. So went there until the sixth grade. Then up to Ivy Street to Ivy Junior High for a couple of years. Spent a year at Essex Catholic when it first opened, but I finally graduated from West Side High School. I went there for three years and graduated in 1962 from West Side.

But when I went to West Side the first year, they converted Ivy Junior High into what is now or was Vailsburg High. So, my sisters, who were younger, stayed up in Vailsburg for high school. I took the bus down South Orange Avenue.

We had the Army barracks at the end of our street on Boylan. Boylan was a dead-end street actually. We had the Army barracks there after the war that they constructed across the street. They would use a vacant lot and put up a long barrack, one floor. It would be an apartment towards the front, an apartment towards the rear. Maybe four rooms in each half. There were several of them around. Stanley Knots who lived on the first floor had a victory garden, grew lots and lots of vegetables. Right across the street from our house there was a single building lot and he grew vegetables and actually at the end of the street there was some more vacant property. All of which have houses on them now, but someone else had a much larger garden. So, we had a little bit of that in the neighborhood.

In the middle of the block was the dress factory, Williams Dress Factory. He was Italian. His first name was William. I cannot recall immediately what the guy's last name was, but all the ladies in the neighborhood had worked in the dress factory. They could all come home at lunch time, feed their children and then go back to work. If any of the kids had a problem, they could run right in the door of the dress factory which was a two-story block building and go find their mother at a sewing machine. I'm sure it was frowned upon, but I guess they had to also understand that you had all the mothers in there and all the children outside.

There was a sporting goods store that we would go to on South Orange Avenue. The A&P was opposite Brookdale Avenue on South Orange. There were a couple of local small grocery stores. Almost every other corner seemed to have a small grocery store. The 31 South Orange took you right downtown. My uncle Al drove the 31.

I can remember a few of our friends moving away. Next door DiFilippos moved to Union. Next door to them, two houses down, Lucianos moved to

Montrose Street. And then shortly after that, maybe that year, maybe the year after then we moved to Sanford Avenue. So, it was changing slowly, but not really an ethnic change.

Calvetti (appointed 1966): We didn't see much of the city because everything we wanted was right where we lived. We had a movie theater there. The Kent Movie was on Mount Prospect Avenue. The furthest we went was the Regent on Bloomfield Avenue. So, we went to the Kent most of the time and Lister's Drug Store. He sold candy three bars for a dime. So, for ten cents you got three bars of candy. Went to the movies for a quarter, for thirty-five cents you had it made. We used to go looking for bottles for the money. Back then they used to have soda bottles and beer bottles. They'd give you money for these bottles, when you returned them. So, you'd go steal them off people's back porches, take them to the store and get money for them.

I used to shine shoes when I was a kid. I was a shoe shine boy. I used to get ten cents a shine. And sometimes if the guy was a big tipper, you got a quarter. Most people only gave you the dime. Sometimes they gave you a nickel extra. I sold lemon ice as a kid too. I had a lemon ice stand. I sold lemon ice. I worked in a grocery store. Lenny's was the name of the place. It was on Summer Avenue. The guy had a truck. People used to come in and they'd make a big order and we would drive it home for them. Not me. I would be the passenger, but I would carry the stuff in. We had a bike too. Some things were close. I would ride a bike with the bag, went to people's houses with a bike. It was fun.

Lawless (appointed 1966): I was born and raised in Newark, great, great place to live. I never had any complaints, no problems. Lived here all my life. I'm from what used to be the Seventh Ward, West Market Street, Eleventh Avenue, Central Avenue. The world started at South Orange Avenue and ended at Orange Street, my world. I knew Bloomfield Avenue was there and at one time we lived by Springfield Avenue, I can say that. But that was it, a very, very small section.

I went to the Newark School system. I went to Seton Hall then I went to Saint Michael's. I can name ten guys on the job who graduated from Saint Michael's. Starting with Jimmy Cody, he was in my class. They had a high school there. I used to take the bus down Park Avenue through the park, Roseville down to Broadway. I only lasted about three weeks at Saint Michael's. That was the end of me at school. My formal education stopped at ninth grade.

Benderoth (appointed 1967): I tell my kids about Newark all the time. You wanted anything; you could find it in Newark. If you wanted to play baseball, football, basketball, no problem. You didn't lock your doors. You didn't worry about driving. You usually had a bike when you were a kid. You walked to all the stores to go shopping, one block this way, one block that way. As a kid we had White Castle by us. We had Dave's Long Bar with their foot long hot dogs and you know it was good. I enjoyed being a kid in Newark.

I was born on South Eleventh Street and Eighteenth Avenue. In 1945 we moved to Runyon Street by Clinton Place. The firemen used to put the hose out for us during the summer, Seventeen Engine.

McGovern (appointed 1968): I grew up Down Neck on Gotthardt Street. Went to Anne Street School, East Side High. From high school, I went into the Navy, from the Navy I went to Western Electric, and from there I came to the fire department.

Down Neck was Irish, German, Polish at the time mostly. And very rarely did Down Neck people go up above the wall. You went uptown to shop, go to a movie once and a while, but other than that you stayed in your neighborhood. That's the way it was. Not many people had cars. You used buses.

I'd say it was maybe 75% white, 25% minority at the time. I would guess, but it's just a guess. Like I said, when I was a kid you kind of stayed in your own little world Down Neck. Who had a car? The guy who had the car, he was your only escape.

D. Prachar (appointed 1968) I grew up in a mixed neighborhood on Alpine Street. The house next door was always black. The house across the street was always black. It wasn't until certain types of black people moved into the neighborhood that a neighborhood changed. Prime example is Willie Curry in Nineteen Engine. His family moved into Sherman Avenue and Alpine Street. They weren't accepted by the people in the neighborhood because it was a big family as far as the number of kids. Willie even says, when he moved in on Alpine Street, if you weren't liked by the Prachars, you got beat up, because my brother used to beat him up all the time. And then finally it became an accepted thing. The Currys were there. There was nothing you were going to do to move them out. So, then your neighborhood started changing. Not because of the Currys, but because it was cheap to live in that area.

Weber (appointed 1969): I grew up in Newark. I'd like to go back and do it all over again. It was a wonderful, fulfilling experience. Anybody that I run into today, I talk about growing up in the city and they look at me like I have a third eye because they just don't understand what it was like growing up in a community, especially the Vailsburg section where I came from. It was a wonderful opportunity. I had Vailsburg Park to my backyard. I didn't even have to cross the street and I had the biggest backyard of anybody.

I didn't spend a whole lot of time east of the Parkway growing up. Back in those days the Parkway was considered the moat. It was almost a racial dividing line. The summer of 1967 when the first riots started, it was in July and I was down the shore. I was at the shore and all I knew about what was going on was what I saw in the news. So, I wasn't impacted a great deal by that. Vailsburg was totally insulated from what happened.

K. Miller (appointed 1969): I was born and raised in Newark. I was born on South Orange Avenue and Twelfth Street. We then moved up into East Orange, just over the Newark line. And then we moved back into Newark up in the Vailsburg section. Newark was a great place. Holidays downtown were spectacular. The Saint Patrick's Day parade down Broad Street was spectacular. Vailsburg was sort of almost a suburb of the city itself. It was just a great place to grow up. Very close to everybody, I knew everybody on the block. Growing up in the city, you knew everybody. You knew everybody's mother. You knew everybody's father. Not just on your block, but the block over and you were fearless too. You weren't afraid to go any place or do anything. Get on a bus and go down to Bamberger's or Klein's on the Square. Just a great place to be.

Saccone (appointed 1969): I was born and spent six months down in the First Ward. I was baptized, made my communion, my mother was married in Saint Lucy's. And I moved up to Steven Crane Village which was built on an old garbage dump. And it was just being actually finished. We were one of the first ones to move up there. I stayed up there until the day I got married.

So, I lived in the projects and I'm glad. I had a good childhood with friends. Because especially in Steven Crane there were always people. You never had to worry. I remember not having a TV set and listening to the Lone Ranger. Then I found out that the kid two doors away had a TV set. At that time, it was a Motorola that they used to put a magnifying glass to make it bigger. And I tell you one thing. I had to make friends with this kid fast. His mother used to take care of me when I was young. I worked with his father and I used to hang on the corner. I used to hear them sing. And he's a friend of mine. He's a pretty big guy now. At that time, they were called the Four Lovers, but now they've been around for over thirty years. And the name of this singing group, rock and roll, their group's name is called the Four Seasons. Frankie Valli and his last name which was still on the door until they renovated the new Steven Crane maybe four years ago. His name was still on the door. His last name was Castelluccio.

As a matter of fact, I could tell you one of the persons that lived in Steven Crane is Cliff Dainty. He lived opposite me about a block away. And it was really a nice place. I mean everybody got along. If you didn't have a bike, you made a scooter. You got an old Coca-Cola box, got a two by four and you made a whole hell of a lot of noise going around at night. You had all these old Italian ladies calling you all kinds of names. Then they would tell your mother and then you would get hit, a swing from your mother and get a back from your father.

What was Newark like? Well, let me put it this way, sneakers were only two dollars and ninety-eight cents. When I grew up Klein's was there and my mother used to take me there. It was only two dollars and ninety-eight cents for sneakers and they were Converse sneakers. And you could always find opportunities for jobs and things like that. So, if you had a paper like the Evening News which was a very big paper, it had a heck of a section on job opportunities. We had a lot of job placement agencies. If you wanted a job and there were so many in Newark at that time, you would go for a job there and they would place you. But you had to give them part of your salary or whatever the case may be. Things were cheaper. Gas was cheaper and the city was more lively. You had more people. I would say maybe on a busy day you might have a million people during the day just coming in and out of the city. At night, downtown Newark was like a Christmas tree. People just used to love to go downtown.

The stores were different. But we were poor. Going back when I was a kid, Kresge you couldn't afford and Hahne's or Bamberger's, forget it. The only thing you saw was the Lionel trains going around. We shopped in Ohrbach's. Orhbach's was the place to shop and Klein's. That's where we got our bargains and that's where you shopped.

Daudelin (appointed 1970): When I was a kid, I thought it was still a very vibrant and alive city. All the schools in those days had all the old city league, so all the athletics. You had all this competition among all the city schools, but you also played schools outside. I guess probably after the riots a lot of people moved out; that's when things became neglected for several years there; but when I was growing up the city was a wonderful place to be.

We didn't interact with other neighborhoods. As an example of how little that happened, when I got put on the police department, I had to go down to police headquarters. Now coming from the North Ward, I thought police headquarters was the old Second Precinct on Orange Street. I had no conception of where 22 Franklin Street was. Because as a kid you came down, we went to the movie. We went to Broad and Market Streets to the arcade. We went to Branford Place, but we never went past Branford Place. There was nothing down there. And the same thing going up to Vailsburg. I was born and raised in the city and when they told us you had to go up to 1010 Eighteenth Avenue, I said, "What? Where?" When I was in high school, my junior year, the football coach told us, "Oh, we're picking up this other team, Vailsburg, we're going to play next year." It was on our schedule. And I thought Vailsburg? I thought Vailsburg was like in Maplewood. I had no idea that Vailsburg was part of Newark. I thought Vailsburg High School was in some small town in Maplewood or Summit or something like that. I had no idea that it was part of Newark.

I remember as a kid, Mike Sweeny was a fireman who lived in my neighborhood. I hung around with his two sons. And him being a fireman, he was off during the day a lot. He used to take us to Boylan Street Pool. And my mother used to say, "Where did Mr. Sweeny take you?" and I used to say, "Well, I really don't know, mom. Nice place, nice houses. It's up in the country some place. It took a long time to get there." He would put all those little kids into the back of his little station wagon to go to Boylan Street. I thought we were going someplace special. We were going to Boylan Street Pool.

Pianka (appointed 1970): I was raised in Newark Down Neck. I spent most of my youth, below the wall, below Penn Station. Mostly white, I knew the black people were up in the Central Ward, but it was two different worlds. Never got intimate with black people until I came here to the fire department.

K. Marcell (appointed 1970): I grew up in the Roseville section. I went to Saint Rose of Lima and Essex Catholic. Growing up Newark was very nice. I wasn't that familiar with other areas of the city. Not that much outside of the Essex Catholic area where I used to go down. I used to take the subway over to Second Avenue and then walk down to Essex Catholic, go to school, and then walk back up, take the subway back again. So, Newark was nice then. It was nice, real nice.

Rotunda (appointed 1970) Fantastic. I grew up in Newark; went to Central High School in Newark. Used to go roller-skating over in Dreamland. Switch buses downtown Newark and stop for ice cream at Branford Place. I think it was Seams or something at the time. Ice cream, a whole bunch of people from school and everywhere else, we'd all meet up in Dreamland. But the city of Newark was fantastic. Couldn't beat it.

P. Doherty (appointed 1970): The old Newark? I grew up on Cabinet Street between Morris Avenue and Prince Street. I went to Saint Joseph's for grammar school. I was baptized, made my first communion, and confirmation in Saint Joseph's. Newark was a thriving city at that time. It was a beautiful city. Went to Saint Michael's High School in Newark. It was a great city, still is I think, but then it started to change. That's in the late '50s, early '60s it started to change. A gradual change, not a rapid change like you had in the '70s.

I grew up around Seven Engine (Hudson and Market Streets). I used to go there, to the firehouse, stop in and ask for a drink of water or use the bathroom. And they would play games on you and all that. Make you line up and tell you how to drink. When you drank the water, curl your lips. It was really like busting our chops all the time. But they were a great bunch of guys. Eddie Vesey was there when I was growing up. A few when I came on the job, they remembered me as a kid, Vesey and all them. My cousin Danny was there too, but that was later on because he came on in '62.

Dainty (appointed 1970): I lived in Newark my entire life. I didn't even know the Central Ward existed. I grew up in Steven Crane Village, which were the projects, but the difference in those projects from what everybody thinks of as the projects was they were two stories. There were about twenty units per building and they were predominantly returning GIs from World War II and Korea. It was predominantly white. It was middle class. There were a lot of factories in Newark at that time. A lot of them worked in the factories. Moms pretty much stayed at home, raised the family. Dad went to work. So, you know that was it. It was a pretty homogeneous type living.

The main street came in. If you looked to the left all the streets were south, like Hawthorne Lane South. I lived on Hawthorne Lane North. There was a building that was called the office. That was where the maintenance staff was, the boiler rooms, the clerks for the projects and stuff like that, but it was very clean, very neat. Everybody got along. You never, really never saw the cops coming in, just on patrol. Once in a while there was a fire box out on Franklin Avenue and Steven Crane Plaza that kids would pull. You would see Twenty-eight Engine which was an old Arhiens-Fox with a big bubble on it. And that was it.

Down the end of the street was a working dairy farm. To my knowledge that was the only farm left in Newark. The guy had black and white cows. And it was a working dairy farm. That was unique. We used to go down there and behind the village was the very, very edge of Newark and Belleville. You walked out the back side of Steven Crane Village and crossed the street, you were in Belleville. The same thing if you went out on Franklin Avenue and walked to the end where Clara Maas Hospital is now, that was all woods. There was nothing there. They built Clara Maas Hospital later on. We used to play in the woods. You would never think it was the city of Newark. That was pretty unique. So, that was my neighborhood. I would say downtown Newark because we lived up, up town so that was downtown. If you lived in the Ironbound it was uptown.

That was my extent of the city I didn't have any relatives that lived there other than my grandparents, so I never saw any other part of the city.

When I got out of high school, my first job was working for a contractor as an electrician's helper because I went to a vocational high school. He was in the Central Ward. I didn't realize that was the Central Ward. It just never occurred to me that part of the city was there.

Melodick (appointed 1970) I am a Newark boy. I grew up here. In 1955 I lived on Camden Street and South Orange Avenue. I was six years old. Do I love the city? Yes, I love it. I think it was the best place to live if you could live here, but things have changed. I know crime wasn't like the way it was later on. I remember walking with my mother and father up and down Springfield Avenue. Went to Camden Street School, went to Alexander Street then I went to Vailsburg High, had no problems ever. Things have changed. Obviously now you have to live other places besides Newark. But if I had my choice, I'd come back here any time to live. It was fun. It was fun living here, something about city life. The people, they're closer. They share. Everybody knows one another. It seems like when you move out to the suburbs, everybody's a distance apart. Everybody keeps to themselves. But to me city life is the best. Plus, you learn. You become street smart and you learn many things about life that most of these kids in the suburbs have no idea. They might be book smart, but not about life.

Perez (appointed 1970): I drove through other parts of the city, but if you lived Down Neck, the whole city is below the railroad tracks. Everything above the railroad tracks is all foreign. We went uptown to Bamberger's, Kresge's, Kline's, Hahne's that's it.

Down Neck was Down Neck. Only one person controlled Down Neck and that was the Mob. The guy that's head of the Mob now for Down Neck was one of my buddies. Second in command was my wife's friend in school. And he was going out with my wife's best girlfriend who's the godmother to our kids. The guy who got shot in Vailsburg and wrote the book *"To Drop a Dime"* we're related to them. I grew up in a Polish neighborhood, but all our friends were mobsters.

Tumultuous Times: The Riots and Beyond

Kelly (appointed 1971): We lived on Ninth Street in Newark by Central Ave. They used to have a lot of parades in Newark back then. They had a Thanksgiving parade. They had a Columbus Day parade, Saint Pattie's Day. So, our neighborhood was really busy. You always heard the ambulance and the fire engine, and the cop cars. Right where we were, you could hear the train. At night you could hear the tugboats from the harbor when you went to bed, Newark Bay there, the ships with the big horns, you could hear. It all depended on where the wind was blowing. And naturally you heard the planes from the airport and the sewer plates with cars always running over them. It was really noisy. So, it was good. Because to this day, I like noisy at night time. It's hard to go to bed when it's real quiet. Comes from the city.

There were so many kids in Newark. Everybody had a group, a gang of kids that hung out together. I'd say we had about ten kids. And right down the street was another group of kids. So, we were always playing ball all the time. We played stick ball and football, go to the park, play baseball. It was all ball. We played ball from morning until night. Wiffle ball, sponge ball, basketball and climbing trees and getting in trouble, but lot, lot of people and lots of things to do. If you couldn't find a friend there, you're hurting.

People used to walk a lot when I was a kid. You could walk anywhere. You could walk downtown because it was pretty safe. There was very little on the mugging. I don't remember any dope going on back then. There must have been a little of it, but crime didn't seem like it was years later. It was pretty safe, the neighborhood. People felt safe walking around everywhere. You could walk anywhere and late at night and then it changed.

We lived on West End Avenue in the Burg during the riots. That was a crazy time. I remember the National Guard was there. We used to see shell casing in the street from the gun fire. I do remember a lot of fires during that time because we used to shop on Springfield Avenue for years. That area was all getting rough with houses burning. There was a lot of torching back then. A lot of hate.

T. Grehl (appointed 1971): I grew up in the Vailsburg section of Newark. Part of my house was in Irvington; my garage was actually in Irvington. My house was in Newark, so I had kind of like the best of everything. I went to grammar school at Saint Leo's in Irvington. Then I played all my sports and spent a lot of my time in Vailsburg Park with the guys from Newark. So, I had a combination of both types of friends, from Catholic school and the public school. Vailsburg Park was where we spent all our time.

We shopped in Newark on Springfield Avenue. The toy store was on Springfield Avenue right down the street from Six Engine (Springfield Avenue and Hunterdon Street). The shoe store was there. The clothing stores, David Burr's, a couple of other ones were up in Irvington Center. The sporting goods store was Duviga's across the street from Bamberger's and it was Hahne's and Kresge's and the five and ten and a lot of little stores. But there were no malls. We got on the 54 Devine and took it right down to downtown Newark. That's where we spent our Saturdays, shopping for our parents for Christmas and for their birthdays.

We did everything in Newark, everything. Movies were in Newark, a little bit of Irvington Center. There was the Castle in Irvington and then there was the Sanford on South Orange Avenue. That was the movie theater I went to with the Newark people. When I went with the Irvington people it was the Castle. But everything was right there. The furniture stores were on South Orange Avenue in Vailsburg. Everything was there. Anything you wanted.

Then when the riots came, obviously that changed quite a bit. A lot of those little mom and pop stores along Springfield Avenue were no longer there. They left because of the change in the city or because of vandalism and they couldn't rebuild or whatever. Downtown Newark started changing when the malls came. When Willowbrook Mall was built, that really hurt downtown Newark, more so than the riots. Because everybody still went to Bamberger's, still went to Hahne's, but when the malls came and they put the Bamberger's up in Willowbrook Mall that's where you went. So, it took away the heart of downtown.

Romano (appointed 1972): Growing up in Newark in the '50s and '60s, it was a good city at the time. I lived in Vailsburg for the most part. And Vailsburg had almost everything you wanted. You really never had to leave Vailsburg. South Orange Avenue, which was the main street in Vailsburg, had every store imaginable, had every store you needed from butcher shops to poultry markets to taverns, fish markets, pizzerias, hardware stores, two movie theaters, two county parks. It was a good city to grow up in at the time. Newark was always a tough city. The Central Ward and the South Ward at the time, I guess in the '50s, I knew very little of that part of town. But for people that lived there, they didn't share the same Newark experience that I shared. Later on, I realized that the city was already in decline at that time somewhat. I guess its peak was in the '20s and maybe the '30s, if you talk to the older generation, if any of them are still alive that grew up in Newark in the '20s and '30s.

Burkhardt (appointed 1973): I grew up in Newark. In fact, my father died recently (2004). We finally sold his house six months ago. He was still there. Getting him out of there, we had better shot throwing you through the window. He just didn't want to go. Grew up in Newark; educated in Newark; went to Vailsburg High School which isn't there anymore. Supposed to go to Essex Catholic, but I didn't want to take the two buses to Essex and two buses home from Essex so I took the easy one mile walk to Vailsburg from Longfellow Avenue.

Vailsburg was all city employees. It was like the Short Hills of Newark. I remember we moved from Woodside Avenue in North Newark. I was in the fifth grade. Sacred Heart School just opened, the new school, and people referred to Vailsburg as the Short Hills. We were moving on up. It was all city employees. It was cops and firemen, on my street alone we had seven cops and probably about five firemen. Schnering, he lived across the street from me. Across the street next block down was your uncle, he was in the Arson Squad at the time. You had Prachar, across the street from them. It was all cops and fire.

Rosamilia (appointed 1973): I was born and raised in Newark. My earliest memories of the city, I lived on an interesting street. It was one of the last streets at the time that had a stable. I lived on Garside, what they used to call first Garside Street between Seventh Avenue and Sixth Avenue. And in the middle of the block there they had an old stable. So, all the horse drawn carts that carried junk or watermelons or vegetables or rags, whatever kind of thing they were doing, they would all come in and out of there in the morning. And at night come back.

In the summertime, the fire hydrants were opened from early in the morning until late at night. And candy stores, it was an interesting place to grow up. There were a lot of people. It was a poor neighborhood, mostly tenements. There were some smaller buildings on the street, but mostly four-story brick tenements on that street which made it odd because that wasn't typical of the housing. You go a block over and it was mostly two family. You go two blocks over towards Bloomfield Avenue and it was single families and two families. In three blocks it went from like tenements to one or two-family homes.

I was only aware of Macy's. My mother used to take me downtown once in a while. We used to shop in Hahne's or something. Other than that, I wasn't really aware of other parts of the city. I don't know when I passed Orange Street. I don't remember the first time I crossed Orange Street. That's the way it was. Orange Street was across the tracks kind of. You didn't cross it unless you were going downtown.

Morgan (appointed 1973): I moved here when I was about seven years old. So, from that point until I got married in 1974, I was a Newark boy. When I first moved here, I was on Earl Street. I lived there for about two and a half, three years, moved to Summer Avenue, then moved to Woodside Avenue. When I first moved there, Earl Street was a predominantly Jewish area, saw a turn over probably in a matter of six to eight months from overwhelmingly Jewish to predominantly black. It was just like, boom. That was probably '61 going into '62. Because we stayed there for maybe eight months after that, finished school. Then I moved to Summer Avenue and I was in sixth grade. Summer Avenue was a whole new experience. We had the Boy's Club around the corner. That was like a home away from home. Quiet neighborhood. Left there went to Woodside Avenue. Same thing with Woodside Avenue. Quiet, at that time I was a little older, so I got involved with hanging on the corner and things like that. But pretty quiet.

Brownlee (appointed 1973): I used to spend summers in Newark, up in Vailsburg. Everybody else went to the county. My mother sent me to Vailsburg to be with my uncle, so he could straighten me out. It was great. We used to go down by this bar. Steal beer out the back door. We used to go to Elwood Park in East Orange. They used to throw us out of there all the time. They'd tell us you're from Newark, get out of here. We played baseball on a field that was right near South Orange Avenue. Not Vailsburg Park, it was up further. There was a bar right next door to the field and a Carvel Ice Cream. It was Carvel or Dairy Queen. It was right next to it almost. We used to go to Stanley Theater, sneak in on the second floor. We'd play basketball over by the projects. My uncle lived right across the street on Munn Avenue. That's where I met Jack Hanrahan when I was a kid. I knew them and Gene Brenner. We all hung out over there. Figler's was the candy store by South Orange Avenue. The Caseys used to live over there. Mike Casey, Jimmy Casey. And I used to hang with them. Good times. A lot of good times.

My grandfather lived on South Sixteenth Street right by South Orange Avenue. And he and my grandmother were the translators for that block because they were German and they spoke German and they spoke English. There were a lot of Germans on the block. The people that lived upstairs from him were Italian. But there were a lot of Italians and a lot of Germans on that block. My grandfather had a candy store in the middle of the block, but that was before I was born.

I enjoyed Newark. I loved Newark. It was beautiful. We used to run along the roofs and everything. We had a good time over there.

J.P. Ryan (appointed 1973): I loved the city when I was growing up. It was great fun. I used to walk back and forth to school on South Orange Avenue. As a kid of seven or eight we thought nothing of telling our parents that we were going to go downtown, get a movie, and we would ride on the 31 Dover Street down and go to the movie and come home. Played a lot in Vailsburg Park except when the Army camp was there during the Korean War. Hardly anybody remembers that. There was an entire Army camp in Vailsburg Park during the Korean War and there were quite a number of soldiers that were there.

Vailsburg was a great place to grow up. I enjoyed it thoroughly. It was loaded with cops and firemen. We lived in the projects on North Munn

Avenue for seven years of my existence and then we moved up to 85 Monticello where we remained the rest of the time, right on the corner of Marian and Monticello. My grandfather lived next door. Denny Carry, Director of Public Safety lived immediately behind us.

I still had a lot of friends down in the projects and we used to go down and play. It was more open spaces in Vailsburg Park and it was easier to get down there than it was to go up to Ivy Hill Park. We thought nothing of walking around. There was a great hobby store on the corner of Alexander and South Orange. Picked up models, used to build models there. My dad used to work part time in Sussex Brake on the corner of Munn and South Orange. So, we were constantly back and forth. That was another reason I was going down to that area to play in the park. The park was great. It was wide open and a nice park, except when the Army was there. They had big search light trucks and everything.

Perdon (appointed 1974): The city was all I knew. I didn't know anything else. We were the type of people who didn't have money. So, even our vacations were like they weren't there. Newark was my whole life. I went to Essex Catholic. I went to a Catholic grammar school. Then I went to Essex Catholic High. Everything was all Newark related. I thought it was really fine. Like I said, I knew nothing else. I didn't even know what Vailsburg was like. That was on the other side of that wall. My life was on that side of the wall. Until I came on the fire department, well I went into the service in between, but then the fire department. That was it. We had the riots, '67, other than that, normal growing up type of experiences.

Bisogna (appointed 1974): I grew up in Vailsburg. I got married. I lived there for a couple of years after I came on the job. I had a lot of friends in Vailsburg. Tree lined streets, a lot of kids hanging out. At the playground where I hung out there were thirty, forty, fifty guys. Sometimes three o'clock in the morning, you'd go by there, there'd be forty people standing there. We always used to kid around, you punched in, punched out. We'd come and hang out and punched a clock, put your hours in for the day. It was a good place to grow up.

We had a reunion not too long ago at Cryan's up in South Orange. I'll bet you there were three hundred people. A lot of them were from my year or right around my year. Just seeing people twenty-five years later, it would have been nice if the neighborhood could have been sustained; everybody buying homes in the area because it was like Cheers. You went to Cryan's and all your friends were sitting at the table. If you went to the next bar, you knew a group of guys there. It was fun to grow up like that, have a place to hang out. Not making bars as being the place to be, but there was more of a social aspect to it. Knowing a lot of people is always fun. Vailsburg was nice. The homes were well kept. It was a working-class neighborhood, a lot of cops and firemen, Irish, Italian.

Ricca: (appointed 1974) North Newark where I grew up on Montclair Avenue right down from Summer was probably the greatest place in the world to live. I'm sure all of us who came from certain sections believe that. But there was Elliot Street School a block away for the playground. Of course, we played stick ball in the street even though the playground was around the corner. Branch Brook Park was two to three blocks away. There was an old church, called the old Italian Church for no other reason but to call it the old Italian Church. That was on Summer Avenue and there were two lots. We played in the church lot. We played there from morning until night. Eventually they knocked the church down and built the thing known now as the Immaculate Conception Church on Woodside and Montclair.

But you couldn't get in trouble because from my house to the lot I had to pass three or four relatives houses, two neighbors who were close friends and a couple of neighbors that weren't close friends, but if you did something wrong you either got reprimanded by the neighbor or got whacked by him, because that's how they were back then. The families were very close. It was nothing for your aunt to wind up and whack you if you were doing wrong. A few times it happened to me. That changed. That's I think the main reason why the cities and even the suburbs aren't what they used to be.

We used to go to the bakery on Summer Avenue with a nickel and buy a loaf of Italian bread. Bring it to the butcher across the street, for a quarter he'd fill it with spiced ham and cheese, and for thirty cents you had two or three guys eating off a sandwich. A huge, big old sandwich and then if you bought mustard, the butcher would keep it in his refrigerator for you, put it on your sandwich when you went in the next time. The butcher lived down the block too.

From Broadway up to I guess Mount Prospect Avenue or Clifton Avenue was considered North Newark. Then above Clifton was considered Forest Hill. That's where you go trick or treating on Halloween because you got true nickel candy bars. If you went out with a girl from Forest Hill you were considered doing good. The rivalry always came between Elliot Street School which is on Summer Avenue and Ridge Street School which is on Ridge Street. I had that go round and round with Bobby Testa over that. That he was one of the rich kids from Ridge Street and we were the poor kids down in the valley. But predominantly, I'd say the neighborhood I grew up in was 90% Italian at the time, from store owners to street sweepers.

People think I'm crazy, but I remember when the rag man came by and had a horse. I'm forty-seven, but the rag man came by with his horse to pick up rags. The umbrella man would come ringing the bell as he walked the street, sharpening your knives and fixing your umbrella. The fish man, the soda man, there was a Jewish fellow who came by, March is his last name. I can't think of his first name, but he actually opened the back of his truck and put steps up and he would walk the women in and out of his truck and sold clothing right from the back of his truck. The Fuller brush man, you couldn't wait for one of these salesmen to come to the house because they would give you a whistle or something crazy, trying to sell your mother a vacuum cleaner or whatever the wares were. I guess as I got into my teens the neighborhood started to change with a little mix of mostly Hispanic.

The Blue Max was the big gang around then. If they came walking into your neighborhood, they had their colors on, it was almost like the Westside Story going back. Where, they would only walk in pairs in our neighborhood. We were only supposed to walk in pairs in their neighborhood, the whole turf thing. When I look back at it, the stupidity of it, but it was just the way things were. Every corner had its own gang. I guess my generation grew out of wearing the colors, the vest with the insignia on the back, but my brothers went through that. Angelo, God rest his soul, with his group used to wear motorcycle jackets and motorcycle hats and not one of them had a motorcycle. But that was the way they dressed. I guess the Marlon Brando look. I don't even know the name of the movie he was in, but Marlon Brando had the cap with the motorcycle jacket.

Back then it was a one car family. You had to take a bus, so the only time I ventured out of the area was on bike; we used to take bicycle runs. Everybody would have a bike, jump on it. I'm ashamed to say I was so used to just being in my neighborhood, I got lost on Mill Street in Belleville. We had a half dozen of us on bikes. We were at Mill Street where it hits Belleville Avenue and there was a pizzeria on the corner. We stood there almost in tears wondering how we were going to get home because nobody remembered the route we took. But we would go down near Seventh Avenue. That was a shopping center back then. It was closer than downtown and the bus was a nickel. We used to call it the cheap Charlie bus. It was the Eighteen. It was five cents. It was independent transit and every Friday my mother would take me and my sister down. You'd go to McCrory's because you couldn't eat meat on Friday if you were Catholic. You'd have a slice of pizza or they had a fish fry and you would go shopping there. But usually on a close run you'd go down by Seventh Avenue and Bloomfield Place where Petskin's is and they had everything you wanted there. You didn't have to go downtown. But a Friday would be the trek to downtown for the pizza and fish fry via bus.

My mother sewed. She's a very good sewer and there was a fabric shop there down near Seventh Avenue. During the week if she needed anything, she'd send me out. Bloomfield Avenue was my limit. I couldn't cross Bloomfield Avenue until I was about fifteen.

Restrictions were put on you back then. The big thing was when you got your license. Being a good Italian, you'd put your parking lights on. You'd hang your hand out the window and give the gangster lean. You would start at the Dairy Queen and if you drove at thirty-five miles an hour you'd beat every light up to Bloomfield where you made a turn. You went to Willie's State Diner, had cake, you came back down and made the loop again. The same people that were hanging on each corner on Bloomfield Avenue when you went up were there when you came down. It was just a series of beeping the horn and waving and seeing who knew the most people. You couldn't wait. It was almost inbred in every kid that I grew up with. As soon as you got your license, pop, your parking lights went on and you just headed for the Avenue.

I got my license in 1970. I wasn't even allowed to be in a friend's car until I was sixteen. My friend Billy Shadle, I'll never forget the kid, phenomenal baseball player. He got a '63 Riviera and that's all we ever did was drive up and down Bloomfield Avenue. And at the end of the night, I'd give him a dollar for gas. He'd put a dollar in and we'd get a half a tank of gas. Because they had the price wars, every gas station was thirty cents, twenty-nine cents, a quarter.

But as a young kid, leaving the area, you didn't have to. You went to school in your neighborhood so all your friends were in the neighborhood. Like now my kids have friends all over the map, all over the town of Bloomfield which is a pretty decent size town. But back then you kind of stayed in your group. It was like the Little Rascals almost. You had a nick name for everybody. People didn't have a whole lot of money then, so it wasn't like now. Most of the time, when lunch was called you headed home. Everybody went to their own houses, ate and fifteen minutes later everybody was back.

The part of Branch Brook Park known as the extensions or the four diamonds as we called it, the four baseball fields, that's where you'd be most of the summer. You'd be in the early morning up there playing ball. There was no Little League. Nothing organized. You'd make teams up. Put a screw in a bat that broke, wooden bat then, not aluminum. You'd tape the hardball together and you played. Then you'd come down after you ate supper. You'd go local, to the church lot, and you'd hang out there for the rest of the night. People sat on their porches so coming in at eleven, twelve at night was no big deal because as long as your parents were on the porch you were allowed to be out. That's how I was brought up.

Daly (appointed 1978): When I was growing up in North Newark, it was majority white. In the 60s it changed. I remember getting a phone call from my uncle and telling us to get ready to get out of the city of Newark. And I couldn't understand what he was saying. He goes, "When your father gets home, have your bags packed, ready to go." My uncle was a sergeant in the Police Department and he was on duty at the station where they threw the mailbox through the window and it landed on his desk. That's when Newark started changing to me. It changed drastically. When growing up, it was predominantly white. There were some black kids around. I went to high school in Essex Catholic on Broadway. I had a mix in there. It was predominantly white, but you still had a mix. But in my neighborhood in North Newark predominantly white Italian, heavy Italian.

Gesualdo: (appointed 1978) Well, everything was regional back then. In those days you had your Italian section, your Irish section, your black section. I grew up in the Italian section, which was North Newark where the old First Ward was as they called it. I remember it being pleasant. I had a good time. Everybody around there was family basically. People next door, across the street, down the block, never any problems. If you had a situation that you needed help, you just knocked at anybody's door. I remember people on the streets at night, sitting on porches, having little groups, not gangs, but little groups of guys that hung together. Occasional problems, you know, sneaking the smokes, the drinking, things like that, but pretty much it was a normal childhood, a lot of athletics, playing stickball in the street and porch ball, football in the corner lot. So, pretty much a normal neighborhood from what I knew until I started branching out and getting my license and finding out what the other sections of Newark were like. I mean, if you go to Vailsburg, it was a trek or to go Down Neck was a kind of experience because it was a totally different environment than you were used to. But I don't remember too many places going back in the late '50s, early '60s where there were many problems. It was a great upbringing. You had all your cousins and friends around you all the time, family. So, it was a good place to grow up. Lot of good restaurants.

Hopkins (appointed 1978): I grew up in Newark on Mountview Place. That's in Vailsburg. It was off of Sanford Avenue, right around the corner from the old Cryan's. It was a lot of fun. Everything was there. You walked to the corner store. You got your milk and bread. Half the guys I came on the job with and a lot of people I knew I grew up with. Half the block was cops or firemen. You had Deluca was a fireman. He was out of Four Engine. Had Roger Bacon. He was out of Two Engine then he went to the Arson Squad. You had Rich Dijewski. He was in Eleven Truck. My father and there were a couple of cops on the block. And it was a small block. It was only maybe fifteen, twenty houses on the block.

J. Prachar (appointed 1978): Greatest place in the world. Had a couple of problems here and there. '67, '68 we had some riots and fires. Got mugged a few times when I was a kid living on Dayton Street. But my younger years were kind of tough living on Dayton Street. We were one of the few white families down there. We were on Dayton Street during the riots. Right across the street from our house was where the old race track was and that's where the National Guard camped out after they brought them into town. So we had this huge bivouac area across the street. We'd see the National Guard come out with the fifty caliber machine guns mounted on the back, going out on patrol. I'm like, "Oh, okay. Maybe we should stay in the house." And I remember playing in Weequahic Park in 1968. My dad was home. I think he was on vacation. We're playing baseball and I remember looking up and seeing this huge, huge black cloud. And that was the day of the Bergen Street fire, Bergen and Avon. And my dad taking off and I guess I didn't see him until sometime the next day when he came home. I think he slept for about two days straight. But I remember seeing that cloud.

Then in '71 we moved up to the Burg and that was the greatest neighborhood in the world to live in. You walked everywhere you wanted to go. It was a great place. You could still play football in the street. Most of the kids I went to grammar school with up there, their fathers were either cops or firemen.

Sandella (appointed 1978): I grew up on Garside Street. They called it third Garside. Going from Sixth Avenue towards Bloomfield Avenue I was the third Garside. So they called it third Garside. I grew up there until I got married in 1980. It was great. It was a real fun place to grow up, a very close-knit neighborhood. The schools, catechism, all that, all those experiences were good. A lot of fun, a lot of experiences, playground activities, a little mischief, nothing really serious. It was just a real nice experience growing up in that environment, in that neighborhood setting. I find it interesting today. It's organized. Everything is organized. The kids don't make anything on their own. We were always organizing things and playing other neighborhoods. It was just great. I loved it. I'm so happy I had the opportunity to grow up in the city during that period of time.

I wasn't really familiar with other parts of the city. I was further up north towards Bloomfield area on First Avenue. I used to go there. I'd walk up to Branch Brook Park, but pretty much the North Ward. I didn't get out of there too much. As a matter of fact, it could be very possible my first day at Six Engine which was probably my second or third shift on the job was the first time I ever went past Orange Street going south. At that time, I was twenty-four years old and I had no reason to ever go past that way.

My little world of growing up was my neighborhood, so I didn't really know too much or care for that matter about the demographics of the city. I just knew that there were issues based on the riots growing up. Different things that were going on between black, whites and it started to affect me in junior high school. At Webster Junior High School, I really started to see that there were different factions out there that felt differently about me and people like me. I really didn't have much of that growing up, believe it or not, in my neighborhood. But when I got to Webster, I realized that this was a lot more serious after the riots. My first year in high school was 1968 at Barringer. It was not a learning experience. It wasn't a learning environment. It was a hostile environment. Constant fighting, blacks and whites. It carried on for quite a while, a couple years at least. So high school was difficult. It wasn't conducive to learning very much during those times. So, the city changed after junior high school. That utopia that I spoke of before, that growing up, being a great experience was kind of tarnished from what occurred in '67.

Zieser (appointed 1978): I grew up around the corner from you in the Vailsburg section of Newark. I lived on Tenth Street until I was about seven or eight years old and then we moved to Vailsburg. My grandmother lived in Vailsburg. My father grew up on Tenth Street in the house that we lived in. It was a two-family house. We lived with my grandparents in that house. My mother grew up in Vailsburg. When we moved to Vailsburg we moved two or three blocks from her mother's house. I loved growing up in Vailsburg. I thought it was a great. It was a good working-class neighborhood. It seemed that over half of Vailsburg worked for the city in some capacity or other. It was a neighborhood that everybody knew one another. You knew everyone's name on the block. You knew what they did for a living. You knew their kids. You see them at church. You see them where ever. If I could do that again with my children, I would have brought my kids up the same way.

When you grow up in the city, when the street lights come on you got to come in the house. And you'd always see one that was later than the others and you'd get in a little trouble. "No, see that one down the street mom, that one's not on." That one's burned out maybe, that's not on.

Since my father was a fireman, he worked ten-hour days and fourteen-hour nights. He always made it a point to come home and eat dinner with the family. He felt it was important. He probably ate in the firehouse too, but he always wanted to eat with the family. So, growing up we would have early day dinner and late day dinner. It was determined by whether my father was going into the firehouse or coming home from the firehouse. So, if he's coming home, it's a late dinner and if he's going to the firehouse, it's an early dinner. And my mother would say, it's an early night tonight or it's a late night tonight. You knew what time to be home to sit down with the family and eat.

Witte (appointed 1978): I was born and raised in Newark, in the North Ward, around Ballantine Parkway and Clifton. Ballantine and Clifton. My childhood was fun. I went to Our Lady of Good Council for seven years. And then I went up to Newark Academy in Livingston for four years. Then after tenth grade my father said, "Okay time to go back. You can go down to Essex Catholic." So, I spent the last two years in Essex Catholic which was good. I got to see a lot of different things.

I thought I knew North Newark, but after getting on the job I found out there's a lot of North Newark I didn't know, a lot of different places. It's a big town. It's just amazing the different places and different things that you really see. Sometimes the conditions are good, sometimes the conditions are bad. It's the people that make the difference with how the place looks and doesn't look. Didn't matter who they were.

Kormash (appointed 1979): I grew up Down Neck. It was great pre-1967. '67 was an exodus out of the city of Newark and the following years after that. Then my whole area, a block at a clip, changed. 95% of the people just left.

I was totally aware of other areas of the city. I used to go to every one of these things, played sports and everything all over the city. Mainly baseball.

Caufield (appointed 1980): What was Newark like growing up? Oh, it was fabulous. It's an experience I wouldn't trade. I have friends I went to kindergarten with that still keep in touch with me and me with them. It was a fantastic neighborhood. When I was growing up there were two sections of Newark in my little map, downtown where Bamberger's and everything else used to be and Vailsburg. And there were no in betweens and there was no Ironbound section no North Ward until I got older. Then we started venturing out a little more. But I absolutely loved growing up in Vailsburg. I absolutely did.

The main road through the Burg was South Orange Avenue and it was Eighteenth Avenue to the south of that. It was side streets, neighborhoods, groups that hung on each corner. Some guys out there just singing Doo-wop music and some guys looking for trouble. There was a little bit of everything going on in Vailsburg at the time. And I grew up on Norwood Street. If you did something that you weren't supposed to be doing, somebody saw you and you paid for it. But even as kids we would help the older women carry their groceries home. It was a good environment to be in. You learned respect. You gave respect. It was a good thing.

Vailsburg was mostly white, Irish, Italian, Polish, a working-class area. Not too much black at the time. Not too much Hispanic at the time, when I was younger. But there were kind of boundaries and there were problems. You pretty much stayed in your neighborhood and other ethnicities stayed in their neighborhood. And if you were somewhere where you weren't supposed to be, you found out about it real soon.

F. Bellina (appointed 1981): I grew up in Newark. I was born in 1958 in Irvington General Hospital. That's where my mother's doctor was. And we lived on Fifteenth Avenue and Nineteenth Street on the third floor. My whole family lived on the first floor, second floor. My grandmother lived on the first floor. My aunt lived on the second floor, my father's side of the family. And we lived on the third floor. I went to South Seventeenth Street School. I lived there during the riots. We had the National Guard on the corner. And I lived there until like I believe it was 1970 or '71. We moved to Vailsburg. I guess my father felt that it was time to go. I was still going to South Seventeenth Street School. I would walk to school. And then we moved to Vailsburg and I felt out of place. When I moved to Vailsburg and I went to Lincoln School, it was not with the same mix. It was mainly white kids. Where I came from, South Seventeenth Street School, it was different. I looked at life a little bit different than they did. I wound up getting into fights. I wound up getting into arguments. I wasn't really accepted. And I didn't do well in school at that point. I really had a hard time there. I went to Vailsburg High School for maybe two years then I quit school. I decided to join the Marines.

Newark was two different cities to me. When I left Fifteenth Avenue, that was one city. When I went from Fifteenth Avenue up to Vailsburg, that was a whole other country. It was like a whole other city that I really had a hard time with. I didn't understand some of the things that were going on. I found it hard to settle in.

Wapples (appointed 1982) I was born in Newark and I grew up there. My impression of the city of Newark as I was growing up was, I just took it as a big melting pot. That people got along and it was a nice place to live. And after the riots came in and ravaged the town, it left a lot to be desired. The town was just left in shambles. Back during that time, I must have been about seven, eight, nine, I saw a lot of tearing up of the local stores and the areas. I remember the Afro-Americans coming together. It was the era of black power, the clenched fist coming up in the air. And let's come together, be together. It was back during the '68 period, '67, '68 period when Martin Luther King was living. And part of the riots that we did have was dealing with his death. Prior to that, in '67 we had an incident in here with a taxi cab driver. The following year, '68 we had a riot after to Martin Luther King's death.

As a child, basically what I do remember is seeing the armor cars coming up and down the street, tanks, the National Guard, State Police. And they brought a lot of problems into this town. They were shooting up at people's windows. They were shooting at windows, shooting up the windows. I saw the police running to the liquor stores, filling their cars up with stuff. And just apathy all the way around with the Afro-Americans and the non-Afro-Americans. People were taking advantage of an opportunity, who weren't Afro-Americans and African-Americans destroying their own neighborhood by taking and ravaging, destroying stores, their means of survival basically. After the riots they had to go outside of Newark to do their shopping and stuff because there weren't any stores really left within the community in which they lived. They had to go a distance to secure the things that they wanted that they used to go a block or two away. So, it wasn't productive. It was counterproductive all the way around.

It was anger. It brought a lot of disharmony within the people. We were going through the struggle of human rights back during that time with ML King. It brought blacks together as a people. But the riots also destroyed their environment, too. It brought people together to some point because they had a struggle, a fight with a common cause. Anytime you have adversity of any kind it brings people together. As opposed to you going in this direction; he's going in the other direction; and she's going in that direction. So, it brought people together, but it did a lot of damage too.

I've seen the city when it was an up-and-coming city and I've seen it when it went down, but now it appears to be coming back in the downtown area. Hopefully they'll do something within the inner city to bring it back to where it was when I was a little younger and the way I remember it being a productive town.

E. Griffith (appointed 1983): I grew up in Vailsburg. It was a great neighborhood. I started out on Alexander Street, went to kindergarten there. At that time, you're five years old I guess, I thought that I walked miles to Alexander Street School. I lived on 99. I probably walked about ten houses to get there. I went there and then I went to Sacred Heart. While I was going to Sacred Heart my mom used to walk me up there. That was a bit of walk. We did a small stint, six months, on Unity Avenue. Different neighborhood, but we were in a house instead of being in a two and a half story frame. Then in '69 we moved up to Ivy Street where I spent the rest of my life, between Eastern and Kerrigan. Really nice neighborhood, great friends, we'd walk to school. You know people don't do that today. Vailsburg High School had just changed. I think it was a middle school or something like that and it had changed to high school. I can remember the football team running up past my house to go practice in Ivy Hill Park. We had two beautiful parks.

I can remember as a kid, my mom taking us around the corner to Mount Vernon Place, getting on the bus, taking us down to Bamberger's to go shopping. That was a whole day, I mean she'd start at Bamberger's and I think we ended up in Hahne's. And at some point, we'd end up at one of the counters where we'd have a lunch or something and you'd spend the whole day. I didn't like it, but you were down there and then you'd get back on the bus and take the bus up and every now and then you'd go past a different street and you'd look over and see a burned-out building. Wow, look at that. And as a little kid, the wheels start turning. But you could do that.

You could walk the neighborhood. Kids went out and played. The street light came on, and as a young kid, the street light came on that was your time to go home. You hung out in the playground. You went in and there was a rec supervisor. You had your little tag. You hung it up. You took out your basketball, your softball bat, or knock hockey game and you turn it back in. People knew you on the street basically from church, going to church. You could never get away with anything because on every block somebody knew your parents and they'd say, "Hey he's doing this." You don't see that now. Now kids do play dates. They set up and they go someplace. My mom never knew where I was. Well, you'd be up in Ivy Hill Park. You'd be in Vailsburg Park. You'd walk all over the place.

There were little neighborhoods, but you could walk all over. I knew that if I walked over to Mount Vernon and Eastern Parkway, there's a group of guys there. Lincoln School had its group that hung out. The back of Vailsburg High had a playground there. There were people there. There was a whole group that hung out on South Orange Avenue. And those were all spots I could walk around and hook up with friends for whatever adventure we were going to take on that day or that evening. Walking up to South Mountain Reservation. Then found out you could take the train and try to get away from the conductors. Running away from them. Well, if I start here and he starts chasing me, by the time we get to Millburn we're there.

By the time I got to high school, Vailsburg High was really starting to get rough, really rough. Matter of fact, my good friend Davy Kraemer, when we left Sacred Heart, he ended up going to Vailsburg and there were stories. He got beat up every day. They took his lunch money and beat the hell out of him. They took his lunch money every day. His family ended up moving to Sparta. And we lost contact and then later on low and behold we ended up meeting back on the fire department years later.

I remember stopping at McDonald's. That was a big deal, coming to Vailsburg, the McDonald's. I played Little League football down at Vailsburg Park. We had to walk down there. Every now and then you wanted to get out of there before dark because it got a little rough. But it was nowhere near what everybody's talking about today. For the most part, the neighborhood was great. I think back, Cryan's and Paul's Tavern which I worked in. I worked in Paul's Tavern, Friday and Saturday. Worked in the Varsity Inn too. It's a neighborhood place and the way I thought, if I could work at the place, well I was out. I was bartending or I was bouncing, I was out with the crowd, but I was making money. That's how I got to know a lot of people. You become, "Woo, you're the bartender." Big deal. But I made a lot of money in that business. I even I did it with the fire department. I stopped it because it just got crazy. You're getting out three, four in the morning and then trying to go to work the next day and that wasn't good. But for the most part I loved Vailsburg.

Giordano (appointed 1984): Growing up in Newark, I remember the early '60s, Franklin School on Park Avenue, Webster Junior High. Very diverse, the area I was in, mostly Italian and Irish. We were all poor, but nobody knew it. We all had families, so it was a lot different for us. You had your aunt upstairs, your uncle down the street, your friend's mother making the food. Most of the people from our area, they didn't have anything. So, you've got people today, they're getting sneakers for three hundred dollars. Our parents said, "You're going to Two Guys. You're getting Keds for two ninety-nine ($2.99)." I'd say with how low the salaries were for firemen in '84, '85 at twenty-three to twenty-six thousand. Can't imagine what our parents were making then. The money had to be so much lower. Like I said, the family structure was different. You had a participating mother, father, grandmother, aunt, the support system was there, even with your neighbors. It was a different time and place.

My school was a traditional public school. Other people went to Catholic school. Seems they fared much better. Things were stricter. It's like going to a charter school today. You're going to do better if you go to a charter school, a big percentage do much better. It's strict so you have to do it. The parents have to participate. It's a funny thing you say with the education. What I saw when I was fire union president and when I was director and got to see where people were. I could tell, just looking through, who went to parochial school, who went to public school. It just stood out. It doesn't make them good firemen. Not all qualified people have it. Either you have it or you don't.

Growing up I only knew my own geographical area of the North Ward, of the neighborhood. I would say from Broadway to the top of Park Avenue, Bloomfield Avenue more over to the Forest Hills section and the Basilica. That was pretty much the area that I knew. I don't think I ever went past Orange Street going south to the Central Ward, West Ward. Maybe at times I was in Vailsburg or Central, Weequahic Park or Untermann Field during high school football or Track and Field or whatever the event was to watch. I was totally unfamiliar. It was a whole new world for me being there. The Ironbound I kind of knew parts of, but not too much. I only knew Ironbound Stadium, guys that we played ice hockey with, Ferry Street and Wilson Avenue. The Ironbound, it takes a long time to learn the streets and things down there. But later on in my career that's where I did the last ten or twelve years of union work.

O. Johnson (appointed 1984) I grew up on South Twelfth Street, 836 South Twelfth Street between Madison and Clinton Avenue. So I know that entire area. I'm very familiar. We didn't have all the games, but we played. Even though I was surrounded by so much negativity and everybody wanted to be in drugs, everybody wanted to be in gangs. That wasn't me. That was my choice that I made. I wanted to become something. Police officers back in the day. They knew all the kids. They knew the kids who were problems. They knew the other ones.

Arce (appointed 1984): I grew up in Newark. I came here in 1965. I was four, five years old. '67 the riots, I remember running into the grocery stores with military and the police. I grew up poor. Being a kid who doesn't know English; I'm poor; is very tough, a lot of emotional stuff going in your mind. I grew up in the four corners of Newark. My family would move every year and a half to somewhere else. I went through about maybe ten schools in Newark. Miller Street, Hawthorne Avenue, Clinton Place, Bragaw Annex, Bragaw Avenue, Webster, Barringer, Burnett Street School, West Runyon. So I went to every school in Newark. I went to two schools in one year. They didn't know my attendance, one day here one day there, from Hawthorne to Clinton Place, until they caught me. It was just terrible. To me it was the worst thing. I only remember two good teachers and they both were mathematical teachers. Everything else was like terrible. The school system was not the best.

N. Bellina (appointed 1986): As I remember I think the avenues were cobble stone and the side streets were brick. Because we used to play on Fifteenth Avenue and it was cobble stone. I'm almost positive most of avenues were cobble stone. I know the side streets at that time, Nineteenth Street, Eighteenth Street, they were all brick. I remember that. I used to take the bus, I think I was eight, seven or eight years old, to see my mother down at Bamberger's. I'd take the number 1 bus down Sixteenth Avenue.

I went to Seventeenth Street School. Fifteenth Avenue School was actually closer than Seventeen Street School. Fifteenth Avenue School was at Fifteenth Avenue and Fifteenth Street. I had to go Seventeenth Avenue and Seventeenth Street because they divided it up into districts and you couldn't go to another school back then. You had to go to the school you were assigned to.

Seventeenth Street School was great at the time. It was a great school, but after the riots in '67, somebody came up with the brain storm in the '68 school year to start the bussing, two busses out of Seventeenth Street went to Newton Street School. Now they're sending me and two busses of white kids to Newton Street School. Now Newton Street in '68, the other side of the street is where all the vacant buildings were that they took down for University Hospital, all the buildings were there. It was vacant. It was nasty over there.

Our first day we went down there they bombed the school busses with bottles and rocks because they knew what was happening. They had to have us eat lunch at a different time because they would have torn us up. This is a year after the riots. They didn't want to see any white kids down there. I think after the riots it changed. There was an article in the paper. After they did that bussing, they said something about thirty thousand white families leaving Newark in one year. You had to because you had to go to this school. Well after the riots happened, they weren't. They left and went to Bloomfield, Nutley, Maplewood. We went to Vailsburg. The schools were involved in that. You were taking out of Seventeenth Street School maybe six buses loaded with kids and they would go. And six busloads of blacks would come in. That was citywide. That went on. When parents see that, "Hey my kid's not going here. He's on a bus, ten miles away in a black school. Pew, I'm gone." And that's why a lot of apartments and buildings got vacated. They were gone. Just packed up and left.

But before the riots happened, it might have been early '67, I would have to go to Saint Ann's, my mother's parish, down on Seventh Street and Sixteenth Avenue. So I would leave to go to catechism at three o'clock from Seventeenth Street School. I'd cut through West Side Park, now I'm on Twelfth Street, and run down Sixteenth Avenue because that was all black down there. Five o'clock came around and you got out. It was dark. I had to run all the way up to Fifteenth Avenue and Nineteenth Street. I can't tell you how many times I got chased. It was scary.

Back in '66, '67 the black area was probably starting below Tenth Street. Then it was getting heavier as you went down. Littleton Avenue, Camden. There were still white people living in there, but it was changing. It was tough. What happened was real quick like right after January, it was me and another kid, Harry Chrystal, a Puerto Rican friend of mine, on the bus with the teacher and the driver. That was it. Everybody started taking their kids out of school. The teacher got back on after lunch. Gave me twenty cents to take the bus on South Orange Avenue and said, "Go home. Tell your mother you're not coming back cause I'm not coming back." Exactly what he said to me. "I'm done." So that was it. I stayed out for a couple of weeks and they got me into Saint Rocco's on Thirteenth Street. We moved to Vailsburg the next year. I was able to go to Lincoln School in Vailsburg.

Ch. Centanni (appointed 1986): In a lot of ways when I was growing up in the North Ward it was a predominantly Italian neighborhood. Really you didn't know there was another world out there. You basically had everything you wanted in ten blocks of walking distance. There were shopping centers, delis, A & Ps, coffee, anything you needed was on Bloomfield Avenue. So that's really basically what I knew of the city. My father was a plumber and I worked with him. So there were times when we worked up in the Vailsburg area, Sanford Avenue area, Orange Street area, but I guess I was either not paying attention or too young to even understand where I was or understand that area. But we did work over there a little, so when I got in the fire department and I wound up on Springfield Avenue, I needed directions to get there. And my uncle was a hot dog guy in Newark. He used to sell hotdogs. So he sent me the directions. He wrote them down for me, gave us a dry run. He sent me to the firehouse with a pretty good way to get there. But to your question, I didn't know the rest of the city existed the way it did. One of the things I did know. My grandmother was a lifelong Newarker. She used to always tell us about Springfield Avenue and Clinton Avenue and how that was like the hub of the world. Downtown, Broad Street, you could get anything you wanted in Newark in its heyday in the '40s. So I knew that part of it and I knew the stories of the riots on Springfield Avenue and all.

Goetchius (appointed 1986): Growing up in Vailsburg, the early years I can remember it was pretty sheltered. I didn't even realize we lived in a big city. I didn't know my way outside of Mead Street and Commonwealth Avenue. We basically didn't leave our four or five block area. And until the '80s we really didn't see a big change. I wasn't there then. I was out of town. But looking back I believe there were definite differences. There was a big step of people going out of town from that area.

I don't remember going downtown to shop. If my parents did shop in an area like that they would go to Irvington or even South Orange Avenue. And even going to a supermarket, there weren't too many supermarkets around, have to go to Irvington. Around Christmas time they might go to Livingston Mall.

I can remember going to that one theater in Vailsburg. Then it was transformed into a like little theater for acting and stuff like that. I used to go there for class things and they used to give things away. There were too many things that were in there, Halloween, things like that.

Lee (appointed 1986): I initially came up from the South in 1970. I was living in the Central Ward right around the corner from Six Engine on Morris Avenue which was notorious for fires when I came up to Jersey from Georgia. We don't see fires like that in Georgia. So, it was like wow. It was really something. My grandparents at that point had raised me and I was very upset because I had to leave and come up to here where my mother was. I had a real negative impression of the city because most of my life I was in Georgia with my grandparents. So, it was an entirely different world even to the point of the way they talked. Down South has a different slang than up here, so it made it difficult for me to fit in because of my speech. So, my initial impression was not that great of Newark.

I grew up in the Central Ward until I was in the eleventh grade and in the eleventh grade we moved into the East Ward. The Central Ward at that time was one of the poorest and most poverty-stricken wards in the city of Newark. Actually, the riots on West Kinney Street were not too far from where I actually grew up. That area never recovered from the riots, so it was pretty rough and pretty tough at a young age coming up in that area. At that time, I had a limited knowledge of North Newark because I had family members that lived in the Walsh Homes in North Newark. That was a project complex off McCarter Highway. So, I knew a little bit about North Newark, but mostly it was Central and East. Those were the areas I was familiar with.

Masters (appointed 1986): I grew up on Avon and Farley, 28 Farley Avenue. I went to Blessed Sacrament School from there. Went to Essex Catholic, took the 13 down to Broadway. And then in the middle of Essex we moved to Kearny. Right after the Martin Luther King riots. In '68 or '69 we moved and that was it. My best times were in Newark, participating in drum and bugle corps over there. It was an unbelievable parish with all the firemen and cops around from Newark. That was when your father or whoever had to live in Newark. And it was just a different atmosphere.

Childhood memories of Newark are fantastic. Come summertime my father and mother would say, "It's a nice day." That's all they had to say. You're out of the house. We would play street football which was like telephone pole to telephone pole. We'd play Wiffle ball. We'd go to the court on Avon Avenue School, play basketball. We had sprinkler caps for the hydrants, believe or not. Every time we used it we used to turn it in. It was just a fantastic place. And the shopping, back then I used to go with my mother to Springfield Avenue. Nobody would bother you, walk to Springfield Avenue where they had all the different shops. When we needed clothes or anything, that was a trip to Newark Slip Company before it burnt down. And Two Guys from Harrison was a trip with the whole family for clothes. Then basically shopping downtown at, back then it was called Bamberger's, Klein's, Two Guys, I mean it was a beautiful place to shop, downtown Newark. People actually knew you because you were a frequent customer. It was a good mixture of people, diverse and nobody bothered you. They looked out for you.

Alexander I (appointed 1987): I was born and raised in Newark. I grew up on Clinton Place. I attended Hawthorne Avenue school. Graduated from Hawthorne and then I attended Weequahic High School. Newark was beautiful. We lived on blocks where everybody knew each other. If I got out of hand or did something wrong, I didn't have to wait for my parents. Trust me, you would get it before you got home. But more importantly, families had respect for one another. We had boundaries and if you crossed them, you knew what was coming, so we were a very disciplined group. We knew we had to stay focused. Get our education. Do the right thing. The main thing was respect and that's what we were taught when we were raised. We grew up with respect. Respecting our elders and not back talking. It's a different generation now days of course, but I enjoyed Newark. It was a lot safer. I thought Newark was a beautiful place. I'll never forget, when my father was at work, my mother would take us downtown Newark. We would see all the farmer markets. We would have picnics by the statue there of Lincoln on the courthouse and things like that. It was really nice.

DeLeon (appointed 1988): I was born and raised in Newark. Born in Martland Hospital, the old building, it's not there anymore. We lived on Bleeker Street and then we lived on Norfolk Street. Growing up in Newark as a kid, it was the greatest place on earth. I used to play on abandoned cars where there was a car fire. I would sit at the steering wheel, turn the wheel, used the brakes, jumping on mattresses.

When I was nine years old, I used to go to this candy store on Norfolk Street with my sister and a couple of kids. I don't know what possessed me to go, but I started running across the street to beat the traffic and I didn't do well. A bus got me good. Broke both my legs, fractured my skull, almost didn't make it. So, it was another lesson that I picked up. Wasn't a good thing.

The city was alright until about my teenage years. I started to know the differences between the suburbs and the urban setting. I know crime was high. My dad had a grocery store on Broadway and he got held up five times at gunpoint. I used to make deliveries on Broad Street, all the gangs used to hang out there. I put myself in very bad positions at times. I could have gotten killed many times. I grew up innocent. I was a quiet kid. I wasn't out there looking for mischief even though there was plenty of it. There was plenty of alcohol. There were plenty of drugs. Plenty of anything if you wanted to do it, but I just never got into that. And I lived in Newark until I came on and then got on the department and moved on from there. My parents have always been in Newark. They've been in Newark their whole life. My mother still lives there. She's going to be eighty-seven in April. She's in the North Ward.

I went to a Catholic school. Maybe that's what helped me. Good Counsel was a block away. I walked to school. The nuns were tough. But I was also like a clown. So, they would take the ruler, bring me out in the hallway, smack my hands a couple of times with it. I had to write on the board, "I will not do this." a hundred times, had a lot of discipline. But you wore a shirt and tie. From there I went to Bloomfield Tech. It was my only exposure to something different from Catholic school. There was no public school from grades one through eight. I didn't know that environment.

My parents lived in the city, but they kept me kind of in the bubble. So, I was kind of clueless. I'm glad they did that because if I had been introduced to something else, I might have had a record and may not have come on the job. All this stuff snowballed. When you reflect on it, you say, "Wow, yeah. I could have been just another statistic, number, or problem and doing everything." That's a tough environment though. I see it now.

Greene (appointed 1988): I didn't grow up in Newark. My father was in the service. I was born in New Mexico. Then we lived in Germany, Texas. Then we came to New Jersey. When we moved to Newark, I thought it was very exciting. It was like a little New York City. I had cousins who lived in Newark. I lived in and went to school in Newark, but I did not know Newark was that big. That was about the only revelation. I guess probably as far north as I had been was on Park Avenue. I did not know how extensive the Ironbound was and as far as Ivy Hill and the Weequahic sections, those to this day I kind of know the streets, but I haven't been on all of them or know where they are or how they're connected. Sometimes you live in a town, but you live in a compartment. You don't really live in the whole town.

Griggs (appointed 1988): I was born and raised, went to school in Newark, everything, the whole kit and caboodle. The city I knew, I was a North Ward boy. I didn't venture past Park Avenue. So I really didn't know the city. Until that day I was assigned to Springfield Avenue. That was an eye opener. Coming across Park Avenue, I wasn't familiar with Central or the South Ward at all. So, it was all new to me. It was like a side of Newark that I never really saw.

I went to kindergarten on Ridge Street. Grammar school I went to Our Lady of Good Counsel. I went to Seton Hall Prep in South Orange my first two years, but then I transferred to Essex Catholic High School which was on Second and Broadway for my last two years. So, I basically stayed in the North Ward. I really didn't see much of the other wards.

I had a great childhood growing up. I mean to this day I continue to see the kids I went to grammar school with. We had a good time. We hung in Branch Brook Park. I've always been in the Forest Hill area. So that was really nice, growing up. It's still nice today, the homes are really nice over there. I can't recall having a bad childhood. I had great times living and growing up in the city.

My mom and dad are from East Ward. That's where they were raised and grew up. I spent time down there. My grandparents lived on Cortland Place, right adjacent to the Elks Club and I grew up there. They would watch me on weekends, so I was a little bit familiar with the East Ward and the North, but the South, Central, and West I wasn't familiar with at all.

Alvarez (appointed 1989): Growing up in Newark was cool. You could go to the playground every day and get a softball game going if there were enough kids hanging around the playground or basketball or something. Or just go to your friend's house, knock on the door or even just hang out on the steps. Eventually some kids would walk by. "Hey man, want to go to the playground?" Yeah. And we'd just go over to the playground or we'd play man hunt at night. Just hang out, it was what I thought was great for growing up. It made me a street wise kid. You were able to figure out how to get yourself out of a problem. Whether it was an argument or sometimes it wasn't figuring it out, it was just duking it out. We had bicycles and if something broke, your tools were vise-grip and duct tape and you made it work. To this day I find myself a lot of times at incidents, whatever it is, not so much fires.

Fires we fight with water, but other things that we're called upon. Trying to help somebody out of something or trying to make something work. Try to fix something just so it works, where you look around, look on the floor. Maybe you find a piece of metal that you could just bend it and shape it and make something work. And it's not being smart. It's just a product of Newark and you had to make it work. There wasn't the money. We didn't live in a disposable world. "Oh, this doesn't work anymore? Let's go buy another one." No, you had to fix it somehow. You stuck something in it. You did this or did that and you made it work. You found a bike in the garbage on the street, "Oh, my forks are bent. I take the forks off of this bike; take the ball bearings out." I'd figure it out and put it back together and make it work.

I grew up in the Ironbound section and I was pretty much restricted to the Ironbound section. I didn't cross the railroad tracks. They call it the Ironbound because it's surrounded by railroad tracks. And as a kid I used to ride my bike all over the place. I was a heavy bicycle rider with my friends. We knew we didn't cross the railroad tracks. If you crossed the railroad tracks, you would come back walking and maybe with a black eye. You just did not cross those railroad tracks because you were going to get robbed. We had plenty of friends that tried that and sure enough it happened to them. You weren't welcomed on the other side of the railroad tracks. Then I started driving after that and I still didn't cross the railroad tracks. We would go into Harrison or Kearny and we had some friends there. I had cousins there, but we never crossed the railroad tracks.

I remember that when I got my first assignment to Fifteen Engine, I said, "Where is that?" And somebody said, "Park Avenue." I was like, "Where's Park Avenue?" And I remember one of the guys saying to me, "Oh, yeah, you're really a Newarker. You really live in Newark and grew up in Newark." And I'm like, "Yeah, I do. I did." And he goes, "Yeah, right. You don't even know where Park Avenue is." And I was like, "Nope. I had no reason. Once

I started driving, the kids that I knew that crossed the railroad tracks, they went to go get drugs. That was the reason for crossing the railroad tracks. They went to go get drugs and I never did drugs so there was no reason for me to ever go on that side of the railroad tracks. So, no I don't know where Park Avenue is, but I can name every single street in the Ironbound section. So, yeah I am raised in Newark and I did live in Newark."

Cordasco (appointed 1989): I grew up in North Newark off of Bloomfield Avenue on Garside Street. I lived there. Actually, when I was a baby, we lived on North Eleventh Street. But then from like two-ish we lived on Garside. It's funny because I had a lot of family that lived on the block. That's the way it was back then. My grandmother lived three houses away from us, then aunts and uncles throughout the neighborhood. I lived there until I wound up marrying my wife who lived on Park Street, six blocks away.

Up until junior high I went to Summer Avenue School which became Roberto Clemente after he died in the plane crash and they renamed it. From Kindergarten to sixth grade, I was at Summer Avenue School. Seventh grade I was at Broadway and it was bad. There were fights every day, Teachers weren't teaching, so I stayed with my godmother who lived on Richelieu Terrace for six months and went to Lincoln School. Then she wound up going through a divorce so I went back to Broadway. Then my mother and father were divorced. My father had a Bloomfield address. So, I went to Bloomfield High School using my father's address.

Daniels (appointed 1989): I grew up in Newark from the age of twelve. I've been educated in Newark. I've lived in almost every portion of Newark except for Down Neck. I went to Camden Middle School on Camden Street. I went to Central. We moved out for a stretch in Irvington. When I was about eighteen, we moved back. This is my city. I was born in Florida. A place called Coco, Florida, not far from Coco Beach. But Newark is my home.

It was tough when I was growing up. First of all, I had a loving mother, a diligent father who worked hard for the family. He was my step dad. He was never really like the kind of father that would take me out to play ball and stuff like that. But he did provide for my family and he did discipline. I learned a lot from him because he was a very hard worker. When I fell short, he would be all on me like white on rice. I picked up a lot from him because you couldn't lick your wounds with him. You had to keep going. And he taught me how to be a man. My mother was always there. She's never been out of my life except for those first few years when actually I moved up here, made a transition, but she's always been there. So I grew up in the area between Camden Street and Fifteenth Avenue and Morris Street. So basically, I grew up in the Central Ward. And the Central Ward, there was a lot of stuff going on. We had abandoned buildings. We had poverty. You had the projects over on Prince Street and all those areas. It was a tough place, but Newark was a tough place back then. In the early '70s, it was rough. In '71, '72, people were getting stuck up, kids were getting stuck up for their jacket. There was a lot of stuff going on, so I grew up right in the heart of that.

And although it was tough, I did have a lot of friends and support even in the environment like that. So, the area that I grew up in, like I said the Fifteenth Avenue blue buildings, even growing up in that area, a lot of families and friends, we kind of stuck together. We were a community. Those things happened. A lot of things happened in the homes, but the kids stuck together. So, I was never lonely. I never felt like I was in danger even though the environment was hard and rough. Things happened to people. I never feared being hurt or killed like kids might feel today. I knew everybody from the bums to all the young kids and who their parents were. And they knew who mine were.

Tarantino (appointed 1989): I grew up on Lake Street and then I moved to Manchester Place. Growing up I kind of only knew a ten-block radius. We didn't go off that ten-block radius. I thought it was the best place in the world. I grew up next to the park. I used to go to the park all the time. Had a lot of good friends, friends that I still have today that I grew up with. Half of those are either cops or fireman and are successful and the other half are either dead or in jail. It's a typical Newark story. My parents were divorced when I was very young. Never owned a house until I bought one after I came on the fire department, lived in apartments my whole life. We were on welfare. It was a typical Newark poor story. So, I always defend the city. Got a bunch of bikes robbed in the city, but never got hurt in the city. This city's provided me a great job, a life style, a career, a focus. The city doesn't owe me anything. I owe the city everything.

I went to Essex Catholic High School. I didn't go to Essex on Broadway. I went to Essex in East Orange. I was the second graduating class out of Essex in East Orange. So you get kids from all over the place. And I had heard of Vailsburg before. You've heard of it, but I thought Vailsburg was another town. I swear to God I thought Vailsburg was another town. I didn't find out that Vailsburg wasn't another town until like my sophomore year of high school. "Oh, you live in Vailsburg. It's right next to Newark." "What are you talking about? That is Newark." So, I really didn't go to Vailsburg.

I went to Sacred Heart when I was a kid. And then I got kicked out of Sacred Heart and I went to Saint Francis for grammar school. But when I went to Sacred Heart there were these two black kids. They were brothers, really good basketball players. They lived at 411 High Street and my mother after basketball practice, every once in a while, she would take them home. And you don't know Newark is that big. It seemed to take twenty minutes to get these kids home. It was crazy.

The only thing I knew of Down Neck was there was a place called Lancer's that's still there that you could go and get quart Alabama slammers and they wouldn't proof you. So, when I was fifteen, we used to drive down there and get quart Alabama slammers. South Ward I had never been to ever. The West I knew a little bit because I had been up to Seton Hall when I was wrestling when I was younger, different matches. I went to the Saint Patrick's Day parade when I was younger one time when they used to have it on South Orange Avenue. But I had never been to the South Ward ever until I came on the fire department.

Petrone (appointed 1991): I grew up right next door to you on Oakland Terrace in the Vailsburg section, 112 Oakland. I saw the neighborhood change first hand. I never got out too much to other parts of Newark until I got into the work force at eighteen. I started to work in the south district at Economy Fire on South Twelfth Street. One of the big differences that I noted between Vailsburg and other parts of the city was it was mostly single-family homes, especially where I lived. So, people tended to take better care of the homes. They tended to look out for one another because you own the house. Most of them were families. You try to raise families, so people took care of each other. You're always looking out for everybody. You didn't see that when I went down to South Twelfth Street right off of Springfield Avenue. It was completely different. But the neighborhood was great. I loved it there. I loved the friends, people I'm still very close to today. I loved Vailsburg and I think Vailsburg was awesome.

Bartelloni (appointed 1993): I grew up in the North Ward, Eleventh Street by First Avenue School, City Stadium. I was there until I was thirty. I loved it. It was one of the best places to be. Made great friends, great people and I wouldn't trade it for the world, no question about it. Great place.

You knew every neighbor on your block. You could point out houses. I can still point out the houses where people lived. The kids at that time had plenty of respect for adults. So, if somebody's father or mother said something to you it was like your mother or father saying something to you. You didn't talk back to them, but I think the thing then was you were in the playground. I was in the playground most of my life. Whether it was basketball, football, box ball, paddle ball, we were always out there with other kids, talking to them, learning how to get along with each other. And in Newark you dealt with different races. We had all different people to deal with whether it was grammar school, high school. So you learned. It was multi-cultural and you learned to get along with everybody. You learned to share. Not a lot of people had a ton of money and obviously nobody really cared what your father did back then. It wasn't important. It was important just that you were out with your friends. If you're playing stick ball, if you had a quarter, if somebody had a dime, you threw money in the pot. But I think that we were together more. Today the kids are in their rooms playing on the video games the whole day. We had to get out of the house.

That was important because you learned how to be social and get along and work things out. You didn't worry about half of the stuff that you worry about today. You didn't say is somebody going to snatch your kid? I don't remember hearing that ever. You were out there. People were looking after their kids or their friends' kids. You didn't think about that. Be home when the lights came on. You had dinner, then you went back out and then you came back home, so I think it was just a great time to grow up in the city.

I was aware of other parts of the city through sports. I was a big sports player. A lot of my friends were. So, we played baseball, basketball in grammar school. We would play South Ward kids. We would play the Ironbound kids. I don't really remember Vailsburg too much, but I remember City Stadium because I used to live right there so I would watch Vailsburg football. They don't have Vailsburg anymore, but I remember Viking helmets coming in. Barringer Blue Bears, that was their home. Shabazz used to come. I can remember all the high schools from the city. So I probably knew all the different parts of the city just from the teams. And then playing sports we travelled to the South Ward. We'd travel east. Newark to us was huge back then.

Ramos (appointed 1994): I grew up on South Orange Avenue between Sixth and Seventh Street. There used to be a reservoir right there years ago. I recall when deconstruction on that started. There wasn't anything there before. There was just a reservoir and deconstruction of that started '71 or '73. The homes they built there are called the Reservoir Homes. I went to Thirteenth Avenue School. That's where I graduated the eighth grade. From there I went to Irvington Tech.

A lot of laughs growing up in Newark with the hydrants being open, kids playing in the street. Kids playing ball in the middle of the street, stick ball. We'd go to Saint Antoninus right on the corner of Sixth Street and play there against the wall with the rubber ball. You'd throw it against the wall. You played outside basically. That was the day.

I recall the first time I saw a fire. The firemen were hanging from the back of the rig there. There was a fire on Thirteenth Avenue, the Sixth Street side. There's a funeral home there. And it was in the summer so everyone was out. It was an early afternoon fire. I would say between two and three o'clock in the afternoon. I heard the sirens and then I look down the street. I see a big plume of smoke. So, I run down the street just like everybody to see what's going on. And I see this fireman running up the aerial with an axe, boots and a helmet. No gear like they do today. This was I would say '75.

So, he ran up, got up there, stood on the roof, and just started swinging away. I said to myself, "Man look at that guy. Look at that guy go." After he ran up the aerial and just started swinging. Just the helmet, the three-quarter boots, and that's it. The t-shirt and the pants and he ran up the aerial and started to go to work. That was very impressive to me. I was very impressed when I saw that. I guess through the sub-conscience that's where it stayed.

The 90s and the New Century

Jackson (appointed 1995): I was born and raised in Newark. It was kind of rough. I lived in the Weequahic section on Keer Avenue and I went to Chancellor Annex, Chancellor Avenue School, and Weequahic High School. At the time the South Ward was bad, but not really that bad, especially during my elementary years. But as we start getting older the area started changing. It started in eighth grade where one of my friends was actually shot. That was the start for me. From eighth grade all the way through high school, I lost friends to street violence. Then you have drugs. God, you know a lot of them didn't get opportunities like the one I was blessed with.

When given the opportunity, it was a no brainer for me because I had lost so many friends to street violence. Some didn't have careers; some didn't go to college. Here today, a lot of my friends that I came up with are gone. Either they're doing a lot of time in jail or they were murdered or a very few are doing positive things.

It was a struggle living here, but you get out what you put in. There were a lot of drugs, gangs at the time, different type of gangs than the kids of today. It was like sections of the block, other areas all hung together. And they would probably be rivals with another section of the city. Back then it was about just protecting each other and the area. Now it's just out of control.

Y. Pierre (appointed 1995): Yes, I grew up in Newark. Actually, Richelieu Terrace, forty-two years we've live on Richelieu Terrace. I went to grammar school at Lincoln School. Then after Lincoln School I went to Irvington Tech. My brother went to Vailsburg. The neighborhood was crazy. First of all, you got to realize we are Haitian. We didn't speak too much English. We mostly speak French and Creole at home. So we had a hard time communicating. And at the time we were the first black family to move into the neighborhood. All the little Italian kids were like, "Oh, where you all coming from?" I tried to explain to them that we're Haitian, but they couldn't understand us because we were speaking half in English and half in French. It was very difficult. When we were going to school, I remember I got put back one grade because I was passing all the classes except for English. I was failing English and English was the key language of the country and I have to pass English. We got into many, many fights because we could not understand what the kid was saying. There's a lot of pushing around. They don't want to talk anymore. Now it's a fight game. So, we start getting into fights. It was hard at the beginning. It was very, very hard. But somehow, we managed and we survived the tears.

I was thirteen when I came. There were six siblings. And none of us have any idea of what we were getting ourselves into. First winter was the craziest. Oh my God, I cannot explain to you how we felt about winter, ice coming out of the sky. We were like, "Whoa, it's time to go back to Haiti." We could not survive that winter. There was no way we were going to survive that winter. We had to go to school. We were wearing coats and it still was freezing. No matter how heavy a coat we had on, it wasn't warm enough. No matter how hot it was in the school and the house, it wasn't hot enough. I'm still not too comfortable with winter because it's still hard. When winter comes it's like, "Oh my God, winter again."

Montalvo (appointed 1996): I grew up on Summer Avenue. We lived at 571 Summer Avenue. I spent a good twenty something years there. Then we moved over to 511 Highland Avenue. And then I moved Down Neck maybe twenty-five years ago. That's my whole life. Originally a North Newark guy and then I moved Down Neck and I've been Down Neck ever since.

Growing up in North Newark was interesting because I slept in North Newark, but I lived pretty much Down Neck. My parents had a restaurant there. I went to school, Our Lady of Good Counsel, after grammar school I went to Saint Benedicts and then East Side. When we first moved into the neighborhood Down Neck, we were one of the first Latino families on the block. The neighbors were pretty cool with us. We had a nice time. My father was a hard worker and he always had us outside cleaning the yard. The neighbors appreciated that. So, it was nice.

Farrell (appointed 1996): Everything I did was in the North Ward pretty much. I wish I had this for my son. I wish my son could grow up on Parker Street in the North Ward of Newark. Because my father being a fireman had his time off. He didn't have a second job really. He worked part time as a gym teacher in my grammar school a little bit, but he was always home. If he's not at the firehouse, he's home in the backyard and it was go outside, play, come in when the street lights go on. I wouldn't change that for the world. It was a ton of friends. The block was always busy with kids. It was seasonal, baseball season we're playing Wiffle ball, football, hockey, basketball, you name it or in the pool. It was a great place to grow up. It really was. And I can remember my father being on the job, summer time, how many gigs pulling up in our driveway and the chief and his driver running out, grabbing a hamburger, hot dog, jumping in the pool, getting back in his gig, and going back to work. They were always by our house, always. My father as very friendly with a lot of guys on the job and they knew where we lived. They knew where they could come by and get a quick burger or hot dog and jump in and out of the pool in the summertime. I grew up around those guys.

Newark was a great place to grow up. It really was. You know the Newark mentality. You could almost know another Newark guy just by talking to him and seeing him. You know the guys on the job who were really born and raised in Newark and those who weren't. It's a unique place to grow up. I went to Our Lady of Good Counsel grammar school, Essex Catholic

High School, taking the bus there. Everything was right here. I owe a lot of who I am today to that. I really do. The toughness of Newark, you wake up that little toughness. You grow up hanging on street corners.

My block was completely diverse growing up. It was great. A lot of Italians, I grew up mostly around Italians, but there were black and Hispanic on my block. We all got together really well.

It wasn't a perfect city. I got jumped numerous times walking home from school. Give me your money. Fifty cents, whatever I had in my pocket. Knives pulled out, "Give me this." My mother had a gun held to her head. That happened. You saw that coming little by little. I can remember the first time locking our doors. We never used to lock our doors.

I don't know if you remember a guy named Tony Imperiale. He was the Don of the North Ward. He protected that place. I remember being three years old, looking out my window. I can still remember this to this day. Three years old looking out my window watching a tank roll down my street during the riots. The riots weren't anywhere near us, but Tony Imperiale had a tank rolling around the North Ward. He was protecting.

I can almost remember that feeling, that change when we first started locking our front doors. Never used to lock our doors. And then at one point, "Hey, we got to start locking our doors now." So that's the change that came, you saw it coming.

Roberson (appointed 1996): I was born and raised in Newark on Howard Street. After the riots, my dad started the Hank Arron baseball league for kids. It's right there on Springfield Avenue and Prince Street. And we've been doing that field since it was rocks and glass. Now my brothers and I run it. The crazy part is every year we had a benefit game with the city administration, Mayor Gibson. So, I've got this old picture of me with Fire Director Caufield with a captain's fire hat, old picture. And look at me now.

Fifty years later and I'm a fireman. So, I was born and raised in Newark, went to Quitman Street School, graduated from Saint Vinny's Prep High School. That's my Alma Mater.

Willis (appointed 1996): Newark was fun. I mean, we had fun playing on the railroad, playing down on the river, down on Newark Bay, the airport, the fire department. Eight Engine was open. It was on the corner of Filmore and Ferry. Celanese was across the street, gigantic factory, across the street at the time. We used to play in the factory, climbing the fence, jumping over, going on roofs. We had the Ironbound Stadium. We played hockey all our lives. All the kids from the neighborhood were hockey players. We were all into sports, baseball in Ann Street School. Independence Park, River Bank Park, I mean anything you can do as a kid, we had it all. We didn't have money, but we had each other. We had fun. We were a community. The Ironbound was a big community. I can't tell you how many people I know, all born and raised down there, thousands, not hundreds, thousands. It's not the same. Newark is not the same. It's not a community like it was. But I think that's everywhere now. I think technology's done that to us. Social media, technology destroyed communities. Again, it's my opinion.

I knew Newark like the back of my hand since I was five years old. We were on the railroads. I played in Oak Island. When we got a little older like around ten, we would travel around. We would jump on a bus or we used to get on the PATH train, go over to New York on the PATH train, go back and forth. But our fun was going, fishing poles and bikes, across the Bayonne Bridge going into Bayonne at the Bayonne Marina and the piers for the port. We'd fish snapper fish, get baby blues and go crabbing. We used to catch crabs. That's what we did as kids. It was like a Huckleberry Finn story. That was us.

At the time you had no Passaic Valley Sewage. That was all marsh. We played in there. They had giant ponds and we used to get Styrofoam from the companies and we had sticks. We would float through. Actually, one day I was caught by my father, he was a longshoreman down there. He saw us and said, "What the hell are all those kids doing?" It was us. I got my butt whipped when I got home. We played by the airport, watched the planes land. A lot of the structures that are down there weren't there when we played down there. It was all marshland. It was nice.

Carr (appointed 2000): I grew up in Newark. I grew up on Prince Street. We lived at 232 Prince Street which is on the corner of Prince and Spruce. So my pop, basically could walk to work. He was assigned to the Tact Squad which rode out of Twenty Engine's old quarters on Prince between South Orange and Springfield Avenues. So, it was nice to know that he could come down there, come back and get back and forth from home safely. Not having to worry. I don't think he even had a car at the time. I think he didn't get a car until a year or two after he was appointed to the fire department.

Growing up in Newark was great. I was able to move around, ride my bike over to Central Avenue on pay day and get a couple of dollars from my father. I went to Fourteenth Avenue School. I went to Marcus Garvey. I went to University High School. I went to Lincoln Elementary. I went to Vailsburg High School and after they closed Vailsburg down, I ended up graduating from West Side High School. The last graduating class in Vailsburg was in 1988. I had to go to West Side High School for one year. I graduated in '89. So, I am definitely a product of Newark.

I'll tell you the things I remember in Newark. I remember when the Pabst Blue Ribbon was in operation. I remember when the lady built the ark over there on Bergen and Fourteenth Avenue. I remember Bamberger's. I remember Two Guys. I remember Sonny Oliver's which was down there on the corner of MLK and Clinton Avenue. Everybody that lived in that area that got married had their wedding reception in Sonny Oliver's. I remember Woolworth of course. I remember across the street in that empty lot on Prince Street they used to have the county fair and the carnivals used to come over there at one point. I remember there were a lot of things that used to occur in Newark. Newark wasn't bad, not to me. It was home.

Highsmith (appointed 2000): I grew up in the Central Ward right there on Muhammad Ali Avenue, 40 Muhammad Ali Avenue until the eighth grade. I finished high school in North Carolina and some college in North Carolina. What I remember about Newark as a kid is Leon White. I remember him with the helmet and the bullhorn riding the bike following the fire trucks. I actually used to throw rocks at him. He used to chase me, but I've come to respect him big time over the years as I got to know him. He just loves helping people. And I've come to respect that, but I was kind of bad as a kid.

Jenkins (appointed 2002): My memories of Newark are great. Growing up we had a home. Never had to ask for a lot, worry about a lot. Didn't think of stuff that happened, like the riot and stuff. I was little so I wouldn't know a whole lot about most of that stuff. No more than I would read in the books. Otherwise, I enjoyed it. I had a good upbringing. The city wasn't bad at all. This was in the 70s, 80s, 90s.

Rosario (appointed 2002): I grew up in Newark. I had a great childhood. I remember when the kids were always outside. I grew up on North Sixth Street for the most part between Park Avenue and Abington. It was in that whole area. We were like gypsies. We moved from house to house until we bought a house. So, I had friends all over. And you know, especially on the fire department, you run into all these guys you used to play against in football, baseball, and basketball from the different neighborhoods. You're like, I remember you, I remember you. But it was great. I remember, time to go home when the lights were coming on.

Figuereq: (appointed 2006) I grew up in Newark, North Newark, Mount Prospect, Elliot, Oriental Street. We moved around. I was born in Puerto Rico. We came over when I was about four years old.

To me it's normal. You hear all the bad publicity about it, but I don't really recall that many bad memories. Maybe I just knew where not to go. My parents didn't let us get away too far, run around too crazy. I was always outside running around the front on Mount Prospect Avenue by 444 by the old seventy-seven steps. That's where I grew up. I was running around there the whole time. Bicycle ride on the sidewalk, playing Wiffle ball, jumping in the back of the garages.

The old seventy-seven steps were at Abington Avenue and Mount Prospect. If you're going south bound on Mount Prospect, you could have made the left and go down just steps. They're just steps. They bring you down to Summer Avenue. They're no longer there. I think a lot of stuff over the years happened and at one point they just decided to get rid of them. But we used to go down the steps to buy fireworks around July time.

Medina (appointed 2006): I grew up on Hawthorne Terrace and then eventually we moved over to the North Ward about '89, '90. We lived in the Central Ward for a couple of years. My first school was Harriet Tubman on South Tenth Street. I was there from '81 to '89, '90. I was across the street from the KFC. I think I was living there when the little plane hit the house there, '84. '83? I was young. The KFC was there, right across the street on Springfield Ave.

It was great. I mean, my mother was a single parent, so she kept us tight in the house. We weren't going running around crazy. So, we didn't see much of what's going on today. But she moved us around. She worked for Essex County and for the City of Newark. For Halloween we went to a party instead of trick or treating because it's really bad. In the summertime, she would buy pools. It wasn't bad. When we moved to the North it was okay. And when you get older you start to realize, "Oh, wow, it was rough stuff." It was really something, but it wasn't bad. It was okay.

G. Pierre (appointed 2013): I grew up in Newark, born and raised. I was born at UMDNJ. My father's family comes from the country of Haiti. I go back to Haiti often. My mother, she was born and raised in Newark. My grandmother on my mother's side lived on Lehigh. I used to live right down the street from the firehouse on Lehigh and Bergen.

I remember there was quite a drug problem in Newark. When I was around the age of thirteen, I was playing with my GI Joes on the curb. I had crack vials. You know the little crack vials? I'm throwing the vials like missiles. My mother came out, saw what I was playing with. She had a heart attack. I had no clue. I was just playing. It felt like the next day we were in North Carolina. That's how I felt. I have a lot of family in North Carolina, South Carolina, Virginia on my mother's side of the family. So, I spent a lot of time travelling around there. My mother took me out of Newark. I moved out with my mom.

From thirteen to eighteen I lived in Gold, North Carolina. I lived in Hopewell, Virginia. I lived in Petersburg, Virginia. I lived in Durham, North Carolina. And then at eighteen I got a football scholarship at Delaware State University, so I moved to Delaware State University. Mind you all this time I still came back home. It wasn't like I left and didn't come back home. I still came back home. I stayed at Richelieu Terrace, my grandmother's house. After college I came back to Newark, back to the family house in Newark.

I'm from a family that's gives a lot. My grandmother always used to cook food. She always cooked big pots. I don't know one night ever having left overs. People would come in the house and she would fix them a plate. That's just how it was. She'd babysit a lot of kids. So people would always leave the house with plates all the time. Give them plates and bring them back the next day. That's what they did.

Rawa (appointed 2013): I was born and raised in Newark. I was the youngest of five kids. Born in the Ironbound on Napoleon Street. Pretty spread out in age. I think there's a fifteen-year difference between us, but we're all really close. Father was a cop. Mom was raising the five kids. My dad, brother, uncle, cousin are all Newark cops. My brother married a female Newark cop. My sisters all work at Beth Israel Hospital. So we're all connected even though everybody pretty much moved out as they got older. We're all still connected here, working in Newark. But good childhood growing up in Newark. Down Neck was good.

Garay (appointed 2014): I grew up on Park Avenue. I lived there for about fifteen years and then I moved to Grafton Avenue. And then I moved to many places because I couldn't live with my mother. So, I moved in with my grandmother. I was bouncing all over North Newark until I was a sophomore in high school when I moved in with my sister. Then I moved in with my other sister and then I went off to college.

I couldn't tell you what Newark was like then. I was always home. I had curfews. I was demanded to be home five minutes after school ended. I used to be a home girl pretty much. Even when I was away from home, because I only got to live at my mother's house for three or four years, I always was expected to come back home right away. At the end of my freshman year in high school, I started working so it was work and school, and work and school, and work and school. And if not, I was at my grandmother's house. All I can say is I used to see guys selling drugs on the corner and in the street. I knew they were selling drugs because that's what I heard conversations from the adults say. That's what I remember as far as Newark, the community is concerned.

I was just familiar with North Newark. The one time I was able to get out of North Newark is when I went to the vocational school on West Market. It used to be called Newark Tech. I knew it by Newark Tech. That's the only place where I used to travel. That's as far as I used to travel, to the central part of Newark.

Corales (appointed 2016): I grew up in the Ironbound section on Fleming and Ashley Street, 55 Ashley Street, apartment 5B. I lived there for twenty-three years and then I moved out with my mom temporarily. She got re-married. Then I came back to Newark when my current girlfriend, the mother of my child, got pregnant. We moved back November of 2008. We moved back down to the Ironbound section to her parent's house. And we currently live on Foundry Street.

This is my city. I love it. I'm a baseball kid and I grew up in the parks in the Ironbound section. Chestnut Street Park, there to this day. I'm there Tuesdays and Thursdays. I do coaching. I coach my son's baseball team. I was always part of a travel team for the city of Newark. That did a lot for me. Where I grew up it was low income, poverty. You see a lot of things you probably shouldn't see. I was given the opportunity to travel with my team and I got myself out of that box and was able to see things that I wanted to go get. I wanted to have and that kind of drove me the right way, I guess. So, I'm still right around the corner from where I grew up. Not too far away from it.

I used to go to the downtown area to do the shopping. I used to have friends on the other side of the tracks because our travel team was all spread around. But I didn't think it was this big. As big as it is.

When we were growing up, I saw a lot of poverty, a lot of sad stuff that you no longer see. It's not like the way it used to. Back in those days it just felt like there was too much stuff going on, a lot of stolen cars. I just think now it kind of calmed down. It's still out there but it getting better.

Cruz (appointed 2016): When I was young, I used to live on Sixth Street. So, I would always see the firehouse on Park Avenue. That was right by my elementary school. I went to Dr. Horton. Actually, a couple of people that went to Dr. Horton are on the job. I used to love the firehouse. Those were ideals to me. It was the coolest thing to just walk by there. That's why I wanted to drive a truck. I would walk around and you would see the trucks in there inside the bay all the time. I used to love it. What it felt like was a sense of security. We're little kids and we're like wow, you know there are firefighters right around the corner. We're safe. When you're little you see them as super human, like super heroes. Then when I was in eighth grade, we moved to Forest Hills and that's where I grew up. Then I didn't see the fire department at all.

Forest Hills was extremely isolated. Both my parents worked. We were a family of nine, five brothers, one sister, and me. So, my parents were always working and our older brothers would be home watching us. We weren't allowed to have friends. Our parents wanted nothing bad to happen to us, so they pretty much kept us in the house. We played sports. In order for us to have fun we would have to join clubs in school or play sports or have a part time job. That was the only way we could actually associate with anyone else because my parents were working all the time and protective of us.

Earp (appointed 2016): I grew up in Newark, in the South Ward. I think it's a great city. When I was young growing up, there were a lot of activities that I was able to get into. I think they're going away from that now. I played a lot of sports when I was young. So, it was great for me seeing that and it built a lot of character for me. Because I played football and a lot of people who were from the city would come out to see us play. I think that was like a really good thing. It made me feel appreciative. Like the city appreciates you throwing out positive things. I think that's a good thing about the city.

Part Two:

Neighborhoods

Conville (1940): But Newark at the time, over in the Weequahic section is predominantly Jewish. Over there it was rather nice, but I think Ellenstein was the mayor and he brought in a lot of black people from the south to be maids for the Jewish people. The black people were living in little spaces over in the Weequahic section. That's how the blacks started to come to Springfield Avenue. That area started to degrade.

Fredette (1942): They called the area around Six Engine (Springfield Avenue and Hunterdon Street) Shmierkase County. That was all solid Germans. Then way around the Polish came up. They were down below Belmont Avenue. The Polish people came up from Down Neck, around Pulaski Street, St. Casimir's Church. Then the Irish and the Italians came in pretty heavy. The Italians went up to Vailsburg. From Vailsburg they went to up Livingston. They're still up in Livingston yet. But a lot of them came from Fairmont Avenue, Camden Street, down in that section.

I remember this guy, Edward Scudder. He lived up on Prospect Place up in North Newark (Forest Hills) and owned the Newark Evening News. He had a fire on one side of his fire place in the living room. We had to stay outside with the hose until they rolled up the rugs, so we could come in with our dirty boots to put out the fire alongside the fire place. We had to stay outside because those rugs were maybe a hundred-thousand-dollar rugs in this big, beautiful home on Prospect Place. He owned the Newark Evening News. We had to wait until they rolled up the rugs and took the pictures off the walls before we put water on it.

Kinnear (1947): I would say it was at least 80-85% white at that time. There was a black neighborhood, which consisted of around Belmont Avenue, Prince Street, and maybe ran down to High Street, maybe from Springfield Avenue or Court Street over to Avon. But it was the black area. Basically, the rest city, as far as I know, was white. I'd say 85% white, maybe even 90% white. North Newark was the Italian section. Vailsburg was where most of the Police and Firemen seemed to live. The section I lived in, the Weequahic section or Clinton Hill section, was mostly Jewish, a lot of rich Jewish. You know, doctors and lawyers. I don't know how we got in there. We were on the fringe though. Weequahic was really south of Lyons Avenue. We lived just a little bit north of Lyons Avenue. We were on the fringe, but that was mostly a Jewish section. I guess Down Neck was a mixture. I didn't go down there too much, so I don't really know.

Masters (1947): When I came on the job in '47, the city was still good. It was still beautiful. The makeup in my day was white, Italians in the North Ward. Every section had its own ethnic group. You go to the South Ward, it was Jewish. East Ward was Polish, Spanish, Portuguese, it was all mixed. Vailsburg was Irish, most of them. It was a nice clean city, orderly. When the riots came, that was too bad. I think the riots were the downfall of Newark because they all start bailing out then.

Grehl (1948): All around Six Engine was mostly Italians, Fairmont Avenue, Hunterdon Street, and so forth. Gradually the people started moving out of the neighborhood. It's like everything else. The great American dream, they wanted a home in the suburbs and they started doing that. As they vacated, it was basically filled with minorities in the Central Ward. The Italian people moved up to Vailsburg and their void was filled with minorities.

Vesey: (appointed 1948) Oh, Down Neck was Down Neck, North Newark was pretty residential, pretty stable. All the Jews were over in the South Ward, South Side. Vailsburg was German/Irish. All the colors were mostly in the Central Ward down at Prince Street, Spruce Street down in that area until they started building the projects. It was ethnic neighborhoods more or less. The city was pretty well evened out as far as ethnic breakdowns.

J. Ryan (1948): Nice city, neighborhoods were nice. They were broken down into the ethnic enclaves. Where I came from was mixed, Down Neck, down by Sixteen Engine (lower Ferry Street). Down there was predominantly Polish, Irish, and German. Then the island park, that was all Polish, there were a few Irish there. Then across the railroad was Dutch neck, that was all German. Up around Eastside High School was predominantly Polish and then across the park was Lithuanian and up around Jefferson Street, Madison that was all Italian. Then up further was a small enclave of Portuguese, up on Prospect Street. Then they got bigger. Over the other end, down by Fourteen Engine (McWhorter Street) was a lot of Italians. North Newark was a lot of Italians. With the old ward set up, part of North Newark was the First Ward when I was on the department. They didn't tear it down until later on when they built the Columbus Homes. That was the end of the First Ward when they put the Columbus Homes up. And in the middle, over by Southside High, was Jewish, Weequahic High was Jewish. That was a Jewish neighborhood. Central, a lot of Irish in Central. Westside, Vailsburg was all Irish. Nowadays it's all black. Except for Down Neck, you got the Portuguese and the Germans. Still Dutch neck is not bad. It's still holding. Dutch neck was over Wilson Avenue, part of Down Neck. Wilson was Hamburg Place at one time. Rome Street was Berlin. In that area, that comprised from the Central Railroad, St. Charles Street, west to about New York Avenue over there. Then it became a lot of Polish, from New York Avenue west from there. They had another Italian neighborhood down by Malvern Street down by Mt. Carmel parish.

St. James was Irish. St. Benedict's was Dutch neck. That was German. St. Aloysius was mostly Irish. They had some German, some Polish. St.

Cashmere's was all Polish. And then you had St. Joseph's Spanish church up on Prospect Street. Spanish and Portuguese over there, Portuguese didn't have their own church yet at the time. Well even the other churches up in the other areas were all ethnic. You had St. Rocco's. That was all Italian, old Fourteen Avenue. You had the one up on Sixteenth Avenue which was mostly Irish, Sixteenth Avenue Sixth Street. St. Ann's, that was originally German though. Then that became Italian and Irish in St. Ann's parish.

The black community was up in the Third Ward, up around Howard Street because before you come up the hill, that was all Jewish, over there on Prince Street all in back there. But they were above Belmont Avenue, the small black community, over on Seventeenth Avenue. I know Howard Street was black. That was only before the war. Then after the war it exploded and took off. More came in. Then they built the projects. They tore down a lot. The old Jewish neighborhood, that's been eliminated, Prince Street, in there. Avon Place, Avon Avenue, that was all Jewish.

There was a small Chinese community. That was Mulberry Street, from Mulberry and all around Mulberry. Not up to Broad, it went down. It went towards McCarter Highway. They only comprised a couple of blocks. Not too many, right behind the post office. That was the big area, down there, over at One Truck (Mulberry and Lafayette Streets) a few in there but it was mostly south of Lafayette Street. Most of them were in there. They had restaurants and all and in the side streets, Walnut Street down there.

J. Doherty (1949): The Portuguese and the Spanish, they started on Ferry Street, down there. Where the Iberia is today there used to an Iberia tavern on the corner on Congress Street and Ferry. And you'd go in there and one whole wall of this tavern was cork board and all the letters are from Spain. But through the '50s, I was a young guy, I could see what the hell was happening. I guess when I went on the fire department, we must have had seven or eight breweries in the city. Ten years or so later, they were all gone. The only one left was the new one Anheuser-Busch.

By and large Newark was a bunch of neighborhoods of different ethnic groups. Because Weequahic you could figure completely Jewish. North Newark and Doodle town, that would be the Roseville section, were predominantly Italian. And Down Neck the remnants of Germans still there and Polish and like I said the Portuguese and Spaniards were coming in. That was after the war. The Central Ward it was black. When I went in '59 to Five Truck, you'd have to search like hell to find a white face living within a quarter of a mile in any direction from Five Truck (Irvine Turner Boulevard and Muhamad Ali Avenue). Yeah, those changes came along.

Masterson (1949): The city was Irish, Italian, I guess mostly. I was growing up with Irish, Italian mostly, but Newark had everything. They had Germans over there around Springfield Avenue. There were some nice Italian neighborhoods at Fourteenth Avenue, over in that area and down the ward, Eighth Avenue, Clifton Avenue. Down Neck you had a lot of Polish. The beautiful part of it was, whatever you wanted to eat, you could just go to those neighborhoods. You could buy from your Polish butcher, your German butcher, your Italian butcher. If you wanted a leg of veal, you'd go to an Italian butcher. If you wanted sausage and knockwurst, you go to a German butcher like A.M. Teller. Everything was first class. In fact, there were places that had homemade liverwurst right on the avenue. It really was a beautiful city.

Baldino (1951): The city had been divided into several ethnic enclaves only because most of the people came from all parts of the world to live near relatives. We had sections of the city that were predominantly Italian, the North Ward, Irish and German, the West Ward, Jewish, the South Ward,

Polish, the East Ward, and Afro-American, the Central Ward. Each ward had a combination of all the groups.

Alfano (1953): There were different neighborhoods. Down Neck had their neighborhoods. They had their German, Polish, and Italians and Irish. And they all got along terrific in most of your neighborhoods. Vailsburg was really always nice. And I think a lot of firemen and cops lived there. They called it mortgage hill. I can remember playing ball in Vailsburg Park. God, we had both foul lines full of people. I played against the Shamrocks and the Temocks in West Side Park and I think the Iroquois in Weequahic Park and the Park AC in Branch Brook Park. I played against all of them.

Gibson (1953): My neighborhood was Irish and Italian and some German. But I would say mostly Italian because I went to Catholic school and it was mostly Italian boys, girls in that school. But then things change. Look today what they're doing which they should have done a hundred years ago with the colored people, get educated.

There always was friction. I got along with them. Some of my best friends were Italian. As a matter of fact, when I was about nine or ten I had a colored friend, Russel Boaty. His father was a mailman. My old man, he didn't like them. Russel's father believed the same as my old man. When he found out that Russel had a white friend, he nearly killed him. So, we weren't allowed to hang out around with each other, Russel Boaty.

Deutch: (1953) The city was a very strong city. It was probably 75% white in those days as far as race. Eighteen months after I got on the job, I transferred to Five Truck (Irvine Turner Boulevard) and there were a lot of white people up on Belmont Avenue all around us. Even on Belmont and Waverly, we had a lot of white neighbors. There was one colored fireman on the job when I came on. He was Willie Thomas and I think he came on in 1951 or '52.

R. Griffith: (1953) When I was a young guy it was broken up into areas. North Newark it was a high Italian population. Then out in the Forest Hill area there was a mixture of Irish, English, and maybe some German people along with Italians. The Ironbound had a little bit of everybody. The Central Ward had a lot of black families. South Ward was heavily Jewish and of course the West Ward was heavily Irish with civil service workers.

Wall: (1954) Nice. Newark was ethnic then. If you were Irish you went to either Saint James or Saint Columba parish. If you were Polish, you went to Saint Casmir's. The Italians, I guess Mount Carmel, but we all sort of intermixed socially. And of course, the guys intermixed by having fistfights in the local parks occasionally. I don't remember anyone getting more than a black eye out of it. Newark was an interesting place.

Freeman: (1956) There were fights between Italians and blacks because they crossed the line. They went across town, especially over around Orange Street, in that area. I think over there, there was always something going on between the Italians and the blacks. There were a lot of skirmishes between blacks and Italians, and also in the school system over that way. Not much where I lived. That was amongst ourselves, because it was one big area, the Third Ward, and not many Italians came over this way. We never had a problem with the Jews.

Griggs (1956): When I was living Down Neck you had everybody down there. I delivered papers on Vincent Street and Manufacturers Place, we had the blacks there. They had a tenement house there. I used to deliver in there.

I used to collect newspaper money in there for the guy. You had the Polish, the Germans, the Irish, the Italians. Heavy duty Italian over by St. James. And then you had a mixture naturally. Years later that changed, I mean the whole complex. You had the Portuguese coming in, rebuilding. East Side High itself was a mixture of different races. In fact, up at Benedict's in my senior year, we got the first black student.

My grandmother's father had a house on Fifteenth Avenue. She was a Hemhauser. The Germans were up there. There was friction between the different groups at times. We had the Polish kids throwing rocks at us at the end of Hawkins Street. That was their territory. If we used one of their ballfields down there, they'd chase us off it. I remember my mother telling me that if a fellow went from the St. Aloysius area over to St. Benedict's which was the German area to visit a girlfriend and that gang over there found out about it, they'd chase him back over the railroad tracks. "Go over where you belong. Get out of here." They were very block wise. You had a group on the block and you had people hanging around that you didn't recognize. Well, they didn't belong there and you'd turn and get the older kids and say who's that? And they'd say to them, "You don't belong here. Go back where you belong." That was the way it works.

The only times it seemed to be a good mix was the Salvation Army Boys Club which invited everybody in.

McGee: (1956) Went in the Army and then came on the job. The city was great growing up as a kid because it was neighborhoods. We're talking about ethnic neighborhoods. Vailsburg was known to be Irish and Italian. Down Neck was known to be Italian and Polish. The South Ward was known to be mostly Jewish, the North Ward mostly Italian. And the Central Ward even back in those days was predominantly black. In fact, Camden Street, which was just a block above Bergen Street, was black when I was an infant.

There were a lot more white people in the City, but they were still divided ethnically in their own groups for the most part. But no major problems, it was a great place to grow up and it was a great place to raise a family I'm sure for other people. A good city, I still like it.

McGrory: (1957) In the '50s or maybe even before that, the Portuguese started coming in. It was different. There were always different people coming in. The city of Newark always had a diverse population. In the Weequahic section, there were quite a few Jewish people. There were Germans, but the Germans moved up to Irvington early on. Italians, Irish, Polish, everyone came in. There were always blacks in Newark in certain areas. After the first war, my father said, there was a big influx of blacks who came into the area. Then after the second war the same thing happened. After that the Puerto Ricans came in the '50s.

Bitter (1959): They had different areas as far as black and white. Where I lived on Bragaw Avenue was primarily all Jewish. My wife is Italian. She went to Weequahic High School. You could count the Italians on one hand, all rich Jewish kids. Down Neck was the most stable part of the city. Black areas were all below Bergen Street down off of Avon and Clinton and Springfield, down in there. Everybody had their own areas like that.

Cardillo (1959): I was in a Jewish neighborhood in Weequahic, my neighborhood, on Clinton Avenue and Hunterdon Street. There weren't many Italians up there. The Italians were in the North Ward. There were a lot of Polish Down Neck. The neighborhoods were good. They were good.

Charpentier: (1959) I would say the city was about 80% white and 20% black. The black people were in their own area, which was the Central Ward.

In 1959 blacks were just starting to move into the Weequahic section, but that was still 90% Jewish. You had Vailsburg. That was 99% white. North Newark was mostly white, Italians. Down Neck, well, that was almost 100% white.

Denvir (1959): Vailsburg was firemen and cops and it stayed that way for a long time, years and years. It was mainly white. Maybe there were some blacks in the projects, a few homes scattered through, but mainly when I came on it was mostly white. But even then, it was changing through the '60s.

Dunn (1959): I lived on a street that was all white and either Irish, German, or Italian. There were a few Polish people and that was your nationality mix. Everybody had gone to Catholic school and your friends were confined more or less to the people who you went to school with who lived on the street. Two blocks away from us was a low-cost housing project. That was also 99.9% white at the time. That was due to the fact that after World War II or during the war people were brought in from Pennsylvania to work in our factories and they lived in these types of dwellings. They again were the same nationality and racial mix as the Catholic school. Most of them went to Catholic school. We had a very vibrant Catholic school of really three or four nationalities of people.

Freda (1959): At the time I came on the job, Newark was predominantly white. I don't know the percentages, but North Newark was all white. The area I lived in was all Italian. Around the Sixteenth, Seventeenth Avenue area, that area was all Italian. The other predominant group would be blacks and they seemed to be located in the Central Ward. There was segregation in those days, very strong. Black people didn't come into your area and you didn't go into their area as civilians. Nobody seemed to really mind it or beef about it. But in essence the black people were trapped in the ghetto. That was a very poor area.

The area around Fifteen Engine (Park Avenue and Sixth Street) when I was a kid and up to my early time on the fire department was broken down into ethnic enclaves where there was no such thing as integration as far as the city goes. There was an Irish area. South of Park Avenue was predominantly all Irish, North Sixth Street, North Seventh Street, and so forth. Go north of Park Avenue, going north on the same street, North Sixth Street, was predominantly Italian. There weren't too many mixes. There were slight exceptions where you'd have an Irish family living amongst the Italians and vise a versa. In fact, there was a black family on Sixth Street, which was like a historical billing. Now this was when I was a kid, but I still remember the woman, Mrs. Washington was her name. Even in those days, she was a highly respected woman because people would draw a difference. They would say she's a nice black person. Her kids went to college and she works hard and they would throw away those stereotypes.

But I remember distinctly as a small child, the Italian immigrants, like my friends' fathers and mothers didn't even speak English. We're talking about people out of Ellis Island. They were uptight. Italians in that era were all funny. They strictly wanted to be about their own kind. There wasn't intermarriage between even the ethnics. But surprising enough, they used to speak very highly often about Mrs. Washington because if you were sick, she would always be at your house. Unheard of for a black person to come to your house in those days, but she would be welcomed into your house. She'd always bring you fruit and juice if she heard you were sick or something. It was very unusual. Like today, you might not think much about it, but that was a conversation piece, that this black person lived on North Sixth Street and was accepted. It was something to talk about. That's why I remember her name. It was a unique thing in those days.

So, what I was trying to express. You had the Italian neighborhood. You had the Irish neighborhoods and the black people, in my early fire department experience, were mostly in the Central Ward. Then they started to spread out in the city more. As the white people retreated from the city, more and more blacks move in and spread out. You had the Jewish section. The Weequahic section was block after block after block of strictly Jewish families. That's the way it was. If you were in a firehouse in those areas, I certainly think it would affect your thinking and operations because you would be part of that social and economic area.

J. Miller: (1959) Very well mixed ethnically wise group of people. You had the German, the Irish, and Italians in various sections of the city. The First Ward was mostly Italians, around Seventh Avenue. That section, even when you were young, you couldn't go in there if you looked Irish. They would question you. Maybe beat you up and tell you to get out of the neighborhood. The black populace was mostly around West Market Street, Boston, in that area. Vailsburg was German/Irish, the North Ward was Italian, and the Weequahic section was predominantly Jewish. It was a very cohesive society. Everybody stuck together.

You could get beat up because I did a couple of times. Got chased out, but in the area where the blacks were there was not too much racial tension. Although when I was about thirteen years old there was a big war in the park over on Orange Street near Branch Brook Park. The blacks and Italians had a big fight. I mean this involved thousands of people with baseball bats and everything. I don't know if it ever made the news or whatever at that time. The news media wasn't around, but it was a tremendous battle. There was a different type of intolerance, not hatred, but it was territorial.

I can recall, I was sixteen years old and I was dating this girl who lived up on South Eighteenth Street. I had to walk from Cabinet Street, over

Norfolk Street, and take the 31 South Orange up to her home. Coming home one evening around ten o'clock I had to walk past the old Robert Treat Grammar School which was situated on I think Fourteenth Avenue and Norfolk Street. Across the street there was a black club. I'll never forget because I was walking by and the guys yelled over, "Hey, man. Hey, Zeke. Your name Zeke?" I said, "No, my name is not Zeke." It was half a block, not even half a block away, from one corner to the other.

The next thing you know I was getting beat up by about ten blacks. Really getting beat up. It was comical because they really weren't hitting me. They were getting shots in, but there were so many of them that they were hitting themselves. It was like a Three Stooges comedy. While they were all converging on me, somehow, I got out through the middle underneath and I could run like hell. I ran away. They couldn't catch me. But there were at least ten of them. They were older, maybe in their twenties, some in their thirties. They were drinking. They were not fleet of foot, so they couldn't catch me. When I got home, I did have a couple teeth that were really loose. Eventually I lost the teeth in the front. That's the only problem I had with blacks growing up with them because there were some in the neighborhood. There was a black doctor I knew. Black kids whose parents were doctors in Saint Joseph's school. There was no really racial tension like we have today. It was a different type of tension, just territorial. Sometimes they got mad if you went into their territory.

The Weequahic section was predominantly Jewish and they stuck to their own. They controlled the wealth of the city probably at that time. They had all the big businesses over there. They just stayed amongst themselves. There were no problems with any kind of race wars with those. And in the school system in the Central Ward, was seventy/thirty as far as the mixture because that was where they mostly congested in the Central Ward. There was no Spanish. There were a few Gypsies living around the area in storefronts. In my school there were maybe 5% black. There were never any problems with race.

You didn't belong in the Italian section if you were Irish. I was Irish and German, so I stayed around Hudson and West Market Street, around Saint Joe's. Everybody stayed in their own territory. We went to our own movies, the Dento Theater, the Core Theater, the Essex, or the Plaza. We never went over to North Newark where the other movies were. They had gangs, the Turo's and the Lucky Elevens. They were all in the First Ward. If you were in their movie, you'd better have one of their jackets on or something like that. You couldn't go in their territory. They just didn't appreciate it. Like the Weequahic Dire, people went there. You could go there. There was no problem, but if you went over to some of the theaters on Broadway near Halleck Street and you weren't from the neighborhood, you could have some problems over there. They'd punch you around and things like that. I heard stories like that, but you'd have to be looking for trouble too or they'd be looking for trouble. And there was always somebody looking for trouble, but I stayed out of it. I was mostly interested in sports, so I didn't get involved in any of that stuff.

A. Prachar (1959): It was very mixed. We had a lot of black, a lot of white, a lot of Spanish. It was probably the beginning of integration in the city of Newark in that area. We went to Miller Street School and South Side High School which were well mixed. So it was a good basis for me when I did go on the fire department because of the mix of people on the job. It was no problem with me to get along with everybody.

Harris (1961): Growing up in the city of Newark, we used to walk from North Newark where the seventy-seven steps are up to Summer Avenue and to Mount Prospect Avenue. We used to go up there. Then nine times out of ten, we'd have to fight from there to Branch Brook Park. We were fighting with the Italian kids because that was their neighborhood. Then we'd come back. You may have to fight just to come back. But that's what we did growing up if we wanted to go to Branch Brook Park.

Basically, in North Newark all your blacks lived below Summer Avenue, Delavan, Summer, Wilburton, and down Oraton Street. Then down in the old First Ward you had about three streets where blacks lived. Like Julius Banks, he lived on Webster Street right next to Anthony "Tony" Imperiele when they were growing up. Before I even came on the job, Emil Nardone was my mailman. That's how I knew Emil before coming into the job. And his father owned a store on Broadway, a candy store. He sold sodas and candy and stuff like that. We used to go in there because the church we went to, Clinton Memorial, was right across the street from Tony's father's store. That's how I knew Tony and Emil, from there. That's how Newark was years ago.

Newark was divided up at that time. We had what we called the "hill." Now the hill was Prince, Spruce, Belmont, Eighteenth, Waverly, all the way down to Avon Avenue that whole area. It wasn't in two blocks on the other side of Clinton Avenue going south. And then you had a lot of blacks who lived off Bergen Street going up to just above Six Engine, Hunterdon Street around in there. Now right on the other side of where Camden Street is, where the school is today, Fourteenth, Thirteenth, and Seventeenth that was strictly another Italian neighborhood all in that area. In North Newark we lived from Clay Street all below Broadway going back to Elwood Avenue. Everybody lived below Broad Street. Coming back, cross town you had what we called the "valley," Pennsylvania Avenue, Sherman Avenue. There was about a ten-block area where blacks lived down there. No blacks lived in the Burg. Forget about it. You didn't live up there. We used to call it "mortgage hill" when I came on the job because all your civil servants, Police and Fire, lived in Vailsburg. We couldn't go up there and get the mortgage. Forest Hills,

North Newark, you didn't live there. The Weequachic section, forget about it. It was interesting.

Haran (1961): The makeup of Newark back then was predominantly white, but there were pockets of African-Americans in the area. They were over in the next block from me. There was no trouble back then and none to be expected. Really, everybody got along. The area that I grew up in was predominantly Italian and Irish, probably mostly Irish.

Elward (1962): Growing up everything's divided along national lines, Irish, Polish. Twenty Engine, down on Prince Street; that used to be outdoor markets. That was the Polish section. Going further west, that was Italian. Going further south, that was Jewish. You could almost mark off the school zones and who went there. Gyms from all the high schools, the gymnasiums, they would tell you everything. You wouldn't have to check on anybody's biography and that was the truth. And you could check where the city was going by going down to the gym and you start seeing. Football, basketball. baseball not too much, but the first time you see a black face. That'll tell you the year. You look at the picture of the sports teams. That will tell you what was happening in that neighborhood. That is the Bible. If you ever want to check the history of a city, you go to the gyms and look at the pictures. You got the year, the dates, everything. And that'll tell you what was happening. Better than somebody's "I think this was happening." You look at that picture. That's what was happening.

Butler: (1963) I had been born and raised in the city and I thought the city was still a relatively nice place to live. At the time I came on the job, it was still predominantly white. I remember when I first went on Central Avenue there was one black family living on Ninth Street between Central

Avenue and Ninth Avenue. Nice gentleman with his family, knew all the firemen. I would say within two to three weeks of being there I was introduced to him. Saw his kids grow up. Very nice, he was a hardworking man. His wife was working. Nice kids, they all went on to be professionals, doctor, lawyer, and a psychologist. His daughter turned out to be a psychologist.

Schofield (1963): You had your old neighborhoods. Like the First Ward was Italian and Down Neck was the Polish. Parts of Newark going to Hillside, the majority were Jewish. But everything just kept on changing.

In 1940 where I lived on Avon Avenue, that was starting to change even in 1940. Bergen Street, parts of Bergen Street were starting to turn. There were a lot of Jewish in that area. In fact, there were a couple of synagogues not far from where we lived. I guess human nature or whatever, people moved out and maybe wanted to better themselves or they saw another opportunity somewhere else. Little by little people just started moving out or moving up, moving up to Irvington and so forth.

B. Cosby (1963): I grew up in Florida. But I came up here after I finished school. Newark was to me very different. I wasn't used to a lot of big buildings so close to each other with a lot of people. It was alright. At first it was kind of exciting because there were a lot of women around, a lot of girls. I could see a lot of girls right next door. I could go out at night and see a lot of people, have a lot of parties. To me it was really nice. It was different, but I liked it. It was just congested to me, but I got used to it. By me working instead of going to school up here, I was only in the streets on weekends and at nights. So, I didn't get the full impact of the kids around my age because I was working. But it was good for the swimming pools and the movies. When

I first came up here there was a lot I couldn't do in Florida that I could do here because you know.

Cody (1964): My neighborhood was predominantly Italian. I was the token Irish kid in the neighborhood. I remember getting beat up a couple of times just walking up Eighth Avenue.

When I came on the fire department, I moved to Vailsburg. I got married. We had a home up in Vailsburg and we used to go downtown all the time. The city was nice. There was a lot of shopping. All the department stores were down there.

Wargo: (1964) I was Down Neck. East Side High was mixed. It was Spanish, Portuguese, Italian, German and Slovenes, Sumerians, Polish, and some black and some Jewish. It was a mix. It was a melting pot. It was Down Neck.

I very seldom went above the wall, except to go downtown. There was no reason for me to go up past Bamberger's. I had no reason to go up there when I was a kid except for maybe Olympic Park or something like that, you would get on a bus. So, I really didn't know what the neighborhoods were. I had heard of Vailsburg. To me that was like Whippany or something. It was that far away, like being out in the country or something. I didn't fully understand what Vailsburg was until I got on the fire department.

Knight (1964): The makeup of the city at that time was all Jewish in Weequahic. There weren't that many blacks. The blacks hadn't moved in over there yet. They were mostly down in the heart of the Central Ward. Up in the West Ward there was an ethnic mix of Italians, Irish, Polish, Germans, and Ukrainians. Where I lived was a mixture, a lot of Irish. We had different things in the city and you had more time to enjoy yourself.

Gaynor (1965): I don't know how you could really either categorize the city's makeup or give it a percentage, but more than the makeup, there were a lot more people. We're looking at perhaps as many as maybe a hundred and fifty thousand decline in population from 1945 or 1950 up until the present time. It may have leveled off in the last few years, but we've experienced a huge decline in population. If you worked for the fire department you know we've also had a huge decline in buildings for them to live in. So, you would understand how that could be. And I would say that West Side High at that time in 1962 was about half and half of white/black, a very small Spanish probably 1-2% as far as school enrollment. But I mean I wouldn't know about other sections of the city.

In my neighborhood it was a lot of Italian, even in Vailsburg or at least the streets that I frequented. And I think the rest was just a real mix, a total mix. It was more homogeneous ethnically speaking, on my particular street. Because you had the Boylan Street Pool and Boylan Street School, the first half of the block was really taken up on one side entirely by public buildings. It's almost as if it was two halves. And then when you went on the second half where there were people on both sides of the street, it was very Italian. Including us, my mother being Italian, my father Irish. But it wasn't like block after block everyone was Italian, Sunset Avenue a lot of Italians, Brookdale Avenue a lot of Italians. Jakie owned a store, Jakie was Italian. Spoke to you in broken English and when he counted, he counted in Italian. But that's our little neighborhood. It's only a block on either side.

In fact, by '67, I came back to the same neighborhood. I went from Boylan Street to Sanford Avenue. At twenty-four I came back to Boylan Street for a year or two. Back to Sanford Avenue, then to Norwood Street at twenty-seven where I bought a house right almost next door to what is now our fire headquarters, at 177 Norwood.

Calvetti (1966): Down Neck was always Polish. There were a lot of Polish people Down Neck when I was growing up. And later on it became the Portuguese section. But North Newark was mostly Italian. In fact, they ripped down the First Ward and they built projects down Grafton Avenue. So, a lot of people went to the projects over there. The projects were mostly white too then, believe it or not. And then they changed over, mostly minorities after that. In fact, they blew up a few of the projects. They're all gone by now.

Lawless (1966): There were various ethnic groups. You had Irish, Italian, few blacks. In my time all the blacks mostly were below Norfolk Street. Down by the projects, down by Norfolk, Prince, Charleston, all of that. I went to Eighth Street grammar school. We had blacks there, not predominant. It was predominantly white. We basically all got along. It wasn't like you separated that deeply into ethnic groups. Everybody got along. I had a lot of Italian friends. I had Polish friends. It was everybody. We got along good. I had black friends. Guys I played basketball with in Eighth Street, in the playground there. We basically got along together. This is the '40s, '50s. I never had any racial problems. Not that I encountered anyway.

Benderoth (1967): Runyon Street was a good area. It was mixed, Jews, Italians, Germans, Polish, Irish. It was a mixed group of people, got along fine. I knew a few blacks there too; they were called Negroes at the time. I had some friends in school. I went to Blessed Sacrament grammar school. I went to Weequahic High School. They were in the area, stayed in the area.

In '59 my parents moved out to Irvington and I moved to Irvington with them. Met my wife, got married, moved back to Newark, a lot of people on the street. I would walk with my son out to South Orange Avenue, buy fresh Italian.

McGovern: (1968) Newark was neighborhoods. North Newark was Italian. Down Neck was mixed. Vailsburg was mixed. I'd say the city was 75% white, 25% minority at the time I was growing up.

Finucan (1969): You know it's ethnic. This is 1991. We have the Portuguese Down Neck and the blacks everywhere else, I guess. A few bastions of white neighborhoods, I don't even know where they are anymore. I guess over around Branch Brook Park, over that way, Lake Street, Ridge Street in there. I think there are some white neighborhoods over there towards the Belleville line. That's about it that I know of, everything else is either black and Down Neck, of course, is Portugese. I don't think we have any oriental sections to speak of. Puerto Ricans over on Broadway, over that way, we have Puerto Ricans.

J. Cosby (1969): I wasn't born in Newark. I was born in Florida, the State of Florida. I moved to Newark in 1958. When I first came to Newark, I really didn't like it because where I lived before was basically one-family homes. I could never get used to living in a house with someone else, like a multiple dwelling, someone living on the top of you and the bottom. It took me a long time to get used to that. At that time. I would say Newark was at least 70% white and 30% minority. I didn't realize that there was a lot of discrimination in the city of Newark. Coming from out of the south you always heard that the north was like paradise compared to the south as far as race relations.

One thing that really stood out in my mind was the newspaper advertisements. I'll never forget it. I remember when we had the Newark

Evening News. There were people who would advertise apartments for rent. Whenever they want a white person for the apartment, they would list the apartment as say a three-bedroom apartment, kitchen. Then they would put in there, "white stove, white refrigerator." What that really meant was that they wanted a white person for that apartment. That's the way they would get around the law. They couldn't put white person, white only. So, they would put that in the ad. That was the negative side. There were some positive sides. I think that kind of situation more or less made me work harder. I'm not the type who would try to buck anything like that. I mean it made it difficult for you, but what it did for me is inspire me to purchase a house. I purchased my first house when I was twenty-four years old. That was my way of solving the housing situation. I just went out and bought a house.

Saccone (1969): 90% of the people that lived in Steven Crane Village came from the First Ward and all because the First Ward was getting congested. It was mostly Italians. A few Polish people, Irish, but mostly Italian people from the First Ward because the First Ward was building up.

Daudelin (1970): My group of friends was all Italian. That's where I learned to hate the word "*medegone*". I was the only non-Italian. The makeup in Barringer High School at the time was I'd say 70% white, maybe 20% black, and maybe 10% others. Out of your 70% white, 50% had to be Italian. When I was in high school, I used to get my name in the paper because I played quarterback for Barringer my junior year. And my name Daudelin, ends in "l - i - n." We'd play somebody and I'm excited and I open up the Sunday Star Ledger. It said "delina." They put an "A" on the end because well, he's got to be Italian. So, I got that nickname in high school, Daudellina for a while. There were a lot of old Irish people and German people up there, but they didn't have kids. Their kids had already moved out.

Marcell (1970): I lived in a section that was mostly Irish. Pat Durkin was over there, Pat Doherty, that whole section was mostly Irish. You went over a couple of blocks, maybe three or four blocks and it was all Italian. But if you went south towards Sussex Avenue it was all African-American. I used to play basketball in the Sussex Avenue playground and it was a mix of Italians, Irish, and African-American. There were some conflicts going on between the races in those days when I was growing up, around '65, '64, '63. You had to be careful because if they didn't know you from the sports, there were other guys that would be looking to urge you into a fight. But if you played sports, those guys kind of just respected you as another player. That's how it was in my neighborhood.

I would say the race makeup of the city when I was in high school was about 30% African-American and not that much Hispanic, maybe 10%. And the rest was mixture of white, mostly Italian, Irish, and some German when I was growing up.

Rotunda (1970): The whole city was ethnic. You had the Irish section. You had the Jewish section. You had the Italian section. You had the Polish section. You never knew how sheltered a life you lived until you grew up and moved out of the city and found out everybody wasn't Italian. Ivy Hill was more or less the Irish section. North Newark was the Italian section. Weequahic was the Jewish section and Down Neck was predominantly Polish. It was all mixed in between, but the predominance of the ethnic backgrounds made it good. I covered the whole city of Newark in the sausage business and then with Coca-Cola before I came on this job. So I'm pretty well versed in the city of Newark.

Dainty (1970): North Newark, where I grew up and I grew up in the projects, Steven Crane Village, was predominantly white. It was I would say mostly World War Two and Korean War veterans, working class, middle class people. I came on the job. I didn't know that the Central Ward even existed. I had to check a map, how to get there. And that was 100% black. I don't remember ever seeing any Spanish or white people living there. Belmont Avenue had some businesses at that time, even though it was after the riots. On the corner of Belmont and Waverly (Irvine Turner Boulevard and Muhammad Ali Avenue) were two bars, one on each corner. Next to the one bar was the Belmont Spring company which manufactured and repaired heavy duty springs for trucks. Down the street was an auto parts store and I believe originally Fisher Bakery or Drake Bakery were also on Belmont Avenue, but they were gone. But residential make up was black. We had the projects behind us and that was really all black. So, I would say 100%.

Down Neck was in the beginning of going from middle class white to Portuguese. But it was still predominantly Anglo-Saxon with a lot of Polish, some German. Vailsburg at that time was still predominantly white and I'm talking 1970, '72, '74. Weequahic, I would say it was probably a little bit mixed. The professional blacks who held good jobs moved in. You had the hospital up there which was one of the big employers. You had your stores. But I very rarely went there. I didn't travel through there to get to work. We didn't have a lot of calls up there. So I can't really say definitively what the makeup was.

P. Doherty (1970): Back then the part of the city where minorities lived was Prince Street, Wallace Street, over in that area, from Springfield Avenue to Avon Avenue, a smattering, not all the way over to Avon Avenue. Mostly to like Eighteenth Avenue, but down a little, in back of High Street, near Quitman. Where I lived was ethnic, but not totally ethnic. It was mostly Irish and Italian. They were mixed, and Germans. Schnerings, the Schnerings lived on Morris Avenue right between Cabinet and Twelfth Avenue. And I knew them all my life, Bobby Schnering, the whole Schnering family. And the Quins lived on Morris Avenue between Cabinet and West Market Street and he was a fire captain. And then you had Sal Padesco, lived on West Market Street right on West Market and Morris. I went to school with his daughter. I knew he was a fireman too. There were a lot of them lived right around the area there. And Mike Smith, he was a cousin of mine, he lived by Eleven Engine. In ten years or so they all moved uptown.

Perez (1970): Down Neck had your Polish section, your Italian section, your Irish section. You never crossed into one or the other. The German section, you know you had your areas and that's it. You cross into the other area; you get beat up. Italians, Portuguese, Spanish, Irish, there were Poles, a big Polish neighborhood, Saint Cashmere's. I was right in the middle of a Polish neighborhood. All my friends were Polish. I never knew Italian, Irish, anybody because everybody was Polish. I knew some Polish words.

Kelly (1971): Certain sections of the city were Polish, predominantly Polish. A lot of the old Germans came from around Springfield Avenue and all around that central Newark there. You went up in the numbered streets; that was more Polish I believe. You had some Polish bakeries there. I know there were blacks down by Prince Street. But it was mostly white people that I can remember. You'd never see a Chinese person unless it was a restaurant or something like that. That I remember anyway. I'm sure there were Chinese people there. But it was a mix. It was a mix of a lot of people. Everybody got along.

T. Grehl (1971): Where I grew up was a combination. It was a mixture of everybody, all different nationalities, all different religions, some old people, some young people coming in, Irish, Italian. The Vailsburg section was predominantly white. From basically the Parkway west, the West Ward, was predominantly white. South Orange Avenue had a little more of an Italian area. North Newark was the Italian area. Over by Weequahic High School was the Jewish area. Down Neck at the time was more Polish and then Portuguese began coming in. I used to go to the doctor down there.

Romano (1972): Growing up in Vailsburg, at the time Vailsburg was probably 100% white, in the '50s and early '60s. I think it was probably the last all white section of the city. I really didn't know too much about the Central Ward and the South Ward. The only time I went down there was to go downtown Newark. Taking the bus and it was just passing through on the way downtown to go to Bamberger's or to go to the movies. That was my only knowledge of it. And not being aware of racial problems as a young boy, young teenager, I never gave it any thought. My first awareness of racial problems was when I went to high school at West Side High School in 1960, '61, '62. And there were a lot of racial problems at the high school at the time. Which I guess reflected other high schools. They were probably the same problems that were occurring at other high schools at the time. Which I learned later was true. So as a young boy in the '50s I was not aware of any racial problems. Later on I was.

R. Stoffers (1973): As I was growing up I had no clue what the makeup of the city was. I never paid attention to it. I just do my thing and I don't pay attention to that. Never did and I mean black, white, pink, orange, green. Ay, you know, buddy, buddy. I'd go from high school with Donny Braxton all the time. Picked me up and dropped me off. Never bothered me. He was just another guy from Vailsburg.

Rosamilia (1973): Every ethnicity was represented in the city. There were Irish neighborhoods, Polish neighborhoods, Italian neighborhoods, Jewish neighborhoods. You had Spanish neighborhoods. Just about any ethnic group had a little enclave somewhere in the city even if it was only four or five blocks. And you could tell by the names of churches a lot. Saint Aloysius you knew what kind of neighborhood that is. Saint Rocco's, you knew what that neighborhood is.

Brownlee (1973): When I first went to Avon Avenue, across the street there was a candy store on both corners, an apartment house. There was a German bakery up the street. The church was still mostly white on the one side. The other side was Jewish. And it was about 60% white and 40% black. And it went quick. It really went quick. The German bakery up the street, she had two German shepherds that sat in that store all day long with her. And then they burned her out. And the candy stores closed down. The one became like a rooming house. The other one was apartments up top. Downstairs was still a store for a little while then it turned into empty. Then it went back to being a store for a little bit and then the whole place went empty. Then they tore that down. The synagogue was gone. The building's still there, but it's a church now. And on the other side it's a Baptist church also. The firehouse is right between two churches which is a wonderful place for a firehouse. But we used to ride across, people would wave and it just doesn't seem like that anymore. It's gone.

Down Neck was mostly Irish and Portuguese. And by South Orange Avenue was a lot of German and Italian. Over by Avon Avenue was a lot of German, Italian, and Jewish. And then further over was a lot of Jewish. And Vailsburg was Irish, German, and Italian. North Newark was Italian. When I went on the job the Central Ward was mostly black and Jewish stores. The stores eventually went down. Blum's Department Store was still on the corner of Twelfth Street and Springfield Avenue. That was my first two alarm fire, Blum's Department Store.

J.P.Ryan (1973): Newark's always been a city of immigrants, which a lot of people find that hard to believe. Whether one group or the other predominates for a given period of time, it always changes. It's a regular cycle in the city. It's just by the nature of the industry that's in the town, the jobs that are available. Certain parts of the city were Italian or German or Polish or Black or just about anything. There were very diverse communities in the city. It wasn't predominated by any one group at all. And it was a very stable and very nice place to grow up. I see it coming back to that now. I really do. I see a large influx of Hispanics and Europeans from places you never really hear about. Newark, New Jersey is the third largest receiving place in the country for immigrants from Poland. Polish as a second language is still taught in the Ann Street and Wilson Avenue schools.

Connell (1974): Basically, Down Neck is what it is now. It was mostly Portuguese. The center part of the town was basically black. Around Bloomfield Avenue, the Hispanic population was moving in and Vailsburg was still basically white. It was still a halfway decent part of town. There used to be a couple of good bars up there guys used to go to on their off time. It was still half way decent. The crime rate seemed to be beginning its climb.

Killeen (1974): In '74, Six Engine (Springfield Avenue and Hunterdon Street) was in a black area, so that was all I saw there. Going up toward the Burg was black. We caught some of the high First Battalion boxes like going up towards the cemetery; it was still intermixed, black and white. And going into the Burg it was pretty white. Because after I got laid off I came back and lived in Vailsburg for a couple of years. And going to the south part of Newark, I always recall that as being black when I came on the job. And down by Ten Engine was black and Spanish. And North Newark by Belleville, that was white and Spanish at the time when I came on the job. Bloomfield Avenue was pretty much an Italian enclave. That part was all white Italian.

Straile (1974): I lived on Chestnut Street, they considered that the Ironbound section, Down Neck and there were a lot of different restaurants and activities always going on down there. So there wasn't too much having to go out of the city anywhere else or into the city anywhere. Once in a while we'd go up to the Broad and Market area uptown to do some shopping and stuff like that. I got to North Newark once or twice. Somebody introduced us to Calandra's Bakery. My wife fell in love with the bread they had up there. So at least once a week or every other week we'd go up there and pick up some bread and some pastries or something. I got around Newark a little bit, but not as much probably as I should have. We used to play some sports up at School Stadium in North Newark. We played some softball and football up there. It was a great experience. It really was.

Daly (1978): I lived in North Newark. North Newark is in the corner between Belleville and Bloomfield. And it was mostly all white. If you want to break it down ethnically, it was Italian. I guess I was the *medegone*. I was the only mick on the block. Everybody else was Italian just about and we had a few German, but my block was mixed up. The majority was Italian, a few German, one or two Irish, but it was predominantly white, predominantly white when I was growing up.

Gesualdo (1978): My area was pretty much 95% Caucasian whatever, Mediterranean. I know when we used to go across Orange Street, that was kind of like the dividing line. That's where the black area started around Baxter Terrace and all that. When they took Eighth Avenue out to build the 280 highway that was kind of like the dividing line. You knew if you went across the highway that there was a pretty good chance you were going to get into some kind of fight or something because you just didn't go there and they didn't come across Eighth Avenue, the old Eighth Avenue. So, at the time I would say probably it was as far as minorities go, however you want to classify them, I'd say maybe at that time it was sixty forty maybe. What they considered to be white or Caucasian or Italian or whatever compared to black and Hispanic. I believe now it's probably up closer to 80% minority maybe 20% Caucasian.

The West Ward used to be all Irish. We used to go up there for dances occasionally by the old Sacred Heart Church. That was mostly Irish white up there. Central Ward was mostly where you're minorities were and the lower end of the North section down around McCarter Highway. So, I would say from the time I grew up in, it was maybe sixty/forty when I was going into the service. When I came out it started growing closer to seventy. Now I'd say it's probably about eighty to twenty maybe minority to white.

Hopkins (1978): Vailsburg was mainly Irish cops then the Italians started moving in. All down by Ten Engine, that's where all the blacks were originally and they spread out to lower Springfield and Runyon and all that stuff. Down Neck was Polish people and then the Portuguese stated moving in. North Newark was mainly Italian and then the Spanish started moving in down Crane Street and all the projects down there along High Street.

Mitchell (1978): By the time I came on the job, Down Neck was a mixture, but it started going more to Portuguese. North Newark was still an Italian area and had started getting Hispanics in there. And the rest of the area was mostly black. Vailsburg when I came on the job, that was turning black. When I was in high school it started changing because I went to Seton Hall, so I could see the change coming up South Orange Avenue on the way to school, how it slowly worked up to Vailsburg.

Kormash (1979): The South Ward was black, West Ward was black, North Ward was Italian for the greater part. Down Neck was Irish, Polish, German, Italian, the Portuguese started moving in after '67. There were Cubans and Puerto Ricans down there too, but not a whole lot. Vailsburg was a lot of Irish up there and different nationalities.

Caufield (1980): The North Ward was mostly Italian. The east side of the city had a lot of Irish there and they also had Portuguese, Brazilian. The other people, I wasn't used to talking to and finding out what they're all about. What they do in their lives. As a young child you stayed to your own. That's how you were taught. You taught yourself as you got older and you started learning new ways that Newark was like the Ivy Hill Apartments. I used to call them the United Nations. You had everybody over there. There were no big problems about it either. They were in the area and got along. I said, "Well, if they can do it anybody can do it." But the military more than anything is what woke me up about that.

It took a little while before I learned the different neighborhoods. I didn't know streets in other neighborhoods. I just didn't go there and they weren't familiar to me. I would say South Orange Center was probably more familiar to me than the Central Ward. When I learned about the other areas of the city as much as I did learn about them, this was Italian; this was black; this was

Hispanic. I never had a problem with anybody. To me you had to prove you're wrong to me. You don't have to prove you're right to me. I never had a problem with anybody. Have I come across a lot of it? Yes, I have come across a lot of it.

E. Griffith (1983): Vailsburg was predominantly white and I remember I went to school with a lot of cops' and firemen's kids. There was some black. There was some Puerto Rican. There were a few Asian kids. One was actually Chinese. His family owned a Chinese laundry. But it was predominantly white, Irish, Italian, German, Polish. There was Ukrainian. There was a whole Ukrainian section in Vailsburg. So, it was a mix, but not like it is today where it's predominantly minority now.

You had black, basically the projects downtown, that type of thing. But I really didn't come in contact with it even when you went down on the bus. You didn't really notice it until later on. I mean, I didn't even know about Down Neck growing up in Vailsburg. I knew North Newark because of the cathedral and the park over there. I knew that was a predominantly Italian neighborhood. I think it was waning, but I knew that south Newark over by the Weequahic area was Jewish. That's what I heard, but I couldn't tell you what that actually meant then as a kid. Italian you kind of got to know in Sacred Heart because the kids were pretty good at talking. They pointed out to you there was a difference. We had gravy on Sunday. What's gravy? But it was a really nice mixed neighborhood. It was a lot of fun.

DeCeuster (1984): The North Ward was mostly Italian, but it started going more Hispanic. Down Neck was the Portuguese before you got an influx of Ecuadorians and people like that. Central and South were predominantly black. In the South you had some of those neighborhoods that actually were a little bit nicer. There was a little mixture of everything in there.

Giordano (1984): I guess since we were trapped in our Ward, I'm going to say we were never really aware of the rest of the city. We just thought the West Ward was all black, the Ironbound was all Polish and Irish. That was just the perception of those. You should have known better who was where. Most of us didn't know that many Jewish people lived in the Weequahic section. We wouldn't have known that as a kid growing up. Maybe people over on different parts of town wouldn't know Forest Hills, a beautiful affluent neighborhood either. It was interesting to see when I did work in Weequahic the beautiful buildings in that section in the South Ward.

Johnson (1984): The makeup of Newark when I came on was still more segregated. The south side was predominantly African-American. You had Ironbound and North Newark were heavily Hispanic. Now the population has changed. It's quite a bit Hispanic in this neighborhood (Avon Avenue) and throughout the city, more Caribbean groups throughout the city. There's just a melting pot, it's heavy melting pot. Upper Vailsburg, past Sanford Avenue is more middle class or people who are middle class up in that area. But you have it throughout the whole city. It's a big melting pot now.

Ironbound, North Newark, the property values are extremely high. So, they're going to demand more resources. We always hear things like, well, they want to close a firehouse down in Ironbound; you know you're going to have to fight because people are there. They're going to be there in full force to say, no you're not. Whereas certain areas are dilapidated; there's no urgency there. That is now beginning to change with the new administration.

Nasta (1984): At that time, the biggest thing that struck me was the neighborhoods and how ethnic the neighborhoods can be. The area where I was living Down Neck had a lot of Polish people at that point. There were some Italians Down Neck, but most of them were in the North Ward and that's where I knew some of my friends. A couple of them came on the job with me. I'm very friendly with Artie Morriello, Tommy Condito, John Agoston. Another great help to me was Chester Soloway who actually helped me out when I lost my lease. His mom and dad owned a house on Adams Street. I met Chester actually through going down and working out every night. We became friendly and when I lost my lease, just timing I guess, his parents had a vacancy in one of their apartments.

Lee (1986): Now the Central Ward is predominantly Afro-American black and East Ward was predominantly Hispanic. Once you cross over McCarter Highway you got a lot of Portuguese immigrants. You had a lot of Polish immigrants. You had some German down there then. A lot of Italians were down there.

Masters (1986): The makeup of Newark when I came on the job was predominantly black and Hispanic. Down Neck and the North Ward were still white. The black areas were still not fully developed in the Central and the South Ward where I lived, where the riots were. Down Neck remained the same, Portuguese with the restaurants and the living conditions down there and the North Ward was changing gradually towards Hispanic, but it was still predominantly Italian. Good area to work, to live and nobody would bother you. The Weequahic section in the Fourth Battalion used to be Jewish. The houses when I first came on and even into the '90s, even to this day they're still beautiful houses. That's a hardworking section there and they keep the section good. Mayor James lives there over on Goldsmith Avenue. I remember his house. Very, very good place to live. Like I said, just the Central where the riots actually were really never got back to its feet back then. Supermarkets were a luxury. They had the Pathmark on Bergen Street. That was it and it's a shame.

Alexander I (1987): I really wasn't familiar with other parts of the city. My mother and father always say to us, "You don't want to go in certain areas." They mainly kept us out of the bad areas. They didn't want us ever to go there. I would say when I came on the job the city was more African-Americans and Hispanics. The Portuguese section was Down Neck. And the Caucasians that were still left were more North Newark. But for the most part it was African-Americans and Hispanics.

DeLeon (1988): All Hispanics went to the North Ward. Portuguese and Brazilians went to the Ironbound section. And the rest of the city remained the way it was. I remember my father, when he bought the house in '72 on Woodside. He bought it from an Irish guy and there still was a lot of Irish and Italians there when we moved there. I was friends with Matty Cordasco and John McLaughlin. All those guys were down there. They were still living around there at that time. And slowly but surely, they're all gone. They all left. Until maybe just Hispanics, even some Puerto Rican descent, but now I see a lot of South Americans. So, I guess the area changes with time. North Ward Hispanic and Ironbound still the same and the rest of the city still remains the same. Now they're selling houses in the Central Ward for five hundred thousand dollars. I can't even imagine in my head how you take that kind of money and invest it when there's still a long way to go.

Greene (1988): Newark was very segregated or provincial. Every ethnicity had a section of the city somewhat. The North was Italian. The Ironbound was Portuguese and immigrants. The West was predominantly African-American. But the city was mostly African-American, Polish, and German, something like that, Eastern European.

Griggs (1988): In the North Ward growing up I was probably the only Irish-English-German kid surrounded by predominantly Italians in the neighborhood, up in my end of the North Ward. Further east it was Latin and to this day it's a heavy presence there. What's happening now I'm not really sure. I grew up on Belmont Place, 82 Belmont Place. I believe there's a lot of Italian still living on the block. But I think it's more of a mix. I know down in the East it's heavy, heavy Portuguese. Even in high school I think that was evident back then. But you had your German, Polish, they were heavy down there. Today it's heavy Portuguese and it probably was so back then.

Alvarez (1989): At the time I grew up the Ironbound was primarily Portuguese. It's changed now to primarily Brazilian and other South American countries. But at the time it was primarily Portuguese.

LaPenta (1989): In North Newark there were some Italians and mostly Puerto Ricans, Hispanic, Latino. There were African-Americans. It was a good makeup, I think. I notice today most of North Newark now, the Third Battalion is really dominant in Latinos, Hispanics, and everything else. You could see the wave going out and the new ones coming in. But you see that all over the city. I see the Colonnade Apartments, the ones on MLK and Broad between MLK and Broad. You never saw a white person or a Hispanic person. It all was really African-American. Now you drive over there. There're white people, there are all kinds of people. You could see them coming in. Same thing up in Vailsburg, over on Ivy Hill, over there, Russian immigrants and Polish immigrants, they're all over the place.

Cordasco (1989): My block, it was predominantly Italian, but there was a mix. Right next door we had some Germans. There were some Jewish people. I remember the first black family that came in. They came from the

South Ward and they were the Bradley family. And they were very cool people. Actually, we were friends with them until we moved out of Newark. They lived on Kearny Street, close to Nine Engine. And then some Spanish people started moving in, but predominantly when I was growing up it was mostly Italian. There were a couple of cops and firemen on the block.

Tarantino (1989): I had a pretty good mix of friends. I didn't have a lot of black friends or a lot of Spanish friends, but there was always a group of us that would always hang out together. So, it would probably be, if there were ten of us, there were six white guys, two Hispanics, and two black guys. We had a couple of Filipinos that used to live in the Colannades that I knew. But other than that, the makeup was probably black, white, Hispanic when I grew up. I assume the rest of the city was mostly black and Hispanic. Because I didn't know anybody that was white that didn't live in my area at all. I knew there were Portuguese people there, but I didn't realize there were so many Portuguese Down Neck. And I didn't know really anybody from the Central or the South so I just kind of assumed it was all black.

Petrone (1991): When I first came on the job, I still lived in Vailsburg. It was probably 70% black by that time. It was where I grew up. When I went to Sacred Heart I think there were four black people in my graduating class by 1983. And two years after that, the class my sister would have graduated with, she didn't stay in the school, but that was almost 80% black. So, the demographics changed pretty quickly in Vailsburg. I didn't get down to the South district until I was eighteen. And it was by that time predominantly black. I never really made it over to the north side of town either. From what I understood it was a lot of Latinos in this area (Park Avenue).

Castelluccio (1991): I'm going to say the majority of the population is African-American and Hispanic for Newark. The Spanish and European, most of them would be Down Neck, but the majority is definitely Hispanic. I think the Hispanics might have actually taken over the numbers from the African-Americans. You see a lot more of them in certain sections like the South Ward or even Springfield Avenue here. You'll see them walking. You wouldn't have seen that ten years ago. They've moved into these communities and are starting to take over. It's a big change.

Baretelloni (1993): We were Italian and the North Ward was known for it. Mostly everybody's name ended in a vowel. I can remember that. You know we had some black kids, not a lot though. Puerto Ricans were starting to come in. I was a substitute teacher when I came on the fire department and I saw the Ecuadorians come in. You started to see different Hispanic cultures come in and it actually changed. In my area, I think we were replaced mainly by Spanish, my particular neck of the woods.

I would say you just had to go by the election because usually whatever group has the most, wins. Up until to this day, a lot of times people vote along their ethnic background. In the North Ward we had Carrino, Anthony Carrino. He was our councilman for years. So, I would say the city probably was over 50% black, maybe 30% white and the rest different makeups.

Down Neck was Italian also and now there's a lot of Dominican people that moved in. There used to be a lot of Portuguese. I don't know if they're there anymore as much. I'm not sure. When we were there, it was Italians down in the Ironbound and Portuguese, but then the Italians ended up leaving. Then the Portuguese came in and then they even started to leave and were replaced by Dominican people. The North Ward, where I was, became mainly Hispanic. You could tell by looking at your council. It reflects the community.

Gail (1993): North Newark was very different back then. It was a large Italian population. I would say Italian/Spanish mix. And so, it was interesting. You're young. I didn't mind moving into an area that I wasn't used to. An inner-city area, sort of speak, where you had to watch your car; you had to watch yourself a little bit. I didn't mind. I kind of embraced it. I thought it was cool. It seems to be happening now. Everybody's moving to the inner cities. It's like there's going to be a resurgence of inner cities like Brooklyn, here in Newark. The whole demographic is changing, the population is completely changing. It's pretty amazing.

Ramos (1994): South Orange Avenue was predominantly black. I was the only Hispanic in my class. I knew of Vailsburg. I would hang out mostly in North Newark where my uncle, my aunts lived. That was more Hispanic in that area. On the weekends I would go down there and hang out in North Newark most of the time. The south I knew nothing about. Vailsburg I knew something about. I mean there was a big Irish population in Vailsburg at the time. But there was this high school that closed down, Vailsburg High. I went to Irvington Tech because my mother didn't want me to go to West Side. Although my brother went to West Side High and graduated from there. He today is a Federal Judge. He became a lawyer who became a Federal Judge. She didn't want me to go there.

It was a different time though. He went there seven, eight years before I did and the school had changed immensely by the time he graduated. I went to Irvington Tech because we moved in 1980 from South Orange Avenue. We moved to Eighteenth Avenue. Eighteenth Avenue and Melrose, right next to the McDonalds. In the apartments there, over the bar there, we used to live upstairs.

Farrell (1996): Growing up in the North Ward, I knew nothing about the West Ward. I knew nothing about the South Ward. I had never been to Weequahic Park. We never ventured to that side. My parents are from Down Neck, so we knew Down Neck a little bit. We knew the Burg a little bit because my father had friends up there because he was born on Boylan Street before moving down there. So, we knew Vailsburg a little. I knew Down Neck a little. I knew nothing about the Central Ward, the South Ward, the West Ward really.

Meier (1996): The South and Central Wards, the West Ward they were primarily African American. North Newark predominantly became Hispanic and Down Neck was still a mixing pot of just about everything, still a lot of Italians.

Montalvo (1996): By the time I came on the job, the Latino population was just starting to blow up in Newark. At one point before I came on the job, the Latino aspect of the community was maybe 15-20%. By the time I came on the job, we were up to 35% and now we're almost at 49-50% of the city.

Willis (1996): I hate people that say they don't see color. I don't believe in that. My friend who was black, I called my black friend. I didn't have to hide or hide behind that. We had the projects in Hyatt Court. We had the South Street projects. We really didn't travel past Penn Station. You didn't travel past there, but we hung with kids from South Street. And I hung down in Hyatt Court, all my friends white, black, Hispanic. We all hung together. My neighborhood was predominantly German, Polish, and Irish. And then on the other side of Wilson Avenue began the Italian neighborhood. But everybody got along. I think as time goes on everybody assimilates. Everybody had their food. That's how you distinguished each other. When the Portuguese came and the Spanish came, they started taking over the neighborhood. People were moving out and the kids assimilated. We all grew up together. We all knew each other. We had Cuban families that moved in, everything. We were a melting pot. And I appreciate it because I learnt a lot. You learned the language. You learned the food which is good because I'm Irish. My mother couldn't cook. Our school yard was diverse in all ways.

Freese (1998): The only thing I knew about the rest of the city was its reputation. I knew the city was the stolen car capital of the world at that time. That was a label it had. I didn't know much other than the stereotypical, kind of wild, dangerous with a lot of stolen cars and thefts and stuff like that. I guess my impression was so bad that when I moved to North Newark it wasn't as bad as I thought. So, I think it was just a stereotype of Newark. Actually, I met a lot of great people, a lot of great families in North Newark.

Newark was very poor, mostly black, some Hispanic in North Newark and some Italian. But for the most part, the majority was African-American. A lot of joblessness, a lot of gang activity, but I just focused on the positive stuff.

Carr (2000): Prince Street wasn't like what people believe Prince Street to be. You had families that had moved from North Carolina that stayed there. You had large families. My grandmother was actually from down North Carolina. She had moved up to Newark and lived up here with her kids, worked up here. My grandfather worked at Sears which was over there on Elizabeth Avenue, that big green building over there. So, he was there for a while and then once they saved their money, they bought a house in North Carolina. They went down there and retired. We left Prince Street, moved to Littleton Avenue, got burnt out of Littleton Avenue, moved back to Prince Street. We were down there for a while. Once we got to a certain level of income, we left Prince Street and then we ended up moving up to the Vailsburg section which was by far probably at that time one of the most blue-collar sections of the city of Newark. Either they were firemen, policemen, postal workers, or, teachers.

Highsmith (2000): I would think Newark was around 60% African-American and the rest others. I don't know what else. As I grew up, I never went to North Newark, knew nothing about North Newark. I never went to the Ironbound section. Really knew nothing about the Ironbound section. And Vailsburg we called Hooterville because of the hooters. Because there were a lot of women were up in Vailsburg. Vailsburg had a reputation for having a lot of women in it. And that's all I know. I never really got to travel. To go up there anywhere, I was pretty much locked in the city.

Jenkins (2002): On the side of the town that I lived on, Vailsburg, it was predominantly African-American. I knew the different sections of the city, but not as well as I do now after coming on the job. Like the Ironbound section, you knew more about Ferry Street or Penn Station. That's about as much as you knew down there. North Newark, I knew enough about that. I attended Bloomfield Tech Vocational High School. I used to take the bus down Franklin Street to get to the subway, the city subway to go downtown Newark, stuff like that. So, I was able to see more of that side of Newark prior to coming on the job.

Kupko (2002): I would say the city was at least three quarters black and then your other 25-30% give or take, Portuguese, South American, Caribbean, Puerto Rican, Jamaican, Haitian, and Malaysian.

The majority of your European population would have been in the East Ward and the North Ward. And the Central and South Ward was predominantly your black population and I think it's still that way today for the most part. Not much has changed in that regard.

Mickels (2002): The makeup of the city depends on the area that you're referring to. It's broken up, the south, predominantly African-American. The north Latinos, more so Puerto Ricans, Dominicans, the east Portuguese and Brazilian. So that's how those sections are broken up. Unlike what many people think, that Newark is all black or African-American, no we have different areas, there's the north, the south, the east, the west and they are all predominantly of those races that I mentioned. Even though we always had some of everybody everywhere, but that was the makeup. And that still is the makeup now.

I was not too familiar with the North or the East Wards. I was familiar with Vailsburg. I was familiar with the South, so the West and the South I was very familiar with, wasn't too familiar with the Ironbound section and up north. Bloomfield Avenue I knew more of as far as going up north, but I didn't really have family or friends up that way. And then the east, you went down there just for the restaurants. I learned those areas as I got my years on the fire department.

Medina (2006): The North was pretty much Spanish. I'm Puerto Rican. Everybody is Puerto Rican, Dominican. Actually, where I lived on Mount Prospect, Freddy Tenore's mother still lives there. He's Italian. His mother had a place for like forty years. So, you still had the Italians, the Irish, so it was kind of mixed. And as you go Down Neck it's more Portuguese and up here on Springfield Avenue it's African-American. Vailsburg you still find Spanish, Italian, white, Polish. So, it's kind of mixed believe it or not.

Figuereq (2006): I lived in the city my whole life and actually it's overwhelming sometimes because I'm from North Newark most of the time. I grew up in the north and most of the stuff that I did was in the north, so now coming into the fire department. We have all the other different areas. I really wasn't that familiar with for example the south and the west. Now I'm here in the center which I have to learn.

M. Bellina (2008): I guess in our area around Clinton Avenue I would say predominantly African-American. North Newark when I was there is Hispanic, more up on Bloomfield Avenue there's still some Italian people.

G. Centanni (2013): When I was in the North Ward there were a lot more Spanish families and the Central Ward is African-American. But then they have that downtown area where there's a lot of work, so there's a lot of people coming in and out of the city all the time. East Ward, a lot of Portuguese still live down there.

G. Pierre (2013): When I first got on the job, the area that I stayed in was predominantly black. That's a real conversation because sometimes we get bound to just being in Vailsburg or you get bound to just being in Ironbound or just being downtown. So, I guess a better way of saying it is where I was prone to be was a predominantly black area. I remember when my family first moved into Vailsburg, there were maybe four or five Jewish families still on the block. And slowly but surely, I don't know when. No one ever saw moving trucks, but they kind of got out of there. Now what I'll also say is on another note, you see a lot more cultures now because you see a lot more Haitians. You see a lot more Jamaicans now. If you go down to the Ironbound section you start to see a lot more Indians. Ironbound was more Portuguese.

Vailsburg has a lot of cops, a lot of guys on the job. When I'm jogging around the block. I see their cars. Everyone knows the Burg. It's like that area of Newark that was like an uncut kind of cream of the crop secret of Newark no one knew about. You could be in Newark, go into South Orange, have a good time with the family, come back. So, that's what the Burg is about. I like that, but the area I kind of like kept myself in was predominantly black. I don't want to say Newark was predominantly black because I didn't get around. I didn't start going to the Ironbound area until college. I used to run into New York all the time. You go into New York. You hop on the PATH train. That's when I was a kid. The Ironbound area, I had a section in my life where I was kind of big at you know the Portuguese spots for Rodizio and the Portuguese cultural center they had down there.

I just recently started looking for apartments and that's when I started really looking at what North Newark has to offer. I'm looking at Tiffany Manor and I'm looking at one of the new office buildings downtown. And now it's not even for the essence of knowing what this area is about. It's more so it's about would I want to live here? How much is rent here? I didn't even get exposed to North Newark until I was like twenty-five, twenty-six years old.

Rawa (2013): The city was predominantly black. Where I grew up it was predominantly Portuguese with a couple of straggler Polish like myself which are all pretty much gone. After blacks it would be Latinos and that's about it. But compared to the way I've seen other people grow up, pretty diverse.

J. Centanni (2014): The majority in the area of South Ninth Street are African-American. In the North Ward where I live is a lot of Hispanics and even the block that I'm on, there're still some Italians left in the area there. Down Neck is a lot of Portuguese and Spanish, but I think it's a diverse mix.

I'm learning the area now that I work in just from being here, but prior to that I only knew the North Ward and some of the East going out down there, a couple of bars and restaurants.

Fortunato (2014): I know the North pretty well. I used to work in Irvington near Clinton Ave on Twenty-first Street. I worked in that area a little bit. Down Neck I really don't know. The Burg I really don't know either, but North Newark, Central Newark I know pretty decent. I would assume the city is mostly Spanish, Portuguese, and African-American.

Corales (2016: The city is sectioned off. You know the Down Neck area you get the Portuguese, the Brazilians, the South Americans, with the Spanish mixed in here and there. Then you go to North Newark and it's primarily Hispanics. Then you go up to the west or the south and it's primarily blacks. It's always been that way I think. I don't think that's changed much.

Part Three:

The City Coming on the Job

Fredette (1942): The city was not bad. The people were not bad. When we would shovel hydrants, they would come out and bring us coffee at three o'clock in the morning. In those days they had to go out and shovel hydrants to make passes for the Arhiens Foxes to get in. They would make a big V in the street. People would come out with coffee and things like that. Then the people in the neighborhood, they used to close our doors. We were the last ones in the city to get overhead doors. We had the collapsible doors. They would come and close our doors in the winter time. The cops, the radio cops would never do that. They would drive right by leave the doors wide open. We would come back; the fire house was cold.

Vetrini (1946): I didn't want to leave Newark, but gradually we had no choice. You couldn't find places in the city. And then with the G.I. loan, for two hundred and fifty dollars you buy a house. And for the two hundred and fifty dollars we went to the credit union, because we didn't have two hundred and fifty dollars. So, I moved out of the city, which was against the rules. We had no other choice.

You even had trouble getting a mortgage when you went to buy a house in the city. They wanted a large down payment. The banks were not giving the mortgages out. You could get a G.I. loan. You could get that. But then you had to get that down payment. Where are you going to get the down payment? We went out of the city. I went out of the city in 1951. For a ten thousand five-hundred-dollar house, I put down two hundred and fifty dollars. I paid forty-two dollars a month mortgage, ninety dollars a year for heating, and the taxes were a hundred and forty dollars a year.

But I moved back in 1960. I moved Down Neck. And then in '61 I moved to Eastern Parkway in Vailsburg.

F. Grehl: (1948) During the war, a lot of people came into Newark. Newark was a great manufacturing city. During the war there were people needed in the factories. A lot of people came into Newark and filled the void of all the people away at war. Of course, when you came home the apartments and dwellings were all at a minimum. They were available, but it's a law of supply and demand. There were a lot of people who wanted it. Instead of getting forty dollars a month, they get forty-five or fifty. After all my pay was only seventy-eight dollars twice a month, the first and the fifteenth.

After the war, a lot of people started coming from the south. That's when they started those high-rise projects. When they started building the one right across from Six Engine it was all white people in there. The school system started getting over taxed. And little by little we had too much density for the facilities that were available.

You just couldn't live in the city of Newark and send your kids to school there. I had to send my kids to private Catholic school in Irvington, because I lived right on the borderline of Irvington. People couldn't live in Newark and send their kids to private schools. That's when they started moving out and getting housing that was fit for their size family. Except for Vailsburg and those sections, Newark was basically apartment house structures and people didn't want to rent to kids. They didn't want to rent if you had animals. When I first had children, I couldn't get an apartment because I had kids. Nobody would rent to me. That's when people started moving here and there.

J. Ryan (1948): I thought it was a good city in those days. Good city, very popular city. I often heard the fellows who didn't come from Newark, who were up around there in the service, it was a good liberty town. Good place to the service men there. I wasn't in service long enough. But it was a good city. Everything was there, uptown.

McCormack (1949): I think that the city started to change right after World War II. All the veterans were coming back from World War II. There were literally thousands of them. Every family had a couple of sons in the service. Every family, there's nothing similar, Vietnam or any other war, that would match the total number of people involved in World War II. Every single household had someone in the service, a brother or father. It was mostly men in those days, but the point is that when the war ended, these guys started coming back and getting married. There was a deluge of guys looking for houses.

The families that these guys left when they got drafted were living in these three-story frames in Newark, in four or five room apartments with their parents, brothers, and sisters. When they came back, they'd get married and very often had to move back into those same apartments. They'd have a room as a married couple with his parents or her parents. There was no construction. There was no housing in Newark. The existing housing was what was there and it was solidly occupied. Nobody was selling houses. There was a tremendous demand for housing for these young veterans. They were getting married. They were starting families and they needed housing.

I remember too, because I myself experienced this. In those days if you wanted to buy a house in the city of Newark because the buildings were old, we were told you had to come up with a 20% down payment. That was mandated if you wanted to get a mortgage, a 20% down payment. The average house in Newark in those days might have been selling for ten thousand dollars. So, a 20% down payment was only two thousand dollars, but two thousand dollars was an astronomical amount of money in those days. Very few guys had that kind of money.

When I came on the job as a new fireman, I made twenty-four hundred dollars a year. There weren't any two-income families. Most of the girls, when you married, left work and stayed home to become housewives. So, we were living on twenty-four hundred dollars a year. Trying to pay rent, have a car if you had a car, and save money. It was pretty hard. These people were desperate. They couldn't find housing. Then these developers came in and started buying up land outside the perimeter of Newark. In Union, in Clark, in Rahway, which were close by. You could buy a house, a tract house. If you were a veteran, they had signs all over the place. "Veterans, No Down Payment." You could buy a house out there if you had a steady job like a fireman. Walk out, look at a house, sign a paper, and move into the house the next day. All these young veterans and their wives were bailing out to get a place to live.

The other thing that sped this whole process up and made it feasible was the advent of the Garden State Parkway and the New Jersey Turnpike. You could jump on the Parkway up in East Orange and be down in Clark or Rahway in ten or fifteen minutes. It was no worse than a commute from Vailsburg to Down Neck, if you lived in Vailsburg and had to go Down Neck. There were hundreds of houses going up in these little suburbs. You could walk in and if you had twenty bucks in your pocket to pay the closing cost, you could move in the next morning. That's exactly what guys did. That's where the exodus came from. People started moving out.

A lot of people honestly tried to stay in the city at the time because the city was home to them. But they couldn't find a house to buy. There were few houses available because Newark was a very stable community. If you did find a house, they'd tell you to come up with 20% down and these young kids didn't have that kind of money. So, they bailed out. That's what started the snowballing effect. I'd say that started right after World War II, in the late '40s and the early '50s. It continued right up into the '60s and then it really snowballed. Faster and faster, as if the snowball were rolling down the mountain and picking up speed. But in the beginning, it was because there was no available housing in the city. You couldn't buy a house at any price.

Gibson (1953): When I was a cop, I got like my father. He was a foot cop for years. He was in the first radio car they had though. But when he was a foot cop, he would tell me stories about how the neighbors would leave the back door open. If you want a beer, go in the ice box and help yourself three o'clock in the morning or something like that. And it turned out like that for me. I had a detail by Queen's Church and I knew everybody in the neighborhood. I used to go sit on their front porch and drink a beer with them. They took me off of Broadway and they put me up in Forest Hill. I'd trip over the scooters and stuff on the sidewalk. But the people got to know me and they'd invite me up on the porch for a beer. I got along good with the people.

And when I came back from the service my parents had moved down two blocks. Still on Broad Street, and they stayed there. After I got on the fire department, I was there with my first wife and my mother and father. As a matter of fact, when I got married my first marriage, we had the reception at the house. It was a three-story brownstone, but it had the three-story staircase and everybody sat on the steps. And my old man bought the beer and the sandwiches and that was it. It was great.

Alfano (1953): I do think the city changed. You know the neighborhoods changed. And let's face it. When the neighborhood changes everybody runs. And the only reason probably that I didn't run was that I had all those kids. I didn't have the money to run for one thing. Not just firemen, I mean everybody, because they want good schools and stuff for their kids, so they got the hell out.

Wall (1954): Newark at that time was almost four hundred thousand. Because when I came on the job even in '54, we were something like three hundred and eighty thousand. We were far larger than Jersey City and now

Jersey City population wise has almost the same numbers as Newark because they weren't as devastated as we were.

Griggs (1956): Newark was great. No matter where you went, at least where I went, I found it good. The time I felt Newark is changing is when I enlisted in the Navy in 1951. I would come back on my weekend leaves or time off furloughs, I could see the city was changing at that time. That was my feelings. And after St. Benedict's, I spent almost a year up at Seton Hall College. I got up there on a track scholarship. My parents had separated; the support was stopping; and my mother couldn't handle what little money I needed, so she informed me that it was time to go look for a job. And that's what I did until I went into the service.

When you're away from a location, like in the service and then you only come back occasionally, you see that things are changing. After I got out of the Navy, I was at the Sherwin Williams paint company. The people I worked with in the paint company, it looked like nobody had left in fifteen years. I'm working with guys with thirty years. It was like a home. Everything ended up getting shut down there. They made a storage area out of it. I mean they did everything there. They had their own varnish cookers. They would make paint for anybody else. They could make it for them and make their own paint. It was big time. Everything was cooking down there. And you had other paint companies. You had Benjamin Moore down the street. At least Benjamin Moore is still there today. But it changed.

Duerr (1958): When I went into the service, I wasn't eligible to drink. So, when I got out of the service, I passed twenty-one. I could drink. So that changed my whole modus operandi. I could go to places I couldn't go to before, but basically the city was pretty good. You had everything you wanted. You had all the stores, the major stores you wanted downtown.

Back then it was a great city. Anything that you wanted made in the world you could buy in Newark. There were a great number of theaters, movie houses. You had the Newark opera house. You had both burlesques and you had movie theaters downtown. You had the symphonic hall on Broad Street. So, there was a lot of entertainment back in those days. You really didn't have to leave the city and go to New York because you had everything available in Newark.

Belzger (1959): My wife used to go to our pediatrician's office with the baby carriage, carry the kids in. He'd give them the shots, give them a full physical, give them cookies and milk and charge us fifty cents apiece. Can you imagine? When I lived on Alexander Street, I didn't have much money. He knew it. My house cost me fourteen thousand dollars and everything I had went into the house and four kids. He used to apologize later on when the kids were a little bit older; he used to charge us seven dollars for a house call. He thought that was a lot of money. He said he had to do it. But I remember the second time he came back because my kids had high fevers; he didn't charge us anything anyway. That's the kind of man he was. That's the kind of people they were.

Nineteenth Avenue was the same way. It was a three-family house, a cold-water flat, but the people were generous. I remember my wife and I were married about seven or eight months. It was February. We were in bed one morning and she shakes me. I said, "What's going on?" She said, "It's snowing in here." I said, "So, what?" I was used to it. The houses never were put together too well. We were in the dining room, but we were using it as our bedroom. Five minutes later she shakes me again. She says, "The snow's not melting." But we were just getting along at that time. That's before I was in the fire department.

It was pretty close to the Irvington line and most of Irvington was that way too. Nice, nice people, although over on Nineteenth Avenue they were no longer Irish and German, but they were Polish and Ukrainian, a lot of different mixtures of people. But Newark was good to me, Newark was always good to me. I think back, we had a lot of good things. My wife was in the First Ward over on Garside Street. She always brags she could come home at twelve o'clock at night. Take the bus and get off at Mount Prospect Avenue, come down Third Avenue, walk on Garside Street and have no fear of anybody bothering her. Nobody would molest her or anything else.

Charpentier (1959): The city was pretty good at that time. We were busy, but the attitude of the people toward the fire department was a lot different than in later years. I mean, before we were the heroes. We got along whether it was black, white, purple, or green, male, female. We got along with all the people.

Dunn (1959): The city at that time in the East Ward was doing fine. There was really no problem. I lived right at the street where Ballantine Brewery was; it employed thousands of people. So, you knew about work; everybody went to work. Everybody's father or family member worked in this major employer. Public Service was a prestigious job. New Jersey Bell was a prestige job. And working in the paint companies on the island was a very prestigious job at the time. Because they had all amassed what I considered a substantial amount of money after the war. If you work and you don't spend your money; you save money. So, everybody had money, everybody had cars. The downtown area of Newark where you went was a vibrant area. We had Bamberger's Department Store, which was our large department store. I never went down to Hahne's Department Store because that was where the rich people went. I went to Ohrbach's.

The racial makeup of Newark at that time, I'd say was probably fifty-fifty. In 1959, the workers of the Ironbound who had worked in Public Service, the Fire Department, the Police Department, in Sherman-Williams, in Stanley Tools, had all made what they felt was enough money to start to vacate and move on. As that occurred all through the city, the Central Ward people, who were black people at the time, were also branching out. Where the white who were leaving the community at the time weren't thinking as much of going to Vailsburg as they were in the 40's. Back then a guy would sell his house on Brill Street and move to Vailsburg. In the 60's they would sell the house in Vailsburg and want to move out further. The guy from Down Neck wasn't going into Vailsburg at that time because he thought there was a racial change coming there. So, he would move.

Freda (1959): When I first was appointed to the fire department, I was stationed in a fire house that was opposite the corner I grew up hanging on, the corner across the street from Fifteen Engine (Park Avenue). As kids making devious plans, I would play some jokes on the firemen across the street. In fact, one of the firemen in that firehouse when I was hanging on the corner as a kid is a Deputy Chief. I remember him. He went on up the ranks and he's a chief. He's still on the job today. So, when I feel old, I just think how he feels.

But the city was a very stable city then. The Park Avenue firehouse was the type of firehouse that you would sit outside on the old wooden captain's chairs. They'd be lined up in the summer right across both bays and people would stop and talk to you. People would come into the firehouse. The neighbors and the firemen got along very well. It was unheard of for someone to break into a firehouse and steal anything. In fact, we didn't shut doors to firehouses then. The neighbors would come out and shut the doors.

There was a candy store next door run by a woman. We would literally go in there, sit there, and talk to the woman and she'd be forcing you to eat lunch with her. It was close enough where if the bell rang you could run next door, a very friendly, stable atmosphere. Crime, crime wasn't a big deal then at all. It was unheard of to have a fireman's car broken into. I can't remember an instance of a firehouse being broken into or anything taken or any problem at a fire with the civilians. Believe it or not, when I went over to Twelve Engine (Irvine Turner Boulevard) the same thing existed. Most of the firefighters there were white. We were in a totally black community. It was very neighbor conscious. We used to sit outside. Again, the neighbors were very close, right in the middle of the ghetto. While I was there, my car was never bothered. The house was never broken into. Nothing was ever taken.

A. Marcell (1959): When I first went on up to Eleven Engine (Central Avenue and Ninth Street) it was a really, really nice place up there. The Presbyterian Hospital was there. The Sisters of the Poor were there. The neighborhood was really nice. It gradually, gradually got worse. I think when I went there, they went out about three hundred and twenty times a year, Eleven Engine. I think the truck went out about two hundred and fifty times, but as the years went on things got really bad.

J. Miller (1959): At the time the city was a very industrious city. It was a very busy, hustling city. Downtown Newark, I think was one of the four busiest corners in the world for populace. At the time I think we had almost four hundred thousand people in the city of Newark. There were over a hundred theaters and dozens of churches and synagogues. I was told there were a hundred and thirty-five theaters in Newark. It was possible because every neighborhood had two or three theaters. That's why the fire department had such a big theater detail.

Gene O'Hara was in the Fire Bureau for a while. When they went down to Washington Street, he'd like to go to the Empire. That was part of the theater detail. He had a lot of stories to tell about that. How you were allowed to go back stage and meet all the stars. They would kid with you. Some of them lived by Ten Engine, across the street. In the early '40s it was a prestigious place to live in that area. The neighborhood was nice and they had a lot of rooming houses. Some of these stars would stay there with friends. I guess Gypsy Rose Lee and a few other ones he would tell us about. He met them all.

There were many restaurants to go to, many Jewish Deli's, German Jewish restaurants on Prince Street, where you got good corned beef. You had Stosh's. My impression was it was a very hardworking city.

A. Prachar (1959): It was no change to me because I'm still in the area I grew up in. The only difference is I had moved out of the area because I'm married. I'm living in the Clinton Hill section. I have two sons, but Sherman and Astor are still Sherman and Astor. It's the place I grew up. As far as I know, the people are the same, the attitude is the same, and it was just a question of leaving my home in Clinton Hill and going to work where I had lived. It was just going back to my roots.

Schoemer (1959): It wasn't bad. It wasn't bad. They still held parades and stuff like that for Thanksgiving, Macy's was there. Not Macy's, Bamberger's was there before it went to Macy's. It wasn't bad.

Smith (1959): There were a lot of wood frame buildings all over the city. The projects on Waverly Avenue, Prince Street in that area, they weren't completed yet. There were still on the side streets going off it, it was all wood frame. In fact, the majority of the city was wood frame.

Carragher (1960): Oh, it was beautiful. It was just starting to slide a little bit then, in the '60s. I lived in North Newark on Summer Avenue and Summer Avenue was a beautiful street. We knew everybody. Everybody around the neighborhood were all friends. Our family was active in church over at Saint Michael's Church in Newark. We had theaters. We had the burlesque shows, bars. Anything you wanted to do you could do in Newark at the time. It was probably in the early '60s when it started really changing. I moved to Newark in 1946 and from '46 until the time I came on the job, I really enjoyed the city of Newark. It was really good.

There were mostly all three-story frames and on Prince Street, Charlton Street. It was all built up. It was not empty. There were some empty lots, but it was all buildings. Three-story frames all the way across Prince Street over to Avon Avenue. Charlton Street was the same thing. It was all three-story frames. The projects were there. Stella Wright was there. They had just built the Scudder Homes. It wasn't open yet, but all around there were a lot of old buildings. One after the other, they were run down, a lot of poor people in them. The worst part of the city was around there. Above Littleton Avenue the homes were considered nice. The bad area was like from Bergen Street to High Street. Actually, it was below High Street in certain areas, too. But mostly from High Street to Bergen Street was a bad area. And from South Orange Avenue, Thirteenth Avenue over maybe to Waverly Avenue that was a real bad spot of the city at the time. That's where they tore a lot of it down. But most of our fires were in that area.

Haran (1961): You could get anything you wanted in the city of Newark back then. There was everything. There was manufacturing. We had a seaport second to none. We had a thriving airport. Today it's an international airport. It's probably one of the four top airports in the country today. Anything you wanted to buy you could get in the city of Newark. With the manufacturing, you didn't have to go anyplace else. In the downtown area, we had big department stores. We had Bamberger's, which is Macy's now, but it used to be known as Bamberger's. We had Ohrbach's. We had S. Klein on the Square. We had Hahne's. They were located in the center of the city and could be reached from any outskirts of the city in fifteen, twenty minutes on a bus. You didn't have to go anyplace else. There were no malls back then. Anything you wanted you could get in the city of Newark. And busy, busy back then. I think when I came on and growing up in the city of Newark, I don't think the population ever hit five hundred thousand. But it came close. Today it's only somewhere around two hundred and fifty thousand, but back then it was like five hundred thousand. Not only that, but with all the stores we had there and all the manufacturing in the Ironbound section and other parts of the city, I think the city used to swell to a million and a half people during the day. We had a lot of people in the city of Newark.

Elward (1962): So, they used to say the quiet '50s, not true. The '50s had great music, a lot of things. Everything changed. Like from my neighborhood, a lot of guys are dead now. Let's see, I get out of school January of '51. The Korean War is on. A couple of guys in my class are killed because they made the unfortunate choice of joining the Marine Reserve. They walked out with a diploma one day and they were in Parris Island the next week. At least we got like nine ten months in between. And that's always a shocker when you're that young and the guy you walked to school with is dead, killed. It blows your mind. So up to around, I give it to 1960 on the money. The city was really moving quick in every direction. The first indication was Route 78. The local priest is telling everybody, "Don't buck out of Saint Rose's. Don't worry that depressed highway will never come through here." My father was a bus driver and he says he respects the priest, but my father was no fool. He says, "It's coming." And once it came it destroyed East Orange. It destroyed the neighborhood. But the truth is after the Second World War, the GI bill was in effect. So, what happened was guys like you and me, it dragged to college.

Because you get out of the service, they were telling everybody to get a GI loan to buy a house which was so cheap. But the houses in Newark weren't moving with the neighborhood busting. The city was in flux.

Dalton (1963): I knew it was starting to change. My mother and father were still living on West Runyon Street and it really got bad. They moved to Irvington. I went back to my neighborhood. I grew up in the Clinton Hill section on Seymour Avenue. That was totally gone, gone. Clinton Avenue was really wrecked up and everything else. I was like wow, in a short time too. That's when I knew instantly. I didn't imagine the fires I was going to see though. I never used to see as a kid a whole block burning. Most of them were vacant, but to see that. That's tremendous.

B. Cosby (1963): When I came on the job the city hadn't changed because I came on in '63, but it was starting to change. Because I think in '58, '59 a lot of blacks had wanted to be policemen and firefighters. They were fighting to be on the job. So that's when they had lawyers. A lot of blacks and firefighters on the job in '58 to '63, a lot of them came on. We all tried to stick together and help each other pull out.

I think it was the year I came on the job or the year after we started having a lot of trouble in Newark. The riots were brewing, getting ready to start. It didn't get really heavy until '67, but it was brewing ever since I came on the job, '64, '65, '66. And one incident would set something else off. It kept accelerating.

I think I had just bought my second house because I had three kids then and I wanted a larger house. So, I bought a house on Vohress and Lesley because I had been notified that were going to take my house anyway for 78.

So, I figured I would move out when I found a house and get settled. That's what I did. But I had to move on the day the riots started because I had my closing. It wasn't planned that way, but the way it happened I had to move when the riots started. Now I had to move furniture and stuff from my other house into this house. Try to bypass the National Guard. Everybody didn't want me to pass and they're walking down the street at night. I had to do this in the daytime when I was off and get back to the firehouse that night. I did double shifts, so it took me about two or three days to move.

Butler (1963): There were a few vacant buildings before the riots. But after the riots, so many people fled the city in fear of what was going to happen next summer or if somebody else was arrested. A lot of them just moved out without selling, hoping they'd sell or people just stopped paying their taxes. Then they were forced out of the building and it stayed vacant. But just a mass exodus of people shortly after the riots I think led to most of the vacant buildings at that time. Now today I think your vacant buildings occur because of non-payment of taxes, which the owners walk away from. They make no repairs or anything like that and people slowly start moving out of houses. All of the sudden one day you have a four family or a large brick apartment house totally vacant. That's where you run into your problems. You run into squatters. You run into the junkies.

Schofield (1963): It was a great town, a great city. I remember years ago as a youngster I lived I North Newark at the time. Walked from downtown Newark through the First Ward and up to where I lived on North Seventh Street by Bloomfield Avenue. I never got bothered. Then after the riots, things just started going down. People started moving out.

Garrity (1964): The city was a great place when I came on. There were places to go, things to do all day, all night long, a great place. I enjoyed the city a lot. Always some place, something to do.

Benderoth (1967): I used to deliver beer and soda in the city before I went to get married and all. The area where they built the hospital that was one of my biggest areas. It really didn't change until they decided to build the college there because they were moving all these people out. They said it was the blacks, but it wasn't. There were Italians. There were a lot of Italians there, a lot of Italians that just came over. They didn't speak English very well. And they had to move too. So it wasn't that they were picking on blacks at the time. The city in its wisdom said they wanted to put University/College there and they did. They took out ten square blocks, a lot of homes, a few businesses too. Candy stores, that was where you get your groceries, where you get your bread and milk and cold cuts and your fresh rolls. It was a big grocery store or candy store whatever we used to call them. We had one near the firehouse. Once they started tearing things down that went and we had no place around Three Truck/Seven Engine (West Market Street) to get food. So, if you didn't bring it in with you, you didn't have it. Anywhere else in the city, you could walk across the street to get a sandwich or whatever. Even Belmont Avenue, they still had places to get food. We didn't. We lived on an island. It was very interesting.

J. Cosby (1969): At that time the city was I would say sort of on the decline. There were a lot of vacant buildings. The property values were very low. After I was appointed, I went to Engine Eighteen on Avon Avenue, I remained in the neighborhood up until 1972. That's when the neighborhood really got bad. There were two vacant buildings on each side of my house. I remember one night somebody set one on fire and I responded to the fire. I pulled up to the intersection of Avon and Fifteenth Street. I looked down the street and saw the flames coming out of the house next door. I thought it was my house. We pulled in front of the fire building. At that time, I had just brought a new car. My new car was parked right in front of the fire building. My wife ran out of our house and moved the car. We put the fire out pretty fast, but if we had been out someplace else, possibly I could have been burned out. So that kind of spurred me to move. I moved from Newark in 1972 to Lakewood, New Jersey. It was a good distance away, but I felt like it was a lot safer.

Weber (1969): Coming on the job, it was a whole new experience to me having grown up in almost a white suburb, to see how the other half lived. It was interesting. It was a growing up experience. It created for me the opportunity to grow up myself by seeing how other people lived. The makeup of the city coming on where I was assigned in the Weequahic section, I always knew that to be a mostly Jewish neighborhood. And that had all changed. It seemed like everything changed in a relatively short period of time. From my graduation from high school in 1965 to my appointment to the fire department in 1969 was only four years and it seemed like the total exchange of the people who lived there.

K. Miller (1969): I was home from college during the riots. I was living on Sanford Avenue. And I can remember laying there in bed. I could hear the popping and the cracking with the gunshots going on down the hill. We were up on the hill and I could actually oversee the city. You could see right down the hill and into the city. Not that I could see anything going on, but you heard the noise. You heard and the radio was telling you about the riots going on, but up in Vailsburg it was like being in another country. We certainly weren't jumping on the 31 South Orange Avenue going downtown, but it still was like a far remote thing.

The city was on a slide. We were heavily dependent upon Federal funds for a whole lot of things. The city was a poor city. The major manufacturers, the breweries had already started moving out before I got on the job. The last one, Ballantine, left when I was on the job. Except for Budweiser, Budweiser's the only standing one now. The major department stores all started bailing out. Just an overall deterioration of what keeps a city running, rate-ables. Went through that period where that publication "America Burning" recognized Newark as having a 500% increase in arson fires. Neighborhoods were burning down, disappearing. It was on a slide. No rate-ables to support what we had going on there. But still with a definite need of emergency response, not only in the fire department, but in police and in medical, EMS response.

McDonnell (1970): At the time I came on the job I lived in North Newark. I was living on Clifton Avenue. North Newark was a white area, Vailsburg was a white area, but the South and Central Wards were pretty much black. I don't think there were too many white people left over in the Weequahic section. The major population change had taken place. The racial make-up was probably sixty-forty. 60% black, 40% whites and a little Hispanic population maybe filled in 5% of that.

It was a city that was in decline. It started I guess to decline in the '50s. Probably hit its peak in the '40s, early '50s and things started to change. The population started to change; the city started to go downhill. We had a big welfare population. People were moving up from down south. The city started to go into decline in the late '50s, continued to the '60s, and with the riots that accelerated. The population change was dramatic after the riots. Things changed dramatically. People left the city in droves. Right after that there was a big, big exodus from the city. There was an exodus of businesses. I think the biggest population change had already taken place by the time I came on the job.

It was probably at that point that the city was just on the brink of almost hitting bottom. It probably hit bottom in the next ten to fifteen years. The businesses were still all of downtown. They weren't empty, but Springfield Avenue, which was a major business street, was probably half empty. The whole Central Ward was on its skids, abandoned buildings galore. The city was definitely in a state of decline.

Dainty (1970): There were factories Down Neck. A lot of factories had closed that employed large numbers of people, but there were small shops, manufacturing shops, things like that, auto body, auto repair gas stations, mercantile stores. But a lot of the very large manufacturing places had closed up. They just couldn't keep up. My wife had a relative who owned one of those factories. You remember when you came off of Route 9 onto 21, there was a big five or six-story brick factory building with a toy soldier on the roof. That was his building. He was one of the inventors of the Teflon zipper. He actually closed up, not because he wasn't making money, but he couldn't deal with not being able to get qualified employees. And a lot of the employees he had were just ripping him off. So, he sold the rights to the zipper and closed up. I guess that was probably the case for a lot of places. They couldn't get qualified employees, skilled employees, for factory type jobs. I know from talking to my wife's grandmother who worked in a fur shop down there in the '40s and '50s. They used to get the raw furs and make them into coats and shawls and things like that. So, there were a lot of businesses down there that for one reason or another moved out or went belly up.

T. Grehl (1971): When I first came on the job it was only four years after the riots. So, the memory of the riots was still very, very visible. Everybody could see it. The Ironbound section below that wall, below McCarter Highway was a stand-offish point. The buildings were burnt out in the Central Ward. There was still a tremendous number of fires. So, the after-glow of the riots was still around. A lot of people were very, very prejudice and had hard feelings. The hard feelings were there. It was obvious that the city was in turmoil. It wasn't ready to bounce back yet in '70, '71, '72.

Romano (1972): By the time the '50s came around and the '60s, Newark was well on its way to decline. And the riots of '67 and '68 I think are what sounded the death knell to the city. That's what spurred the great migration, if you want to call it white flight. They called it white flight. And the city was left with a large welfare population, a large population of people in poverty. Businesses had left the city. Tax revenues were gone. All the major businesses are gone by that time. Especially after the riots, so by that time the city was really well in decline.

Burkhardt (1973): Vailsburg started to change probably, I'm going to say, like the mid-'80s. Vailsburg hung on for a long time. Then once Vailsburg started to slip, I mean it came down quicker than the shuttle. Vailsburg is probably the worst section of the city right now. You've got all kinds of mixes up there. You just don't have the poverty people who are in the Central Ward. They didn't go to Vailsburg. They went to Irvington and Maplewood. They went west.

R. Stoffers (1973): When I got on the job there was a hostile atmosphere in the city. Resentment, the man opposing us, whether you're a cop or a fireman, you're considered the same I guess in that aspect. You're authority.

Not as hostile now, towards the firefighters. I think that calmed down a bit. There were a lot of middleclass people in the city later on. Whereas before people had that rebellious attitude and it didn't matter who you were or what you did. I think that changed. Of course, I've seen the cops chasing the cars. They did shoot out the back window of my wife's car. They did put a gun to my head and try to rifle my pants and ask for money on payday. I had eleven cents; they didn't take it. I mean it changed a little bit with the construction even on Avon Avenue and the side streets. There's more middle class in there. And I think you get into a middle class you get a different mental attitude. Now we have people who are looking to make a living here instead of people who are looking to grab. I think that changed the attitude.

Rosamilia: (1973): By the time I came on the job I was aware of the other side of the city. I didn't have a car when I worked at Saint Dominic's monastery, so I used to take the 6 crosstown. And I was aware of it then because I had to get onto a bus and it would drop me off at that monastery. It was almost a whole block there. I think at the tail end of it there were some houses on Twelfth Avenue, but that big old brick wall was almost a whole square block. So, I was aware of what was going on. Plus, my mother was a seamstress. She worked right on Ashland and South Orange Avenue. She worked right there and I was aware of that too. But I didn't do too much traveling around the city. Everybody that I knew, family, friends, and so forth, they were all right in the same neighborhood.

When I come on the job, the makeup of the city must have been close to fifty-fifty because two years before that Mayor Gibson beat Mayor Addonizio in a really close race. And so, I'm saying the racial composition was probably somewhere near fifty-fifty, maybe a little less than fifty-fifty.

Coale (1973): I knew Newark as a young man. Growing up there were no shopping malls and we would come to Newark once or twice a year. That was the place to go shopping in the '40s and '50s. There were no other malls until later on. And then unfortunately the riots came along and that was the end of the city as far as I could see. It changed.

Langenbach (1973): The city was the pits when I came on the job. Belmont Avenue was like a war zone. It still was all the vacant buildings. There were still some things left. I think there was one, maybe two bakeries behind the firehouse. I know the pillow factory was back there. There were a couple of white bakeries back there, German, whatever they were. But everything around us was burnt out pretty much.

Brownlee (1973): When I came on the flight was on. Everybody was leaving.

J.P. Ryan (1973): The city had changed dramatically. It honestly had. It was in a state of decline, rapidly. The first summer I was on there were several riots in the city, civil disturbances I suppose would be the proper terminology.

Connell (1974): My first impression wasn't really that great because most of the meetings and stuff were held at six, seven, eight o'clock at night. It was always dark out and it was almost always on Eighteenth Avenue. At that time, it was still a fairly decent part of town and it impressed me like being nothing like I thought it was going to be. It appeared a hell of a lot better than it really was.

Langevin (1974): Well, the city was a little culture shock. I never really worked in a big city, didn't know my way around. The area where I was assigned to was basically black. It's mostly residential homes with some light industry, retail mercantile. It was a little bit of everything to deal with.

Banta (1974): What did I see when I came on the job? Devastation, vacant lots, nothing but vacant lots and vacant buildings, basically the center of the city was nothing more than vacant lots and vacant buildings. At that time, North Newark, Vailsburg, the Weequahic section, and the Ironbound section were pretty decent.

Perdon (1974): The area around Springfield Avenue was beat up. The people in it, they kept you busy. That's why you were there. There was a lot of crime. You saw all kinds of stuff with the projects. The projects were in full force then. They were in full bloom. If you weren't there for the garbage, you were there bandaging somebody up or they're coming over to the firehouse with gunshot wounds. There was the knee cap bandit. Shooting everybody's knee cap in the elevator and they'd come hobbling over to the firehouse. On Springfield Avenue, you had Bill and Ted's Sportsman's Bar across the street. There was a row of stores there. One was called the Slave Ship. They were on that side and we were on our side and they pretty much, even the project people didn't bother us. In the firehouse when you were there, the people right around there. They were all right.

Killeen (1974): When I came on the job, my impression of the city was I knew it was full of fires compared to the surrounding areas. It was noisy. There was always something going on. It wasn't a slow city like I grew up in. Like in my town, in Belleville, it wasn't small like that. There was always something going on. And that's one of the reasons I wanted to come here, because it was exciting. That was my view of the city when I first came on.

There were a lot of fires. It was exciting and there was always something going on.

Bisogna (1974): I lived in Newark when I came on the job and I thought it was a good place to live. It was after the riots, so there was a lot of destruction in the Central Ward. Driving through it to go to high school, you saw a lot of changes. It was pretty disgusting, but I didn't have to get off the bus. The bus took me to Essex Catholic, which was on the other side of town. It was still pretty decent over there too at the time.

Working on Prince Street and looking around, you saw there were a lot of abandoned buildings at the time. I got to see old homes that I would have never seen that are gone now. Like on Clinton Avenue, there were some brownstones there that were absolutely beautiful. Like the Scott Mansion. I've been in there several times. That's an impressive place. A lot of money went into that place. If they ever open it to the public, you've got to go take a look. I'm sure a lot of it has been vandalized over the years, but they had statues next to the fire places. It had two or three fire places, it was gorgeous and the central staircase, you go up the front steps and go down a long hall with a couple of parlors off both sides and then you're in the middle of a circular staircase with a vaulted ceiling and a skylight on top. Natural light comes down. Very, very impressive home is what it was.

The area has much improved in the last twenty-five, twenty-seven years, a lot of changes. For a while it was the Great Plains there, by Five Truck you could just look for miles. Turn your head you could see nothing but high rises. A lot of stuff was knocked down. There was block after block vacant, just dirt. But now there are townhouses. It's amazing. The last time I went down Irvine Turner it's a whole different area. It's really something.

Camasta (1974): What was my impression of the Newark? New York, the Jersey version of New York, the bad section of Linden, where I grew up. Probably over a period of time the impression of Newark was, "God how'd they get so much wood in one place." I still can't understand how they built so many buildings so close together. I looked at it that way. The people, didn't matter as far as them being minority or the fact that they had the urban disturbances. Of course, the industry impressed me because there was a lot that I could relate to with my father being the fire chief in Linden and Linden being such an industrial town. So, the industrial hazards and the industrial fires, I was able to relate to them from my father a lot easier. That was impressive and the fact that we had everything that my father had when it comes to refineries and that kind of stuff.

Partridge (1974): By the time I was thinking about working in Newark I had a pretty good handle as to the city itself and what was going on there. It was absolutely cultural shock, absolutely. But interestingly, I had actually gone to school with black kids in Glen Rock, from the earliest days, grammar school right through junior high school and senior high school. So, I knew a lot of black kids and had friends and so forth. But it was still culture shock because Glen Rock's a different place from Newark no matter what color you are. And maybe for those kids it would have been culture shock too. I don't know. To see the conditions in the city and the mayhem that was going on at the time. It was a very dangerous place. It was a very active place and there was always something going on. Whatever was going on was nothing I had ever seen before. Clearly it was culture shock.

Ricca (1974): At this time, North Newark was the Italian section with Broadway black and Hispanic. The Archbishop Walsh projects everybody swore was the ruination of North Newark because we found at a later date that a high rise is a bad type situation to put people into. You know that from the Hayes Homes, the Stella Wrights, and all the projects that are gone right now.

In a minute I'd go back to living there again if I could have it the way it was. I guess we all would. I bring my kids through. My daughter just graduated college. When she was two, we moved from Newark, but when you ask her where she's from, she's from Newark. She's proud of it even though she only lived there two years, so she doesn't remember. She thinks she does. But Newark just carries a stigma with it for some people. When you live here and you grew up here, there's a pride that you came from Newark.

It started changing in the early '70s. During the Newark riots I was in summer school at Essex Catholic. That was in 1967. And there was a sniper in the building. The Brother came on the loud speaker and told everyone to leave via the Summer Avenue exit and not to take any buses down on Broadway. He never told anybody that there was a sniper up in the school. Could it have been a story made up by some of the kids? Possibly, but I left by Summer Avenue and ran up to Mount Prospect Avenue to get the 27. I noticed right after the riots my friends started thinning out. The old saying was, "Where are all those good Italians from Newark? Belleville and Bloomfield." That's where people took off to and that's how the neighborhood broke up.

I ended up with a lot of Hispanic friends. Good people who moved to the area where I lived in North Newark to get away from being in the projects and everything. They were working people. Their parents worked just as hard as mine did, raised their kids the same. One kid, his name was Archio, I'll never forget, his mother would come out and hit him in the head, if she heard somebody curse in Spanish. Because he was the only Spanish kid at the time, if she heard Spanish cursing, she knew it was him. She'd come out and she'd chase him around.

But right after the riots I noticed it, realized it. The older people were dying, selling their houses, and their sons and daughters were moving. Or people would flat out move, take loses on their houses at the time because I think real estate was bad. I guess that's from '70 to '75, I think the neighborhood changed drastically. The *bodegas* came in. The old Italian butcher died and his shop was sold off to Hispanic.

Straile (1974): I thought it was a great city. There was a lot going on. A lot of people coming into Newark at the time. A lot of things being done. And it was a change from Jersey City, but I liked it so I wound up living there for quite some time. At that time, I would probably say the city was maybe 50% Caucasian and 50% African-American. That's what I would guess. I really never looked into it that way because I always treat everybody the same. That's me. I hold nothing against anyone for who they are, what they are, what they believe in. I just go with the flow.

Hopkins (1978): When I came on where we worked (Springfield Avenue and Hunterdon Street) was a shit hole. Vailsburg was nice. I mean it was changing. Blacks were coming up South Orange Avenue. Jordan Baris was selling all the homes and people were just getting out. Basically, when we come on the job it was eleven years after the riots and to tell you the truth it seemed cars that were on fire in '67, were still left there. We had that up and down Springfield Avenue. We had Sayre Street where they used to light cars up all the time. And all the side streets had burned out cars, abandoned buildings, stuff like that. You go Down Neck, it was nice. Vailsburg it was nice, upper Vailsburg. Lower Vailsburg was starting to change then, but it was still holding on. Then you had North Newark which was nice. Where we worked it wasn't too nice.

Mitchell (1978): I guess it started changing more where the Portuguese start taking over Down Neck. The rest of the city just changed completely as far as the ethnic background, all over. And it started really going downhill.

J. Prachar (1978): I knew the neighborhood I lived in in Vailsburg was a lot different from the rest of the city because I went to high school in Essex Catholic. So, I used to take two buses. I'd take a bus to downtown Newark and a bus to North Newark. So, I knew the center part of the city was bad as far as high crime, lots of fires. I knew my life in the Burg was a lot different than somebody else's life down there. I already knew that. And I think most of the guys that came on with me knew it too. And we were prepared for it.

Zeiser (1978): When I came on the job it was, I guess, a little surprising because growing up in Vailsburg you think the whole city's kind of like that, but it's different. You don't realize how bad the bad sections were or how different they were. They're only really blocks away. You'd drive down from Vailsburg which at the time was a great place to grow up. You drive a half mile and houses are burning and it looks like a ghetto. The Parkway was a pretty distinct line. You knew when you were in different areas than you were used to.

Brown (1979): I don't know what my impression was at the time. I never really thought about it. I guess I must have liked it because when I came on the job, I was already working for the water department for five years. I was all over the city, so it was all right. My impression didn't change after I got on the job. Like I said I was working for the water department, so most of the weird things I saw as a fireman, I saw on the water department. When we'd go to repair a pipe, we'd see people living in abandoned buildings,

The racial makeup of the city was pretty fairly balanced at that time. Most of the neighborhoods were mixed that I remember. I grew up Down Neck as a kid and everybody got along with everybody.

Kormash (1979): I couldn't believe how many fires. When I first came on at Seventeen Engine, I couldn't believe the number of fires that were happening. I read the newspapers enough prior to coming on. Very few fires were even printed in the paper. And then I later found out that to a degree Newark was sanitizing stuff to try to build its reputation back up. That the newspapers were controlled to a degree, but the number of fires was unbelievable.

Reiss (1979): I drove an ambulance in Orange and East Orange. We were in Newark quite a bit also. Going to the hospitals in Newark, I was pretty familiar with it. I had also ridden with Engine Nine for about two years. So, I was pretty familiar with North Newark especially. I lived on Montclair Avenue all the way up between Summer and Broadway, right down from Chief Ricca. That's where I was living when I came on the job.

I had no problems there at all. I used to walk up to the subway up by Heller Parkway. I never had any problems walking up there or walking on the streets there. That part was pretty good. Seven Engine (West Market Street), there was really no problem around Seven Engine. Nobody really bothered us there. Eleven Engine (Central Avenue) was a lot worse by the time I went up there in about '83. The neighborhood was getting pretty bad. There was a lot of crime. We had a lot of trouble with the neighbors. There was a lot of battling going on between the firemen and the neighbors in that neighborhood.

The numbered streets were problems. They were not particularly friendly to the fire department.

At that time, I would say Newark's makeup was maybe still 50% white and maybe 50% of all the minorities, but there were a lot of Hispanics moving in. It was not so much of a black minority. It was more Hispanics moving in. And Down Neck eventually became sort of Central American South American more so than Hispanic. Of course, that was in the middle of the moving into the becoming a majority black city. I don't think it was at that point, but it was getting close.

Caufield (1980): The city had changed slightly by the time I came on the job. You did see a more diverse neighborhood when I came back from the Navy. Not a problem for me. It wasn't a problem for me or anything, but it was a problem for a lot of people and you saw a lot of things in your life. The neighborhood pretty much though was still working class. People still respected their properties and respected yours as well. The neighborhood had changed. When I came on the job, I started seeing more of how Newark operated as a city instead of just as my little Vailsburg. I started seeing the Central Ward. I started seeing the North Ward, the South Ward, the East Ward and the place it was different. It was eye opening. It was eye opening and I recall the '67 riots as a kid. This was before the service, as a kid and that was just wow.

F. Bellina (1981): I wasn't familiar with other parts of the city. I actually thought that when they said Bloomfield Avenue, I thought that was Bloomfield. I really didn't know anybody from that side of the city. I just knew where I was from, Fifteenth Avenue, the kids I grew up with, who all moved out before I moved out. They moved to different cities. They didn't move within the city. We stayed in the city. My father and mother and grandfather and great-grandfather were in the city. They didn't know anything but Newark. They were all from Newark, in fact that area Fifteenth Avenue, Nineteenth Street. So, my impression of the city at that time was there were two different cities. One that was in trouble and one that wasn't affected by the riots. And I felt they were privileged. I looked at it like they had money. My mother worked at Bamberger's. My father worked in Lionel trains. We were never taught that there was any difference. We were taught that people are people.

E. Griffith (1983): When I came on the job, Vailsburg was a smaller section. We were the last white family on the block, actually, in '87. So, it had changed. It was predominantly minority. I wish the Vailsburg I grew up in still existed. To see it now, it's sad. I just took a ride through there. It's sad, really sad. It's night and day. Because today I don't think the kids can go past their curb. There are guns on the street. Places are burned down. The houses are falling apart. The infrastructure is really collapsing. Now they're building up the center of the city and that's changing, but it's nowhere near as safe as it was back then. It's different. People aren't as close. You go to fires; you get there; and people don't know the neighbor. They don't know who's who and they live on the same block. That was never the case back when I was growing up. So yeah, it's night and day.

DeCuester (1984): It took a while and then I started seeing on Park Avenue, a lot more structure fires. It took a while though. It didn't just come off hand, only after years. Sharpe James had just gotten elected when we came on. We were just going back to the same buildings that were on fire. So, in later years when Sharpe was knocking the stuff down, we weren't going back into the same buildings. We knew where all the holes in the floors were in the buildings because you went back to them so many times.

Giordano (1984): I would say things start to change, but really not drastically, from when I was a kid until when I was at least twenty-one and then hired on the fire department at twenty-eight. There were still neighborhoods. They were decaying somewhat. Some getting abandoned houses. A lot of people were moving out of the city, but it really didn't change that much. The schools were still the same. Areas were kind of the same. The North Ward probably the biggest changed was the demographics went from an Italian neighborhood to more than 80% Latino. That's what happened when the Hispanics came in there. They changed the politics of that area and everything that went with it. A lot of the stores moved out or turned to Spanish owners. The city decayed a lot over time, but things were still civil at the time.

Arce (1984): My impression of the city coming on the job, is I didn't care about anything then. I just do what I have to do to do my job as best as I can. I treat people the same way. I don't care if you're poor or doing well and all in between doing drugs or whatever. I treat people the same way. I don't care about color. I didn't know anything about races. Not one thing until I came to the fire department. I never got involved with that. I stay away. If I do my job consciously, it keeps me away from the other nonsense. If you can make it in the streets of Newark, you can make it through anything. And thank God, I made it.

Nasta (1984): I moved into Newark, got an apartment, to get on the job. I grew up in South Hackensack. It was a pretty big culture shock going from South Hackensack to Newark. South Hackensack is a very small town. It was a town of only around two thousand people. Obviously moving to a big city like that, it was a culture shock. It was more diverse than I was used to. My first apartment was on Monroe Street, Down Neck. When that lease ran out, I moved over to Adams Street, move one block. Down Neck at that time was a great place. If there was any shortcoming, it was parking. Couldn't park your car anywhere. Before I got on the job, I did a lot of riding around the city trying to learn, especially the locations of the firehouses, different neighborhoods. I had some friends that lived up in North Newark. I spent some time up there hanging out with them. So, they taught me a lot.

N. Bellina (1986): When we go into the '80s, when I started driving, I started buffing. I had my buddy Al and a bunch of other guys. We'd drive around, take pictures. Going down these streets with a camera, but no one ever bothered you. You had to park kind of close, but not too close. You didn't want to get boxed in. So many times, you were down the block. When the fire was over, you had to get back to your car with a nice camera bag on you. I think a lot of buffs really didn't get bothered back then with them robbing your camera. You go now you could get your camera robbed. But getting on the job, my attitude towards the city got a lot worse because I never made contact with the people buffing. When you get on the job, you're starting to make contact with people in their houses, in their apartments. You're seeing a lot more than you would see out in the street. So that came into play and it's pretty bad.

Chief Centanni (1986): What I think was startling was the amount of depression and vacant buildings and destroyed houses and how the people had to live. Now my area was in a transition so if you left our Bloomfield Avenue area, went to Orange Street you started seeing some of that change. You had inter-racial different groups moving into the area, but until I got on the fire department, I couldn't believe the differences. When I came on, the Sixteenth Avenue area was blocks of vacant buildings and drug houses and abandoned cars. So, I was like holy crap it's like the wild west over here. That was an eye opener.

A. Masters (1986): By '86, the city was developing. And by that I mean there were different areas that were being designated for townhouses, condos. The word on the street was it was all by Broadway, Oriental, Mount Pleasant. There was talk that developers want to come in and put in new living places across the street from Essex Catholic. It did come true. The only downfall with that was a lot of it was burnt. There's a new school over there on Broadway and Harvey. We were busy back in the '80s from day, afternoon, night. It didn't matter. A lot of good jobs, a lot of good experience, and then the Deputy would call for demolition and once he said that we knew there's going to be a new house on it. They burnt it down to develop it.

Alexander I (1987): For me to come on the job and get put on Irvine Turner like I did, in that area, that was a shell shock to me. Because I didn't even know the city was like that, so my parents really hid a lot from us, the bad parts, but that was a shell shock.

When I came on the job, the city at that point was going through a serious change. There were still what you would call the race wars. I remember when I was in high school, we had a football game over at School Stadium. Me and a couple of my buddies, we were over there. Just out of nowhere we got attacked by Italians. So, there were a lot of race wars in different areas going on.

DeLeon (1988): To me it was a great city. I'm going to buy a house on Lake Street. And I'm going to do my whole career there because it was quiet beside the park. I'm not going anywhere. And as I got more insight into how things really were, especially with property taxes, that wasn't for me. It was a turning point. I can't live here. The school system is tough. I have a couple of kids. When I realized what my parents did to protect me, I was thinking along the same lines for them. I can't introduce them to this. I can't have somebody come at eleven o'clock at night to my house to tell my son, "Okay let's go hang out." Because I know what the end result is going to be on that. And that would have hurt their record. There's just too much opportunity to get in trouble. Still is today.

Griggs (1988): After I came on the job, just riding around on runs seeing all the vacant property. That was wow, remnants of 1967. You heard about it, read about it, but to physically see it, it was like, wow. I live in this town, but I wasn't really exposed to that. So, it was something to see.

Alvarez (1989): When I got on the job and I visited friends that were at other firehouses, I saw the devastation in Newark of all the abandoned buildings, burnt out buildings, the empty lots which is something we really didn't have in the Ironbound section. I was blown away. I never saw that part of Newark. I was like, "My God, this is like a war zone. This is a ghetto." When we were in the Academy, we were bussed over to I don't know the name of the street, but we were doing overhauling in an old abandoned building. We used to be able to do that. And I remember standing in the middle of the block and being able to look through empty lots in the middle of all these blocks. I could see for six blocks. I could see a street six blocks away just from all the empty lots. If you positioned yourself in the right place, you could just see right through the middle of blocks for six blocks just from all the old burned building that they knock down. There were empty lots there. I recall one of the funniest things that I wish I had a picture of was the firehouse on Turner Boulevard, Twelve Engine and Five Truck. There were four blocks that were completely, completely leveled. The only buildings on these four blocks were the buildings of Twelve Engine, Five Truck because they were two separate buildings that were right next to each other and the liquor store next door. And that was it on these four huge blocks, not little blocks. They were on one corner and the rest of the three blocks were completely, completely empty and burnt out. To me that was mind blowing because I had never seen that and it was just unbelievable. So, I thought the city was in great shape from where I was growing up and then when I eventually exposed myself to the rest of the city, I couldn't believe it. It was just like things you see in movies.

Cordasco (1989): The city was in bad shape when I came on the job. I went on the police first in '85. When we first came out of the police academy, we went to the third precinct and it was literally falling apart. They used to have a cell block up there, there was asbestos. They actually had it walled off that you couldn't even go up to that part of the building. With plywood, with two by fours covering it, even the part they were using, stuff was falling off the ceilings. You couldn't go in the basement. You're lucky if you had two working typewriters in the precinct. It actually got to the point where guys started buying their own typewriters to type. There were no computers back then. You literally had to type your reports, especially for arrests and we used to have to rewind the ribbon to find a place that had active ink because it wouldn't show up on your report. They didn't want you to walk, but they had no cars and you wound up having to walk because they didn't have enough cars in the precinct working. So, the city was in pretty bad shape at that time. Just going down to City Hall when we had to get sworn in in the council chambers, just walking into City Hall we were shocked. This was City Hall and it was in the same condition as the precinct we went to. Stuff falling off the ceilings, plaster, paint, cracks. It's the biggest city in New Jersey and you're shocked.

The same conditions were in the firehouse. My first firehouse was Engine Fourteen, the basement, you couldn't go off the bottom step just because of all the water even though they had the sump pump. It was all moldy. The bathrooms were original. The windows were original. Didn't look like it had been painted in God knows how long. If there was any damage to any part of the building, it took forever to try to get it fixed. The door broke in the winter and we were joking and it wound up being true. It took them to the Spring, with a tarp. We were tying it with a rope and going out. And back then they would go into the firehouses and rob stuff. You couldn't leave anything in the firehouse even in your locker because if you were gone for two, three hours, they need five minutes. The conditions in the firehouses were horrible. And the other thing that I found shocking was they had the diesel pumps right inside the firehouse and you could see how they converted it from when they still had the horses. You could see where they had the animals and the barns. We didn't have a drain on the apparatus floor. They had one in the kitchen where they used to keep the horses.

LaPenta (1989): Newark was in bad shape when I came on the job. One thing that surprised me was the number of vacant buildings. I know there're vacant buildings everywhere, in every city, but I guess being on the job and going to the same five-story brick walk up five, six times. I'm talking two-alarm fires, three-alarm fires. You burn the roof off on a three-alarm fire. And then in a month there's a two-alarm fire on the first floor. This building's still standing and they're all over the place. I was really shocked by the number of vacant buildings. I just couldn't believe it. Why don't they knock these down? Then you hear all kinds of stories. The city gets money, whatever. Who knows what the story is? I mean there're so many rumors. You don't know why, but in the end it's always money. They don't have the money to knock them down. It's cheaper to burn them, let the citizens handle the urban renewal themselves.

West (1989): I wasn't raised in a city and certainly wasn't used to that lifestyle, the hustle and bustle of it all. City living is different than suburban living for sure. But I loved it because it was new to me and being a fireman, you saw so much, so many different things. It was certainly a culture shock, but it was fun to be part of and I couldn't wait to get to work every day and see what was next.

I have to be honest with you, I don't know if I even recognized the culture/makeup of the city I came to work in because it was something I didn't even look at. Race or different cultures really never got into my way of thinking. I didn't see it that way. I didn't see blacks or whites or Hispanics. I never thought about it. You sort of get thrown into it because that's what city people are used to, but when I came here, I don't think I even noticed it to be honest with you.

Petrone (1991): When I went to work on Avon Avenue it was different, quite a bit different. I never minded it. Like some of the guys didn't want to work there. At that time, Newark was the stolen car capital of the world and Avon Avenue was a hotbed of stolen cars. They would come up and do donuts in front of the firehouse. So, it was different. A lot of guys didn't like it because we didn't have any parking. We had to park on the street. A lot of trouble with the cars being broken into. Cars getting smashed by stolen cars.

Pierson (1991): It was pretty wild, particularly around the firehouse in the Central Ward. It was an eye opener. Things were going down day to day. Even the show next door at the liquor store, with people standing out front.

Bartelloni (1993): The city was starting to change, more crime. I lived in the North Ward. It was fairly safe, but it was starting to get a little worse. I think a little more crime ridden. You saw people starting to get mugged. You never saw that. People were staring to move. People were moving to the suburbs. We stayed because my grandparents came here in 1940, when they bought the house. And that's where we stayed. We lived there, but then my mother got mugged one day and I told my father, "That's enough. It's time to go." So, it did change. I think it was kind of gradual, but it was changing for the worse.

I used to go downtown and shop every Christmas. Me and my friend Sal Fischetta. We used to take the subway because I was near Ting a Ling's on Bloomfield Avenue. Take the subway downtown and we'd shop. Nobody ever bothered you, but once I got on the fire department, I was at Ten Engine (Sherman Avenue and Astor Street). I never even knew where that was. I didn't know where the firehouses were, but that was a pretty rough, crime ridden area. I wasn't familiar with that because we really didn't have that type of activity except maybe on Park Avenue by First or Sixth Avenue. That was starting to get rough.

Castelluccio (1993): When I first came on the job, my father-in-law was still living on Heller Parkway and that's where I was living. He was a deputy chief of police in Newark. It was a nice area, but even he had his unmarked police car stolen twice out of the driveway on Heller Parkway. You had to be careful, but it was still a tight knit community in that area. So, I felt safe in that section. When I first came on, I went to Twenty-seven Engine. It was Down Neck and that was a pretty decent, nice area. The crime wasn't all that bad. They seemed to have a tight knit community also. It was when I went to Avon Avenue that I started seeing some of the more run down and poorer sections of Newark. I was a little nervous in the beginning, but once you start working there you just grow accustomed to it and its second nature. I don't feel threatened even though I probably should.

Gail (1993): I got an apartment in North Newark and started paying rent and I moved in. I was single. I was in college, so it actually worked out pretty well. You know, I enjoyed being on my own. And then I got a roommate, another firefighter that came out well on the test. He was looking for a place to move to. He was losing his place and I said I could use a roommate to help with the rent. He moved in with me. And we had a lot of fun. I actually embraced it. I liked it. I enjoyed it.

I enjoyed working here as a firefighter. When I got assigned, I worked in the southern section of Newark. It was a little rougher than the northern section at the time. That section had the stolen cars and definitely a lot more drug activity and a lot more violence. I thought it was kind of cool to be a firefighter in a tough area. You got a lot of action. There were a lot of fires. You saw a ton of things that you would not normally see. I felt safe with my crew. I didn't feel unsafe at all. I did enjoy saying I worked in a tough neighborhood. It was kind of like a badge of honor. That was my attitude way back when I was young.

Ostertag (1994): My first impression was wow. I've been in some pretty bad parts growing up and so was cautious. It was like wow, rundown, a very rundown city, but this is where I want to be a fireman. This is where I'm going to catch work. This is where I'm going to get to live my dream on a big city fire department. This has potential. This is where I want to work. But I was very cautious when I first got on the job.

Richardson (1994): When I came on, I had never really dealt with city life, the urban like this. That whole inner city, I didn't know anything about it. So, I came in and was wide eyed and just okay. The guys kind of joked around. I'm pretty pale skinned to begin with and they're like "You're whiter than bread." I didn't want to let on too much that I didn't know anything about the city, but I never claimed to have grown up in Newark. I never claimed to know anything about Newark. I was pretty up front with that right from the beginning with everybody. So, the culture shock was amazing. It didn't scare me because basically you were told you're a fireman. They don't mess with firemen. Nobody messes with firemen in the city. And I guess since the riots there's never been an instance that I ever heard of I think in any city that there's been violence against firemen. You had confrontations, but you didn't have violence. I remember hearing the stories about the Prince Street projects, how they were stealing the gold chains off the guys and then taking their boots so they couldn't chase them. But that was petty stuff. If you didn't display that or you didn't turn around and flash a lot of cash or be flashy, you were mindful and respectful, your issues were very far and few between.

Jackson (1995): When I came on the job, Newark's population was probably 60-70% African-American. Another 10% Caucasian and maybe 10% like Brazilian, Portuguese and the immigrants. But the makeup I think was majority African American.

Y. Pierre (1995): After I got out of the Marines, the city wasn't much different. There was a difference, but you couldn't see it because in the whole time I was in the Marine Corps I was always coming back home when I got leave. So, I would come back from time to time. The change was actually taking place with me when I was in the military. As I'm coming back and forth, you would hear that your friend moved. There're a few more black people in the neighborhood. You know it's such a change. Then you see a few more black people in the neighborhood and finally there were maybe three white families left. I remember that vividly because the chief of police lived on our block. He was one of the last families to move out. And I remember Joe Rolli, an Italian kid, we became friends. He used to live next door to us.

Then they moved. And after that there weren't any more whites in the block. It was just all black. It's just a different vibe.

Things changed again. It's changed again. Now it's a bunch of people coming into the neighborhood with bad attitudes. It's just too much of a change. And coming as kids, going through all those changes, it was something that we were not expecting. We were not expecting this kind of thing to happen so fast. I remember before I was in the Marine Corps I was going to technical school where there were maybe twenty guys that were black in the school. By the time I graduated in 1980 the whole school was black. We had a female in the school. Before we didn't have any females. I mean all those changes just happened so fast that I almost couldn't keep up with it. Just couldn't keep up with it.

Farrell (1996): What was the city like when I first came on? The North Ward obviously changed. The demographics have changed. After the 60's and what they call white flight, everybody leaving. I watched a whole block change. We were one of the last ones off our block. I still have family in the same house. My cousin, her husband and kids still live in the same house I was born and raised in. We still have that stronghold there and they still have a lot of friends in the North Ward in the city. I left just before I was done with college. I was twenty-four years old when I left Newark. And I moved back into the city later on after I got divorced. That's when I decided to take the test, after I got divorced. I moved back. That was the opportunity for me. I was back in the city.

In the last twenty years I don't think the makeup of the city's changed that much. Where I work is different. I see Newark differently from the South Ward. Whatever white people are left in the city are going to be in the North Ward or Down Neck. There's a big Hispanic population over there and I watched that happen as I grew up. The South Ward is different. You look at

Newark through different lenses over here. It's much different. I don't remember growing up and having the gangs as much. The North Ward I'm sure had their little Hispanic gangs back then.

Meier (1996): I was never really in the Central or South Wards growing up. I was familiar with North Newark a little bit, mostly Ironbound. So, when I got into the city there were a lot of places of the city I didn't know. Newark's a big city. Like other cities in the United States there's blight and poverty and wealth and everything a city has to offer. So it wasn't that I was unfamiliar with that. I never spent any considerable time in those neighborhoods.

Rodrigues (1996): My impression of the city? That's a good question because coming from the country to the city I was looking up at the buildings. I was like "Wow, how many stories is this?" The impression back then was a little negative in a way because I could see what's going on. A lot of fires and arson happening. The crime rate, I don't know how high it was, but that was the negative thing. The positive part was, listen I have a job in one of the biggest cities in the country. So, it had negatives and positives at the same time.

Freese (1998): I lived on Mount Prospect when I got on the job. 604 Mount Prospect was my address. I stayed there for a couple of years after I got the job and started making decent money. I ended up buying a house on Lake Street and then from Lake Street we had to move on. My girls were getting a little bigger and we were thinking about school. And to be honest with you if it wasn't for my daughters' schooling, I would have still been living in Newark. I would have still been on Lake Street.

Carr (2000): By the time I came on the job, I think people got really busy. They brought a lot of jobs to Newark, quite a few jobs to Newark. Prudential has about four, five buildings in Newark alone. The airport has improved. The Port has improved. They added the rail system in Newark. A lot of charter schools started popping up in Newark. There have been a few downturns from where we had risen at one point. Ras has done a great job with rectifying that, making sure that the people were safe. Especially when that arena came about, they really made sure the people that were coming to see the Devils game and any other type of event that they had at the arena, they made sure that the people were well taken care of.

Jenkins (2002): It was a good city to me. When I came on the job, I'm on my own. I'm my own man. I had my own house. I'm still living there and I think that it's still a great city. I was never part of the group running down this or that. The city got a bad rap. If you're familiar with the city then you know where to go and where to stay away from.

Kupko (2002): I attended Kean University. When I went to school my father had the idea to keep my options open and apply for the fire exam. So, I moved back in with my grandmother who owned several properties in Newark. It was actually an easier commute for me to go from Newark commuting than Edison commuting when I was in school. Plus, I had my own apartment there so there was a little more privacy. I also took away the burden of my parents paying for room and board in a dormitory on campus. So, it worked out all around for me at the time.

When I came on the job, the city was still accommodating. I assume people feel safer sort of speak in the Ironbound section, especially the out of towners. Most of your restaurant industry and things, most of the things that would attract somebody from the outside, are there. There was a stigma always up the hill. My grandfather even told me war stories of them being on top of the train tracks during the riots with rifles. Trying to protect their property down there, but you have some stereotypical beliefs in your head of the dichotomy between the lifestyle that was up on the hill from before and after the riots. And then the lifestyle that the predominantly Portuguese population was trying to maintain on the other side of the tracks.

Mickels (2002): I got divorced in my mid-twenties and my grandmother still lived in Newark. She lived on Hansbury Avenue, Hansbury and Maple. She was getting older and suffering from some medical problems. I didn't want to be by myself after the divorce. My grandmother needed some help, so I moved in with my grandmother. I stayed there for about twelve years. I lived with her for twelve years. And that's when I found out and took interest in the fire department. During those twelve years when I came back to Newark.

My impression of the city when I came on the job was, we have issues in Newark. We have poverty and people that just are underprivileged, not having necessities. There were a lot of abandoned buildings. I always was in Newark, but I got a better look at the city driving around or riding around on a fire truck. I always thought there was a need for first responders, police and fire, EMS. There was always something going on in Newark, buildings catching fire, whether it was vacant or occupied, crime activities, so I felt Newark still needed to be controlled and well taken care of. I felt that that's what I was there for, to assist in helping to do that with public safety.

Rosario (2002): I love my city. I went into the military for six years and I came right back. Growing up in Newark, it's a really tough city. But I met my wife here, my best friend. My kids were born here in the city. They say you always come back home and this is my home. When I came back it was a little better than it was when I was growing up. It was a tough town then, but if you had the right crowd you survived. It was a little cleaner.

K. Alfano (2006): Prior to getting on the job, you have to live in the city, so I lived down the Ironbound with my brother. It took us almost five years to get on. So, I was in the city. The only thing I knew about the city was when I had to stay here for four plus years. I knew Down Neck and I traveled a little bit. I knew Down Neck, but I knew a little bit about the different parts of the city. Since I've been on the job, I've been up in the Vailsburg area, but I come to visit the city on my off days. I would say other than Down Neck, where they put the stadium up, I think it's kind of been the same the last ten years. I really don't see too much changing.

Dugan (2006): I was in the Army from '97 to 2001. When I got out in September 2001, it was just before everything kicked off. I moved Down Neck to New York Avenue. Lived there for six, seven years and I moved out maybe a year or so after my probationary year because I wanted to start a family.

As a kid I was Down Neck. When I came back from the Army I noticed where there was a candy shop, now there's a bar instead. When my father and I went fishing, he would go down to Weequahic Park and look for worms. When we would do it, every once in a while, we'd come back up to the car and there'd be all fingerprints all over the windows because somebody was trying to break into it. I think the laws they had made with the car thefts have definitely changed. Because I remember as a kid, the donuts they used to do on Sanford Ave right here in front of the firehouse. This was like a huge donut spot. So that's something that's definitely changed. I don't hear people doing donuts in front of the firehouse anymore. But it still is a pretty dangerous area when it comes to gun violence.

Medina (2006): When I came on the job, I knew the city pretty well. I grew up in the North Ward, so I knew that pretty well. And I boxed on South Street, so I knew that area pretty okay. You go deep in Ferry Street there's no problem. The Central Ward area up to the city line here, my aunt lives on Twentieth Street, so I sort of knew the big areas like Springfield Ave, Avon Ave.

M. Bellina (2008): I think coming on the job gives a unique experience. You get an insight into the city. You get to see that average people don't understand what's going on. You don't hear half of what goes on in the city on the news. So, you could become jaded to certain things that go on here or you could become sympathetic or somewhere in between. It's something that I value. It makes you appreciate where you come from. It's a different place. Even us, being here twenty-four hours, without having certain apps on your phone like for fire and police, you still don't know what's going on in the city until you get an alert and you're like this is going on here. It's the different perspective. My dad always told me, you're going to see and do things that you'll never be able to explain to someone that has no experience or knowledge. Even other firemen that are from a different city, it's really going to be tough to explain to them. And it's true.

G. Pierre (2013) As you get older, you start to put things in place and see what's going on. You watch movies and think and figure out what's going on. You watch news and you still hear Newark in the news while you're in North Carolina or Newark on the news when you're in Pennsylvania.

I think when I first returned back to Newark, Newark was in a worse state than it is today. Gang violence was prevalent when I came back. I mean walking to the corner store, I said, "What's up cuz?" I didn't know that was like a gang term. I was down south. So, down south at college, everybody's cousin. Everybody's friends. So, it's like, "What's up cuz?" I'm looking around. What's wrong with all those dudes. I had no clue how real it was until I got back on ground zero. The gang violence out here was crazy. This is in Vailsburg. This is like right around the corner from my house. Vailsburg used to be one of the topnotch areas in Newark at one point in time. If you could come to the Burg you'd feel like you were in Shady Acres compared to downtown somewhere. So, the gang violence was real. It was out of control then. Since then, things have kind of calmed down.

Rawa (2013): Down Neck was predominantly a Portuguese neighborhood growing up. It shifted. Now it's more South American, Brazilian, in a short amount of time. It's incredible to see how a small section of the city can change like that. It's not what I remembered. I have my nieces and nephews that live next door now. I don't see them have half the childhood that I had. They're never outside playing. Their parents, also a cop, don't let them go out to the park or ride their bikes anywhere. There's like a constant state of paranoia which I get. But that's not a childhood to live.

I only knew Down Neck. Riding in Rescue, I'm driving through parts of the city and these guys weren't from Newark, so they looked at me. "How do you not know where you're going.?" I'm like, I'm from the Ironbound. I never hung out in the West. I'm not used to this. I went to high school down on Martin Luther King Boulevard, but that's about as far from the Ironbound as my experiences went. My view of Newark hasn't changed. I'm proud to be from Newark, but I guess when you see the way things work sometimes, you get a different understanding, as a city worker. Nothing bad, but you see different politics. In that aspect you get a different view of the city that you're used to.

Garay (2014): When I came on the job, I used to look at it like it was a huge, huge city. Now that I'm on the job, it's become smaller. It's odd to describe. I know it's huge. It's the biggest, but because I've been to every firehouse, it's like, this is not that big of a place. At that time, the city was mostly minorities. Mexican Americans, the Mexican community has grown in North Newark abundantly. South Americans, before there used to be a lot of European Portuguese. Even the Hispanics in North Newark, but they've gone away. They've gone elsewhere, to other towns. Near-by towns actually. The South American community has grown. The African American community has grown too. So, I've seen the difference in that aspect.

Cruz (2016): Now that I'm in the fire department I've seen parts of Newark I've never seen in my life. I had never been to Avon Avenue until I worked out of Eighteen Engine. I hadn't been to Clinton Avenue. I would know Ferry Street because when I was young my mom would come to the fish market to get fish. Other than that, for me it was either Forest Hills or Park Avenue.

Earp (2016): The city is getting more diverse from what I've seen. Just in my neighborhood alone, I see a difference. It was a majority of black, but now I see a lot of Hispanic. I see a few white or if you prefer, Caucasian Jewish people in the neighborhood. I think it's getting a little more diverse. Especially downtown Newark, the new structures they're building. A lot of people are coming from the city or the Hoboken area to live in Newark. So, it's changing. Before it was a city that people didn't want to live in. Now that it's getting better, you see different people moving here. You see different eateries. You see a lot of Asian food, a lot of island food. Different food you wouldn't normally see in the city of Newark, it's coming in now. So, it's getting diverse. I think it's a good thing. I think it's a beautiful thing.

Part Four:

Changes in the City

Vetrini (1946): Well, after the riots there was an exodus of white people. That you can't deny. And there was a drop in property values around the city. The businesses that folded down during the riots not too many came back on or near Springfield Avenue. Some of the schools were closing down, the parochial schools, they were closing down. And businesses, if you wanted to get satisfactory shopping you had to move out of the city to the malls. The stores that were down about Broad and Market were folding up. Bamberger's closes, Ohrbach's closes, Klein's closes, Hahne's closes. That was big. It had a very detrimental effect on the city. There's no two ways about it. Those were about the major things that started to change in the city.

Kinnear (1947): I think the city started to decline before the riots, but that was the big turning point. It only made it worse for the people living there. They burned out their own stores. They burned out the places where they could go shopping. They did change our attitude, a little bit, not that much. I remember going down to Twenty Engine after the riots and talking with them. That question came up and most of them said no, it wouldn't change their attitude. I don't think it really did at first. Going to a fire; trying to put it out; trying to save people.

It changed just in personal relationships, outside of firefighting, where you didn't feel they had the same respect for you that they had before. So, there definitely was a big turning point as far as relationships went. I guess, the city continued going down after that. Not because of the fire department, but because of what happened and the time it takes to heal those wounds. A lot of stores were burnt during the riots, but it continued, yes. I guess from '67 to the year Six went over five thousand. That was 1981.

There was a period when we would pull up to a fire involving multiple buildings. That subsided after a while. The firebreaks made a big difference, but that took a number of years to create all those firebreaks. I tend to think there were people working, sometimes starting those fires. Most of them had to be arson. They really wanted to start big fires and they did start big fires. I think that's part of it. Most of your fires that just start from carelessness burn one building. You don't get four or five fully involved before the first company even gets there.

The urban decay expanded from the one section where most of the blacks lived. That was the section by Charlton, Prince, and Waverly Avenue. It just spread block by block. It seemed to be that when one black family moved in people panicked. Maybe the first one or two black families that moved into a block that had twenty houses on it didn't cause the panic, but when it got to be three or four or five, people said, "I have to get out of here." It was wrong, but that's what happened. If they'd have stayed, it might not have changed things. I can't say too much on that, but the decay spread from the core. And it just widened and widened and widened.

The fires spread the same way. The fires were occurring in hundred-year-old buildings, so you're going to get some fires that are more serious than you would see in say a twenty-year-old building. But the number and the seriousness of the fires went beyond that.

The number of fires in the Hayes Homes certainly couldn't be blamed on the building. The building was modern, brick, with elevators. You still had a tremendous number of fires in there, careless fires. I don't think the building itself had much to do with it. I think the people were more careless. In those buildings you had garbage chutes, but you still had a fire in the garbage in the hallway. I don't think the buildings as much as the people had to do with the number of fires we had. Because I think if you pulled back, probably, you had as many fires in the projects as you had outside the projects. The city's population changed. There were more people from the country moving into Newark. Maybe they were more careless with matches.

I've got to say I guess that's a factor because it happened that way. Why? I don't know why. I don't know why when these country type people moved in, they were different. Why couldn't they adapt to the city way of doing things? I don't know. Maybe where they lived in the country, they just threw their garbage out the window in a compost pile or something. Why they couldn't adapt to living in the city; putting the garbage in the garbage can and taking it out twice a week, I don't know why. It always amazed me why that happened.

Sure, they were poor. Maybe that had something to do with it. Maybe they couldn't afford something, but you can afford a garbage can or if you can't afford a garbage can; you can walk out with a paper bag. You can drop it down the garbage chute. But you can't put yourself in their shoes and think like them. What do I know about how they grew up or what they were taught? It certainly had a lot to do with the decline.

I think they made it too easy for people to come to the city, too. I think they could come in and get on welfare or relief without any residency requirements. They'd come in and they'd get money for not doing anything, for not working. Of course, they needed it, but there was no obligation with it really. There was no "We give you this money, you've got to keep your apartment clean." or "You've got to sweep the streets." or something like that. That was a big thing. There should have been an obligation with what they were given. Something they had to do to earn it. I think that was probably a big thing.

F. Grehl (1948): When they put up the projects, it cut down on a major source of fires down there in the Central Ward from where Kinney Street made the turn there at Morris Avenue. From there down, all the way down to almost High Street. That's where the Central Ward was. It ran basically from Thirteenth Avenue over to Avon Avenue. That's where all the basic work was. As they started tearing these sections down, there was a lull before the projects became a problem. Of course, in the projects you didn't have the major fires, but you had the constant going to the things. The workload shifted lower and it moved elsewhere.

It's not nice to say, but the people were not educated enough or didn't care enough. They just took their problems to another section of the city. Now that section got busy. Particularly over in the First Battalion, they got very, very busy and parts of the Second Battalion, down South Street, in there. It just kept moving. It expanded to the point today where you have enough basic fire breaks with vacant lots here and there, throughout the city. You still get major fires, but you're not going to get five, six, eight buildings at a time anymore.

The city changed dramatically education wise. It's done a complete reverse. Weequahic High School was probably the best high school in the city of Newark. 94% of the students went on to graduate from universities. Today, I don't think you have 10% if you have that. In my time a lot of the schools didn't have that college degree thing because as soon as we got out of the high school we were drafted or those that just went out preceding us were drafted. So, you had about a four-year span where nobody went to college until after the war was over and the G.I. Bill took over. It was tough. But I do know that Weequahic High School was probably one of the best.

McCormack (1949): What I've seen is a significant decline in the population of Newark. It seems to me we have a lot less people. It was a teeming city. The industry has moved out for a lot of reasons. Some of them were economic. They'd go down south because they got economic breaks, tax breaks. Thousands of jobs probably left this town like that. In many ways it seems to me the blue-collar echelon has moved onward and upward. What we have left here is, more or less the poorer people in society. I don't think there's as much money in this town as there once was. In that sense I would say economically, I don't think we're as well off as we used to be.

I don't know if the economic decline can be directly tied to the fire rate. That's a whole series of things. In the first place the housing stock in Newark was old. When those three-story frame buildings were built, they were slapped together very fast to house waves of immigrants coming over in the eighteen-hundreds. So, I doubt they were built to the highest standards of perfection when they were built. They lasted a hundred years through generations of families. Eventually, they wore out. There were other factors involved along with the wearing out process of the buildings. They were owner occupied in those days, one or three families in the house. So, the owner was on the premises. Very often he rented to his family members. His sister had the second-floor apartment or his brother-in-law. Maybe his son or his daughter would take the third-floor apartment.

I remember when I was a kid growing up, I had friends whose mother and father lived on the first floor; the oldest married sister lived on the second floor and rented from the father; and the third floor was occupied by a spinster sister of the mother or something. It was all family. They obviously were going to take care of each other's property. They worked together and cooperated. Obviously, there was a family connection there and there was a sense of responsibility with maintenance and so forth. A lot of things like that happened that were conducive to these buildings being maintained.

The city was stable. As a kid when I grew up in Newark, whatever neighborhood you lived in, the whole neighborhood was like your family. People weren't prone to move around a lot in those days. Your next door neighbor very probably would be your next door neighbor all your life. You grew up knowing the people next door. All the way through your childhood, your adolescence, and your young adulthood the same people lived next door to you. The same people lived across the street from you. The same guy ran the corner store. Your mother brought her groceries in the same butcher shop. It was all like a family. Everybody knew everybody and everybody was friends. I don't know when that all changed, when that type of cohesiveness started to dissolve, where people just started to break that up. I would guess it happened during the '60s some time. During the Vietnam War era when there was so much turbulence and turmoil. Everyday something new was happening. Protest marches and war troubles and everything else. So, it was all kicked into the picture somehow.

Owners left their buildings and rented out three floors to total strangers, a lot of things happened. People were less concerned; they didn't care. They had a social attitude that they were probably getting ripped off by the landlord who was rich and lived someplace else and was taking advantage of them. You know a whole bunch of factors that run the whole spectrum of things. I guess it all snowballed. It was a whole series of things, not one little thing. When something starts rolling downhill it seems to go faster and faster and faster. You can pick out all kinds of reasons for it. Which is the major reason? I don't know. I think that the owners living on the premises of a building made a significant difference.

G. Alfano (1953): Well, the riots didn't help, the riots didn't help. It's like a girl that got a bad reputation. Even if she turns good, she's still got that bad reputation. Well, the city of Newark, it had a bad reputation. For instance, when you went to the Poconos you sat with somebody and the first thing they'd say to you is, "Where're you from?" I'd say, "Newark." Newark! Whoa! It was like I had the plague. I said, "Yeah, were you ever there?" "No, I wasn't there, but Newark is shit." The reputation is hard to overcome. And like I said to this guy. You were never there. You could go to Forest Hills, Lake Street and Highland Avenue and all them. Where would you see nicer houses? Or even Weequahic or even Vailsburg, really. Great neighborhoods, but the riots definitely gave them a bad reputation and it was damn hard to overcome. And even today, if people here knew, it's like you have the plague.

Wall (1954): In '59 the city was very stable. The fire rate started to escalate before the riots. I'd say in the early '60s fires began to grow in Newark. We had some pretty bad fires, fires that extended well beyond the building of origin. And of course, by the time the riots hit it was "go to hell" day. On top of those fires, we used to get a lot of incinerator fires in the high-rise projects.

Things started to change very rapidly in the mid '60s. The fire load was constantly picking up, very busy time for fires. People were beginning to move out of the city even before the riots. The city was changing in character and you were beginning to get areas that were depressed. Among the indicators that I always looked at was the false alarms, which went off the board. We had a tremendous number of false alarms that Newark really hadn't experienced before. It would seem to be a breakdown in moral character or whatever you want. There was a steady climb that we didn't notice at the time.

Here was a real indicator that something was going on that we didn't have a handle on. It got to the point where Director Caufield was very, very upset with the false alarm rate. He stated publicly that he was going to bring the false alarm rate down. And he did. For a while there you couldn't call it a false alarm unless you found the kid hanging on the box. Now if he wasn't hanging on the box, it was an unnecessary call or a call for assistance or whatever.

Freeman (1956): The condition of the city had deteriorated. It just got worse and worse. You might say it was succession. The blacks succeeded the Jews and then Spanish people succeeded the blacks, which they're still doing today. So, the whole thing was succession. The Portuguese succeeded the Italians Down Neck. The succession was all over the whole city where you had mostly blacks. It's 85-90% black now. Then the city started going down. You had more fires in those years, in the '60s, '70s. The crime went up. You couldn't walk the streets.

Then you had the projects. They built the projects. That brought crime. You can't put poor people on top of each other like that. So, you just got a bad element in the city and it just kept getting worse and worse and worse. You couldn't enjoy the city like you did before. It just got worse and it's still bad. As this succession developed, the people were poorer and poorer. There was less and less money in the city.

Over in the Weequahic section, where you had blacks succeeding the Jews, they bought the houses over there. That's still a good section. It's still good over in the South Ward, except for the projects and things in there. Then they ran Route 78 up through there. They took a lot of buildings down for that. But I would say it's pretty stable over there.

The real estate part of it is pretty good. People generally are keeping up the houses. There are some bad houses where people don't have the money to repair and make it even look better. But the neighborhoods are bad too. When you go over there, the neighborhoods look good, but still, they're bad. You can't walk the streets over there, a lot of bad, a lot of crime over in that area also. Maybe closer to the Hillside line it's not, but still, I'd say generally speaking it's bad all over, maybe with the exception of Down Neck with the Portuguese. That's a little city in itself. But even there I noticed you get a lot of false alarms down there now. And you're getting a few fires down there now, where before you didn't. So that's also getting bad.

I would say the fire rate is definitely tied to the economic condition of the city. Just look at the Third Battalion years ago. They weren't even busy. The Fourth Battalion was the busiest battalion. Vailsburg? You didn't get any fires in Vailsburg. The Weequahic section wasn't bad. Down in the valley near Sherman Avenue, Wright Street, and Brunswick Street, we had a few fires down in there. Those are row houses so it went right through from one cockloft to the next. It just got worse.

You had Mayor Carlin. He was way back then. I guess that was around the '50s, Carlin was in. Then you had Addonizio; he preceded Gibson. Then Gibson came. I would say the city had a lot of money back then during the Carlin and Addonizio administrations. The city was really in good shape. But then that changed. Two Guys closed and now Hahne's is closed. Klein's, Klein's closed first.

I had a business downtown then. I had a plant shop. I can't believe I was in business for seven years down on Halsey Street. Between West Park and New I was down the basement there. I was in school then. I was in Rutgers nights, I had the business, and I was working on the fire department. I had people working for me.

But the city just went down, down, down. You were afraid to walk the streets. People would get mugged. The Police Department wasn't that great. A lot of the guys moved out of town. They could care less about Newark. When you live in a city, and you work here, you take a little more pride than you do if you lived out of the city. You just do your job and go home. You don't take pride in things. I work here. I live here. Most of your firemen and policemen live out of the city.

I would say during the Addonizio administration the city started to decline. We had a lot of money then. But it seems to me from then on things went down. You had the riots in '67. I think that precipitated a lot of stuff. With the riots the city took the nosedive. You had projects before then. It had started going when they were built. But you still had a viable community even then because you still had all your stores on Springfield Avenue. You still had some stores on Prince Street, although a lot of them had closed with the Jews leaving. Jewish businesses had closed because you had a poorer city then. People couldn't spend the money.

After the riots, it really went down. All your stores on Springfield Avenue closed. A lot of people who didn't get attacked closed down and the community had no place to go. The people just beat up on themselves, burned stores and the whole nine yards. I think after that it really started going down.

So, the city has changed radically from when I was a kid. The economics have changed from say a lower middle class to working class or poor, people who can't afford anything. Fires increased after that.

C. Stoffers (1956): I don't know what year you could say it happened. It was starting when I came on, but it wasn't that prevalent. The only housing that they put up for the veterans were these barracks.

Once the decay hit one building in the block then the others would start and everyone would start bailing out. Then when they put up the projects, the people would be putting in to go into the projects. Who wanted to live in an old three-story house?

McGee (1956): The change that would be noticeable to everybody started immediately after the riots. It was gradual, very gradual prior to that, but the riots were absolutely the culmination of the people's decision to move out in droves. That drastically changed the character of most of the neighborhoods. Just now, which is thirty years later, these neighborhoods are starting to be more cohesive again, in their own different ethnic backgrounds.

I still live in Newark. I live in a predominantly black neighborhood. And yet my neighbors and I have no problems at all. Everyone gets along well, but that wasn't true when the transition period was going on. There was resistance by the white people when these new groups were moving in and they moved out. There were settling problems of the new people moving in.

All these things caused a lot of problems in the city which just by time alone and by integration itself have started to work themselves clear again. It's not a bad situation.

Central Avenue around the firehouse was a fairly stable, mostly Irish neighborhood before the riots. That changed after the riots. People were moving out prior to that, but they left in droves after the riots. This was done within two or three years, a major, major change.

McGrory (1957): The change was drastic. There are so many reasons, economic reasons, that you can't put your finger on any one thing. There was no place for anything to go. The city didn't do any building. There hadn't been any major building in the city since the very early '40s. Business, factories, all kinds of industry started to bail out. After World War II, when they saw the population starting to leave the cities, they started to bail out of cities like Newark. Newark is not any different than a lot of cities on the eastern seaboard. The old factory towns and the old industrial cities all went the same way. But, if anything, Newark went there first.

It was more than one thing. I still don't think we understand because if we understood, it wouldn't have happened to all the cities. There was a big influx of different peoples into the city, which changed it. I think most of it is economic. It really changed the city. But I think Newark's problem was not enough area to really spread out.

Duerr (1958): Well, the major change occurred right after the riots. Up to that point the neighborhood around Eighteen Engine and Nine Truck was predominantly Jewish, alright. And you had streets along Madison Avenue where there were a lot of doctors and lawyers and teachers that taught at South Side High School and various schools. So, it was a pretty prominent area. Right after the riots that all changed. All those influential people moved out and their space was taken up by other people. And so, fires started to increase. The mood of the neighborhood became a negative aspect towards us, the firefighters. We weren't looked at in the same vein as we were when the other people lived there. We became a liability more or less. When we responded the younger generation would throw bricks and stones and bottles at you. When you got to a certain location sometimes, they would have all this stuff on the roof and they would throw it down at you as you got to the corner. You had four engines and two trucks there.

So, everything's changed and the change occurred right after the riots. It changed for the worse not for the better. The neighborhoods started to change. People started to move out and you had a lot of women moving in with children. You never saw any husbands or males there except on the weekends. And that's how they lived. At that time, we used to have the spring-operated doors in the firehouse. And once you pulled the release and opened the door and you left the firehouse, the firehouse was open. So, you'd come back and the televisions would be gone and there'd be mustard and ketchup splattered against the wall. The whole situation changed and the city came and put in automatic doors which alleviated some of those problems. But I would say the basic changed occurred right after the riots when the city started to change the composition.

Charpentier (1959): There was a definite change in the city. The attitude of the firemen towards the people and the people towards the firemen changed. Before that we were very aggressive getting in there and after we were very cautious. Because a few incidents even after the riots where we were still being pelted by rocks and bricks. They were booby trapping buildings and sucking us in, cutting holes in the floor and putting linoleum or something over where you step. You'd go through the floor. Or they put nails through a piece of wood that would come down when you opened a door.

We had to be extra, extra careful for our own protection. Before, we were there to help them. After, we were there to protect ourselves because we were the ones who were going to get hurt.

The majority of fires were vacant buildings that they purposely set on fire to draw us in and to do bodily harm to us. But that was not amongst all of them. The attitude of the majority of the people forty and up did not change. They knew we were there to help them. A lot of times they would even intervene and say to the younger ones, "The firemen are our friends. Don't hurt them. They're here to help us, not to hurt us." But the majority of the people below forty were out there for revenge against us, for what I don't know. We didn't do any damage to them. We were there to help them and they were out there to do bodily harm to us and take the equipment.

During and after the riots there was theft of equipment. It made no sense; they were just stealing it to steal. Stuff that they had no use for. All right, the hydrant wrenches they could use to open hydrants, but a lot of the other equipment was useless to them. They were stealing masks and everything. Without a refill on the tank, what good is the mask to them?

Denvir (1959): After the riots, people started to really leave. I'm trying to think of when my mother and father moved. They went down the shore. That would be after the riots. Probably '67, '68 they moved down the shore, which I was glad to see. Maybe even '70, but the riots didn't touch them. It was down below. They kept it to the inner city. It did deteriorate fast after that. Everybody was just looking to get out. Get away with what they could.

Freda (1959): I think the big change came about when the influx of narcotics hit. That's what caused all the problems with the crime around the firehouses; how the city became destabilized; and where the crime rate went up. The other factor was a lot of firemen had moved out of Newark already, but I saw no reason to move out. I was very happy living in Newark, had a family in Newark. My wife could walk out on Roseville Avenue at night. Newark had a very good school system. The big thing then was if you lived in Vailsburg. If a fireman or policeman was really doing well, he bought a house in Vailsburg. That was the ultimate. You really admired people who did that.

My view of the city changed after I was promoted. It changed because I was dealing in a different area. I went from a suburban white firehouse to a service in the ghetto, dealing with the hardships of the ghetto. That changed me and my outlook a lot. I saw the disadvantaged people and how they were treated. And of course, you meet more of criminal type elements in the ghetto, people who probably don't like you because you're white, maybe for good reason. As I think back, they probably had good reason and I mean that sincerely. You start to change. You have to fight not to become a racist. If you don't understand that, you will become one.

Prior to the riots, the Central Ward along Belmont Avenue was a very busy area, very functional area. There were people out on the streets, cars going up and down continually. It was very, very active in the social atmosphere there. After the riots that diminished rapidly; a lot of businesses were burned out. A lot of houses were burned out. People black or white moved the hell out of that area. They wanted no part of it. I saw a vibrant area sink down to a very lowkey area. I saw the social attitudes change of people both black and white.

After the riots, Newark really started to go down. Right after that, business people wanted to get out of this area. There was a sharp rise in fires after the riots. We started having a lot of business fires. We could assume a lot of them were arson because these people were insured in those days. It was common to see businesses burning down, especially along Springfield Avenue and Clinton Avenue and a few on Belmont Avenue. We knew what it was. Everybody knew what was happening. People wanted to get out of Newark because the riots left a bad taste in their mouth. They didn't want to do business anywhere in the city. They were fearful to be honest with you. How do you move out of Newark if you own this building and nobody is ever going to buy it? There was a rash of business fires after the riots and most of it was arson.

Actually, stores in those days had a good fire record. All the sudden, these stores are starting to burn down, a Molotov cocktail thrown in the store. I didn't believe it to be honest with you. I knew it was arson. Not in every single case, but the great majority of them were arson because they soon moved out to the suburbs. They didn't open up in Newark. Their store burned down. They got the insurance money. It would be logical if they were doing well and wanted to stay there, they would reopen the store. No, the store never opened again. They moved to the suburbs.

Then you started to see a preponderance of boarded up stores in the Central Ward. That's when it started happening. Where you start to see stores all of the sudden covered with plywood and empty. In many cases, they literally abandoned them without paying the taxes and the city assumed them. To this day (1991) there are stores in that area that are boarded up since the riots. That people abandoned and left after they were burned out, after the riots.

I don't know where people bought stuff because the supermarkets were gone. There was nothing there. The infamous grocery store next to the firehouse burnt down and never reopened. The only one that survived there was the liquor store and he was boarded up well before the riots. He's there to this day. Anyone else that wasn't boarded up was burnt down and a great majority of them never reopened.

I don't think so much because of the money, because I think these merchants were making a lot of money. I think it was more or less out of fear after that. That store on the corner, which did a brisk business never reopened. Just to give you a taste of what happened. A lot of stores on Springfield Avenue never reopened after the riots or the other mysterious fires that followed. Some of them have reopened, but there were some really high-class stores on Springfield Avenue. There were a couple of block areas there that had bridal shops. I mean tailors who would make bridal gowns. People would come from all over to go there. It was a very vibrant area. They're gone forever. They never reopened. All these things never opened. Supermarkets that were burned down during or right after the riot left. There wasn't too much around.

Another thing that happened after the riots, the government paid attention. The governments tried to pacify the people. They started building a few pools and they started paying more attention to the all-white police and fire departments. It was tokenism. Were there big social changes? Of course not, they were literally afraid of people getting mad at them again and just starting another riot because riots started to break out around the country then.

Smith (1959): When they had the riots, the attitude changed all around. After that there was a lull like a dread silence. Then the neighborhoods changed. The people who lived there left and the people who came in were not like the people who lived there before. Because basically before it was a community, a black community just like you had Irish, German, Polish communities. They had their churches. They had the stores, taverns, and everything else. But it was a community. The kids went to school and there were two parents, a mother and a father. After that it changed. You got into the neighborhoods basically what you have now. Then it went downhill.

Elward (1961): But Newark before the riots, I'd say the city was fairly calm when Kennedy came to office. Calm but tight. There was a time when I was a kid, I would go all the way over by Weequahic to go to a party. When we came back from service, I was back from service in'53. Just in that little time, you could see a radical change. I mean radical. And it was almost inevitable that something was going to happen. I mean there were other things that have never been reported. There were some blow outs down by Branch Brook Park. But from my side of the block, you could still walk the street. After we moved to Seventh Street, we used to walk up to Fourteenth Street and sell Irish Sweepstake tickets. Never had any fear. But I would say when Kennedy came in, you could almost feel, this is permanent. This is going to be a permanent change.

Highsmith (1963): After the riots there was no animosity towards the fire department. I wasn't afraid to walk down the streets or go anyplace or anything. After a while I brought a home and moved to Elizabeth with my family, but everything I did was in Newark. It's just that I moved to Elizabeth because I could not find a home in Newark. And Elizabeth was my home. I was born and raised there. But Newark, it started building back up, slowly but surely, as far as buildings are concerned. But people's minds did not build back up. People still wanted to lean on things. They didn't want to go out there.

Calvetti (1966): I think everybody bailed out after the riots. A lot of white people put their houses up for sale and left. Especially if they were mortgage free. They don't have to worry about anything. They just left. That's what killed the city, the first riot. And then they had that other riot in '68 when Martin Luther King got killed. You know that was only a day or so. That's all that one was. Then there was another one in '72, the Puerto Rican uprising. That was only down in the Seventh Avenue area.

Benderoth (1967): The city did change and I never noticed so much the black and white change. It's just that all of the sudden it changed. When I came on the job the city was probably fifty-five white, forty-five black. The day after the riots the white people moved out because they could afford to do it. Hey, I don't blame them. I eventually moved out too. Better schools, we could see the school systems.

After the riots we didn't walk anywhere. We moved to Vailsburg then just to get off of Nineteenth Street because it became a bad neighborhood. There was a black woman who lived across the street with a little boy. This kid was dressed to the nines all the time. She disappeared during the riots. We disappeared during the riots. We all came back. She went to Plainfield to her mother's house. "I ain't staying here," She said, "These people are terrible." That's what she would tell my wife. She moved soon after that.

I went to Robert Treat Junior High School on fire calls probably five times a week. And that was just my tour. I remember saying to the principal one time, "I think I want a diploma." He said, "What?" I said, "I'm here as many times as your kids are here." I'm talking two o'clock in the morning. He looked at me and walked away. I was working the night we condemned half of Robert Treat Junior High School. It was raining, all of the sudden there's a crack. They wound up taking half a wing off. The city changed.

McGovern (1968): Gradually after the riots, the city changed. In the late '60s, early '70s you have mass exodus out of Newark. People were giving away their property to leave. Then for the next ten or fifteen years it went downhill with all the abandoned buildings and all the fires. People just didn't care anymore. They left. They were afraid to live in Newark. They had good reason to be with the crime rate. I remember the night of the riots. I wasn't on the job yet. I couldn't get back home. I was at my future wife's house. She lived in Bloomfield. I couldn't get back into Newark. They just closed everything off. So, I had to go back, spend the night at her house, and try again in the morning when things were better. But that's the way it was. It was a war zone. Newark was a disaster back then.

K. Miller (1969): I did see a change after the riots. A decline in the city as companies and merchants left the city, ones that decided there was a better place to be and ones who were actually burned out during the riots. I remember Springfield Avenue going all the way down past Bergen Street, all the different stores and clothing stores and after that they were gone. Those stores were empty. That's the ones that weren't burnt down. They definitely took the hit. And then downtown started to deteriorate too; the bigger companies started to leave. And you no longer went down there. You started to find other places to shop. Then all of the sudden the malls started popping up. Livingston Mall. And you start traveling out to those areas, other than downtown. It's a heartbreaking thing to watch.; to watch the city go the way it went.

Rotunda (1970): The riots were 1967 and everything started changing very, very rapidly. Bergen Street, Chancellor Avenue, from jewelry stores and fur shops just went to junk shops. I was in that area and I was only a kid at that time, I was not that high on the seniority list of Coca-Cola. I was third highest paid man in Coca-Cola. You had to have seniority to get those routes and I didn't have that, yet I used to do business there like you wouldn't believe. But it was a working route. You had to work. You didn't drop off a million cases all at one spot. You had a lot of small stops, but they all did well. It was a hell of a neighborhood. Then it was changed.

E. Griffith (1983): There was change. You heard about it. I was young when the riots happened, but there was a change coming. You heard stories of this and that. People started to move. After the riots you started to see a flight, people started to leave. Then things started to move. There was some racial stuff going on. Woo, black families are coming and stuff like that you heard. But then yet I went to school with not many, but a few black kids and there was never really an issue. I mean I ran track with black kids in grammar school. My whole deal was if you're rotten to me, I'm rotten back at you. That was just really the way it was. But you heard things and people are talking. Right, wrong, or indifferent, I think it was all spurred on by the riots. And it's just moving west. The problem was moving west, whatever the problem was.

Part Five:

Renaissance?

Cahill (interviewed 1991): The Ironbound rejuvenated, that was the most astounding thing. We went through all those years of all this social spending and social justice and all that. I don't think there was one dime of Federal money put into the Ironbound section. It was a perfect example for anybody who wanted to study the welfare system as opposed to capitalism. There it was right in the city of Newark with a wall separating it. You just had to walk under the wall to see a thriving economic community. Walk back on the other side to see a decaying rotting community with Federal dollars all over it. Socially that was the biggest impression that I've had. Watching this transition, as the city went down the Ironbound went up.

Dunn (interviewed 1991, 1997): Everybody seems to be striving for a better life for themselves. If you work hard and you amass some money; you want to do something with that money. It just doesn't seem to be the place to put your money for a good investment, with the city. In 1991, that seems to be changing now. I see people doing that. I see the Hovnanian complex going up there. If you told me that ten years ago, I'd say that it wouldn't work. But because of circumstances outside the city of Newark; taxes, commuting, smaller families, less children, more professional people, it's working. I guess their marketing experts know that and that's why they will spend the money. But for a long, long time there was no construction going on in the city of any type. So that was one of the defects of the city.

You encourage people to build up a benefit, so they can do something with their money. Then you say, "If you stay in this context, you can't do what you want with your money." So, the younger generation moved out. The older generation was much shrewder than that; kept the three-story frames; have a ton of money today; and they buy a house down the shore when they want to go visiting. But again, that's because their families were raised and they've gone through that thing.

I would venture to say today that the people who stayed on Brill Street, of my ethnic group that was there when I started, are mostly overly wealthy people for where you see them living. But their aims were different. They got locked into a house because their mother lived on the first floor yet and she didn't want to move. So, they wound up buying a house on Ortly Beach for ten thousand dollars that's worth three hundred thousand dollars today. They always said when mom dies, I'll be able to go. What they never considered was the fact that the house on Brill Street was now worth two hundred thousand dollars because of the income producing potential.

I lived on Ferry Street right across the street from Eight Truck and Sixteen Engine all my life. I never thought in the backyard I would see new homes going up and today there are three new homes going on that property in the mid two hundred thousand dollars. But for fifty years you could have brought the lot for two thousand dollars, yet nobody wanted it. So, whatever has changed, something has changed in the community.

Being I was recently transferred back Down Neck; I see how vibrant Ferry Street is. The things that you would look for today, friendship, camaraderie, neighborhood, are all back in the city, in the East Ward. I don't know about the rest of the city, but right now I see that in the East Ward. I'm surprised when I stand on Congress Street at night and not see anybody go by who I know, even though I'm out of the city like twenty years. I think everything stayed the same in the city and it didn't. The population has totally changed, for the better in the East Ward because you can see what they've done down here as far as putting money back into the community.

At the present time, we're doing the New Jersey Performing Arts Center. The people who are running that facility are mostly suburbanites. It was interesting to see their shock to see the Newark Fire Department and Newark Police Department respond in such a positive fashion to their request for assistance concerning temporary occupancies, the shows. I think they perceived us as house wrecker type of guys, the cops that beat up the people type of guys. Instead, when we sat down at this informal meeting with the people from the Arts Center, they were so surprised and couldn't give us enough accolades on how well everything had gone on their first premiere show which was the Hard Hat concert. There was one radio car damaged that night and that was from a wind storm, broke the windshield. Even the officer who had to write the report chuckled, "Nobody's going to believe the wind broke the windshield." But it was a heavy thunderstorm came through. It broke the windshield. There were no rocks. There were no crowds of nasty people or anything like that. This guy says, "When they read this through the system. They'll figure somebody threw a rock or something at the radio car and it wasn't. It was a wind storm."

They're trying to do a tremendous job over there to revitalize the city. On the board right now is the river front redevelopment program which is the Arts Center and River Bank Park becoming a baseball field. Will that happen? Now, it will take five years to see. But they are spending money and I think the intention of the people over there is to make sure it is a success because there's a lot of money here. If it fails, it isn't going to be the city of Newark that fails. It's going to be the State of New Jersey that fails. They don't want that to happen.

Finucan (interviewed 1991): Things have hit bottom and are going back up. That's my view of the city. We've seen the worse. The city has turned a corner. It's part economics. I have to give Sharpe James credit. I think the city is doing okay. It was at the absolute bottom of the barrel. Newark was the laughing stock of the country for years. We were the asshole of the world and everybody knew it. Even comedians like Johnny Carson would make jokes about Newark. We were at the bottom and I honestly don't believe we're at the bottom any longer. I think we've crawled out of the bottom and we're crawling out now, but that's all we're doing. We're just crawling out. And in our limited span of what you can see in your career on the job it's a slow process. But I believe we're crawling out. We're out. Getting out, reaching daylight.

The last recession affected the city, but not fatally because Newark is in a much better, much stronger position than we were. Newark was lean and mean. We were at the bottom. We had nothing. We had no credit. We had no big work force. We had nothing. There was nothing to lose. We were at the bottom. The economy hits, so what? What are you going to do to me? You can't get blood from a stone. There's nothing there to give. So, yes, we are in a recession now. There's no question about that. A recession does affect the city, but you only lose a lot when you have a lot to lose. Newark was lean and mean, lean and mean and that's about it. We had a tiny police department, a tiny fire department. We had no services. There's nothing there anyway. We had no businesses in Newark to fold up. We had nothing. It was like Japan after World War II when it was bombed out and like Germany. You've got no way to go but up. And any little glitch in the cyclic business affairs of the country, we're just going to roll through.

We'll improve faster in better times. We're in a recovery right now. It's going to be very anemic. It's not going to be the boom times like in the '80s, but it will get better very, very slowly. And that's what I see for Newark. We're going to get better very slowly. We're going to constantly improve year to year. That's what I see happening, witness, two buildings within earshot of where we're sitting now.

I think the work load is way down. I don't think it's way down, I know it's way down. There are statistics that prove that. We're way down. Everybody, even your busiest companies, Six Engine, I'm sure they're not doing the fires they used to do. It's just not out there anymore. Things have hit bottom and are going back up. That's my view of the city. We've seen the worse. The city has turned a corner.

J. Miller (interviewed 1991): I think that it's bottomed out and Newark is in a period of rebuilding, a renaissance, especially as far as the industrial and educational point of view Down Neck. There's a lot of entrepreneurship going on, big high rises. We're certainly going to need more fire companies to fulfill their needs. More inspectors, the Bureau will have to increase. Everything will have to increase because there are just a lot of people coming into the city. It has a lot to offer. We are centrally located. You can go to New York. You work here or live here or go to New York or vise-a-versa, whatever you want to do.

There are some bad sections of Newark where a lot of people don't want to live because there are drug pushers and crime. But that's always going to be. That's the biggest deterrent that's going to stop the people or stop the growth. Once you can stop that decay, the illicit drugs and the crime that goes on in the city, then the city will come back.

The foundation of any city is its police and fire, sanitation. Without that foundation, nobody can survive. Once the police department gets things under control things will improve. We've always been under control. The fire department has always been there. No one can ever say that we have decayed. I think that's the case in our department. It's only gotten better as far as equipment and putting out the fires. We put them out. The police department, I can't speak for them because I'm not there. I can only read what is in the paper.

D. Prachar (interviewed 1991): I think the city has now turned a corner and they have the decay under control. A couple of projects like Gateway, to revitalize downtown, brought a lot of business back that had left. Uptown

Havonanian, University Hospital, it's going to take a lot more, but you take areas that they always said were next to burn. Vailsburg, South Newark they didn't burn. The reason why, single family houses. They took care of the property. You didn't have Joe Smut come in and write all over your walls and everything. Where your decay started down below, your three-story buildings, your apartment houses, your projects. The millions of dollars wasted there. You didn't have that.

That was always the thing. Vailsburg is going to burn next or South Newark. Sure, Vailsburg did burn some, but not that much. Not the upper part where you have the one-family houses. You may find some abandoned ones up there that are boarded up, but you're not finding the burnouts. It turned around. Drastically, it did a one-eighty. It's coming back up and you can't say so much it's the mayor or the city council or the fire department or the police department because it's a joint effort by different organizations. Maybe it's your Chamber of Commerce along with your mayor. Maybe it's your mayor along with your fire director or your police director.

Now, to see how far we've come from the riots; to see downtown, I call it the glass city, the buildings going up, the colleges. How they've come along to the point where they're building more and more dorms to bring kids into the city. No matter what ethnic group you are.

People saying to me "How could you work in a city like that?" My first answer is, "When's the last time you've been to Newark?" Okay, go up town, Belmont Avenue, Springfield Avenue by the projects. That's still the same. Come downtown. Heavy security. A prime example is you could walk all the way from Penn Station all through the Gateway buildings, not even walk outside. I know people who work in the Gateway Buildings that in the last couple of years have just started walking outside. Didn't know there was a place like Ferry Street where you could eat in restaurants. Didn't know there were markets on Mulberry Street where you could go down and get fresh peanuts.

You don't have the shopping area downtown, like Kresge's, Klein's, and Bamberger's that you had years ago, so they don't venture up that far into the old downtown site. But they do come out of buildings now. There's a different life style out there. Where years ago, you would walk out, you didn't worry about getting mugged for a dime. You didn't worry about some homeless person trying to get money off you for a cup of coffee. You had them, but you didn't consider them homeless back then. Different life styles, but now you see things change. You see the new buildings going up on South Orange Avenue, Springfield Avenue

Denvir (interviewed 1993): Now they're rebuilding and everything. They're doing a good job there downtown. And eventually that's going to come all the way up and branch throughout the city. I was down in Trenton last week and what a good job they did down there. Really, it really looks nice. The parts that I go to. I didn't really see any slums where they used to be. It used to be black. It's mixed racially. The neighborhoods seemed clean. The streets seemed to be cleaner with a lot of new buildings. I think Newark's going to be like that. Like Down Neck, the Portuguese did a great job Down Neck.

F. Grehl (interviewed 1993): Will Newark level out at the point where it is now? I will never see it. It's possible at a point. The population may stay steady at two hundred and fifty thousand, but there are more and more of the educated people moving away. It's going to be a totally uneducated group. Do you know Prudential is practically out of the city of Newark? They have two floors or three floors in that whole building. And only for corporate purposes, to be able to stay where they are and not change. Big personnel, that's all. The rest of it they moved all out of the city. Why? They can't get the people. They didn't want to work there. So, if they can't get employees, what are you going to do for the future? We haven't even started to improve the school system to get them, haven't even started.

McDonnell (interviewed 1999): Calling Newark a renaissance city is almost a fraud. I think that the decline in the city pretty much stopped, the fires certainly. You don't see the city being burnt. The whole central part going all the way up to Irvington is gone. It's not good, but it's status quo. There's a chance now that if they got leadership, the city could change around and maybe start to become a good place to live again. The fires lasted, lasted until the late '80s. It was like a twenty-year war. People think of the riots, but the burning kept on for twenty years. Then it started to slow down. It's probably slowed down to almost a normal pace to what it should be.

I don't really see continuing decline, other than there's still a lot of crime. That's probably their biggest problem right now is crime. Now at least you see good things happening downtown. Things are getting better. Out in North Newark where I still go, I don't see things really dramatically getting worse there. The blight seems to have almost stopped pretty much. It was a like a plague spreading. You could see it. You know it's over there and next year these couple of blocks will be gone.

There are so many things in the city that need to change, the schools and everything, before things can go around. But I think the decline, the rapid decline maybe hopefully hit bottom. It doesn't seem to be that inevitable. You knew this will be gone in a couple of years. Now that seems to have stopped, hopefully. Now maybe things can head in the other direction.

J.P. Ryan (interviewed 1999): It's changed. I see it changing again. The change is dramatic now. It's much better than, certainly, the years of decline and stagnation. It's coming back. The Ironbound section and many parts of the city are springing back to life with new housing. The housing was old and really it was made cheaply. Three-story frames, it was the land of three-story frames. After all the years of dragging kerosene up for the kerosene stoves, the back porches were saturated with kerosene, dried out, there was a lack of maintenance, and their close proximity, all facilitated larger fires that we saw in the past.

The town's changing, demographically. It's changing dramatically, for the better. New housing's going up, which I never saw before. Heavy investment into the infrastructure of the city, entertainment places. The city is being revitalized. It truly is and it's been a lot of work by a lot of people.

If it isn't a renaissance city, I really don't know which one would be. It's logistically probably one of the best cities in the country. It's surrounded by access highways, has an international airport, main rail yards, rail lines. The Northeast corridor goes through here. Has a seaport, very active, largest, busiest container seaport of the east coast. There's so much going for it, can't help but be an engine to drive for good.

Goetchius (interviewed 1999): Now I can see signs of improvement. Like Broad Street is on a roll, the city's on a roll. Yes, from twelve years ago, I wouldn't say it was all Sharpe James' doing, but the city has changed a lot towards the good. But on a local community level, neighborhood level I still don't see any real good changes. I see a lot of unhappy neighbors, a lot of citizens that are still afraid to leave their doors open. And even though we're living in a seventy-thousand-dollar house and they're building a pre-fab house right next door and I'm sure their property values are going up there's really no neighborhoods. Like the neighborhood I'm in at Ten Engine (Sherman Avenue and Astor Street), they're doing a lot of building. A lot of lots that were sitting there for years and years they're filling. But it's not a friendly neighborhood unless you're going there to pick up a stolen car or drugs or a lady of the evening. The city has gone up, but not on a like a citizen level. It's really getting on the map. But I think you're going to need to have a real community-based level of the neighborhood to have a real city.

Banta (interviewed 2000): If you look at the city today, the building that's around the city is ridiculous. It's basically where ever there's a vacant lot outside of maybe the Central Ward, there's going to be a new three-story frame. Most of them I assume are going to be owner occupied. I think the city overall will become a positive place. The city right now is going through the building of the arena, the New Jersey PAC center over on Center Street, and Bear Stadium over on Broad Street. They're a part of the life blood of the city today. I think the nucleus between those buildings; the nucleus of a new downtown is in place or will be in place with the completion of the arena. And if we can put in better stores in the downtown area, maybe turn some of those blocks into nice condos; I think you can make this a hub for the yuppies. With the transportation centers that are here between Penn Station, the PATH, and the railroad at Lackawanna and Broad, the nucleus is there and I think if it's done right and the development is done right the city as a whole can be rejuvenated.

Ricca (interviewed 2000): The city probably bottomed out at some point during my time on the job, but I see a big reconstruction of the city. Hopefully, if it keeps on going the way it's going, it'll be back to the heyday that I remember or better yet, back to the heyday that my parents remember, walking from North Newark to downtown on a Friday night to go to a movie. It was a good hike. As the crow flies it's got to be two, three miles, but that's what people did back then. The city is definitely on its way up, but I think it hit bottom at some point. One of the reasons why we moved from Newark was because of the schools. Jokingly I asked my wife, "Would you like to move to Forest Hill. The kids are in college now. I don't have the responsibility for school. Would you like to live in a mansion in Forest Hills for a hundred fifty thousand dollars?" And she has entertained the fact. That she wouldn't mind. I mean Forest Hill is beautiful. Weequachic, close your eyes and get dropped off there and you'll think you're in Beverly Hills, some of those mansions. But I definitely think things are working for the better.

More and more people are working together too. Though it may not seem that way, but I think people of all nationalities work together a lot more now than they did in the past. A lot of the people in highly elected positions didn't strive to have the city come back. At times they wanted the city to be depressed. That was a bad time for the city. But I definitely think it's on the upswing. It's not declining.

Bisogna (interviewed 2001): When I came on in '74, there were a lot of abandoned houses. The biggest changes in the city are the projects. A lot of the projects are gone and where the abandoned houses were there are now town homes everywhere. It looks a lot better than it did. Vailsburg doesn't look better than it did. That's pretty nasty up there. Down Neck is a viable community. That's beautiful. I don't have that much experience Down Neck, even getting on the job I wasn't down there that much except for going out to eat later on. In the '70s, I really didn't even know it was there. I knew there was fire department down there, but it is a community where there aren't that many fires. They're a hardworking industrious people living down there now. If I lived in Newark, I think that's where I'd go. You walk around the street there at night and it's a nice place to be. People are hanging out. There are a lot of restaurants and the stores aren't all barricaded up like downtown.

The city's come along way, except for Vailsburg. North Newark stays pretty good and the south section is still pretty nice. The homes are in decent shape. I think it's better any time you have one family houses where people can have private ownership. Even if they have a landlord, they want to cut their own grass and show the neighbors that they're good people. It's hard to let your grass grow when people walk by and say, "Ah, look at you. Are you a bum? Cut your lawn." You have to have some kind of pride. The townhouses are a good idea because everybody has their own door, opens to the street. You want to pick up the litter in front of your house. It makes you feel good to have the front of your house look good. The projects were a failure because there were so many people in the same building. You didn't care if you threw a pack of cigarettes on the ground. If you littered, somebody else will clean it up. There's no pride of ownership in a big high rise like that. I'm glad to see a lot of them are gone. There's still a few of them around.

They had to have places for people to live, naturally. They just can't blow the building up and tell them, "Hey, look go back to Georgia." or whatever. But the city looks a lot nicer now than it did twenty years ago. I'm sure if you talked with an older guy, he'd say, "Fifty years ago, then you should have seen it." Then again, the Weequahic section and Vailsburg were nice. North Newark's still good though, good looking. I don't know about the quality of life as far as crime. There are still a lot of car thefts in Newark.

McGovern (interviewed 2001): There's a big change in the city, now with the new construction. I don't know what the future is going to be for the fire department. I won't be around to see it. But I think the city is really changing. The city is moving right now. A big influx of money and the police department keeps getting bigger and the fire department keeps getting smaller. But I think Newark's the place to live now. Like Hoboken, Hoboken was a sewer at one time, now it's booming.

Pianka (interviewed 2001): Without a doubt, the city's come back. A lot of people wouldn't know it, but it's come back tremendously.

Langenbach (interviewed 2002): By the time I made Captain (1982), the city is starting to make a move up. I'd say, in the early '80s, you could see it's starting to turn around. You still have the vacant building fires all over the place. But you could see little glimmers of hope that things are starting to change a little bit. I think they had an aggressive policy that I wasn't aware of then of knocking down a lot of the vacant buildings. So now we ended up with whole neighborhoods that are gone. So, we lost a lot of work. Yes, things are starting to get a little better. We went through the Puerto Rican riots in '74 for a couple days. But after that everything was calm. Then the workload started going downhill. We had that spike and then it just went down. I don't think it ever came back after that.

Now everything around is new. They're building, building, building. Everything's coming back, but we still have the same old problems. I saw the people as victims when I was a fireman in the firehouse. They were all victims. Now that I'm in arson, I'm looking at them as perpetrators.

The arson rate is an interesting paradox. As the number of overall fires go down, the number of arson fires go up. A bigger percentage of the fires are arson than they were before. The vehicle fires went through the roof. I mean this is like the elephant burial ground for cars. People brought their cars from all over New Jersey, New York, Connecticut to burn them in Newark because they thought they could get away with it. So, it was an interesting paradox. We did a good job of keeping track of numbers and forecasting things. But you see the numbers of fires kept going down, down, down, but the arson kept going up, kept rising. Either that or we were just better at picking up on the arsons.

I don't know if I have hope for Newark. I did and then I shake my head. I look at things that are happening and I'm not so sure. For the administration, the mayor especially, to put so much stock in this new arena as being the save all of Newark, I don't know. Things are going to happen here, again, dynamic things in the next couple of years. Re-evaluation, they're going to come in and re-evaluate the property. What that's going to do, I don't know. So, to take all that windfall that you got from the Port Authority and sink it into an arena instead of doing it for taxes seems crazy to me. I'm impressed by what I see. I mean every vacant lot has a new house going up onto it. So, a lot of money is coming into the city. If that momentum stays, terrific, if it doesn't, oh man, God help us.

Gesualdo (interviewed 2003): I'm going to say probably the fires started scaling down in the middle, late '80s. I can remember, studying for the Captain's exam and thinking to myself, "Ten years ago, it wouldn't have been this easy." I really had a lot of admiration for the guys who passed their exam in the middle, late '70s when you were hopping. Sit down and read for five minutes boom you're going out. Come back, read for an hour, I thought to myself, I probably wouldn't have been able to study back then. I need time to sit down and read. I don't remember being disturbed that many times. Probably in the middle, late '80s it started calming down a little bit. We were down to maybe about sixteen seventeen hundred runs then. And then they took out some boxes here, knocked down the Kretchner Homes, and now we're down to like fourteen. So, I'd say around the middle to late '80s it changed.

I think the city is probably stabilizing. As far as recovering from the '60s, I don't see it happening because I get the feeling sometimes that the city of Newark wants to isolate itself from the rest of the state and from the rest of the world almost. I feel that the people in the city aren't as informed as they should be, don't make an effort to be more involved in anything other than the city of Newark. I think everything is becoming political. Half the city's probably on the city payroll, so I guess that has a lot to do with it, either sanitation, fire, police. I think they limit themselves. Maybe it's because of whatever indoctrination or whatever was preached to the minorities back in the '60s. Thinking that it's our turn now; I don't see them growing socially. It's a kind of a cocoon type situation. Newark is the only thing that matters. It could be because they only had control for the last thirty years or so and that kind of newness hasn't worn off. The politicians and people don't know that they have the ability to make things work outside the city too. That's the only thing that I feel about the city. All these renovations and improvements downtown, yes it looks nice, window dressing, but there's still cancer three blocks away. That's got to be fixed. No matter what decorations you put on it, you still have to get to the people who count and the kids without places to go and things to do.

T. Grehl (interviewed 2003): Up on Springfield Avenue around Six Engine, the Post Office is brand new. There's no more Gershenbaum's, there's no more Red Star. It's all gone. The community's changed. It's changed. I drove by there the other day and other than Almor Furniture, it's all two and a half story buildings, beautiful. I think it's Sharpe James Apartments if I'm not mistaken there now. That's the name on it. It's magnificent. There's no more of those ugly thirteen story project walk-ups right across the street. That was a nightmare. We went from the high rises and the broken down four-story frames with the wood falling off the porches to brand new homes.

The fire rate has gone down. It slowly started to decrease. Smoke detectors and certain laws were changed, that really helped a lot. Our height was in '81 which was the year we did five thousand runs. Then it went down every year. It peaked at that and then went down. I guess everybody came down. I believe Seven Engine is now the busiest, probably with I'm going to guess and say twenty-six, twenty-seven hundred runs. So, it's cut 40%, 35%, quick math, but it's down.

Fireboxes, no more fireboxes either, that had to kill some of the workload. You can't find a firebox to pull in the city of Newark if you tried. Quick detection too, that's another thing. How many times do you hear 9-1-1? We have the 9-1-1 now, where the people call the police. Everybody in the world has cell phones, so if anybody sees a car fire, an accident, a little small fire with guys burning garbage in the background. They get on the cell phone. They call 9-1-1or they call the operator.

When I first came on in '71, it was right after the riots basically, a couple of years after the riots. The central part of the city was going under repairs etcetera. A part of it was abandoned. Down Neck is probably still the way it was. I just think the city has really come around. I mean Vailsburg is still basically the same other than with a different mix of people living there. Down Neck has more construction than ever. And the Central Ward, where I put quite a few years in, it's no more three and four-story frames. It's all two and a half story new construction with sprinklers. It's amazing. You go through there and it makes you laugh. All the sleepless nights and all the running back and forth and all the buildings that we lost that we broke our butt trying to save. It's now either empty lots or beautiful new construction. We could have saved the city a lot of time by just letting it all burn at once. It could have been this ten years ago.

Mitchell (interviewed 2004): The city began to improve economically. The fire load went down plus a lot of them were burnt out. They rebuilt a lot of middle type homes. When they built them, they're a little better fire proof and the people seem to be taking more care of them because there are a lot more homeowners than just renters now. That's a big difference.

Calvetti (interviewed 2005): Well, the riots killed the city a little bit because a lot of people moved out. And then it was bad for a few years. And then they had like a renaissance. They're tearing down houses. Putting up modern houses. Taking out the projects. Giving people something to look forward to, to live in. And I think it's changed for the better, the city. It's getting a lot better. It's getting like it was in the old days really. People own their own house now. And they take a little bit of pride in it. I hope.

K. Miller (interviewed 2005): I started to see some improving. I don't know that much about the city's enticement to get new construction there, whether they were given tax relief. But a lot of structures started to get built and for the better. Hovnanian projects went up with the sprinkler systems in them. Only two, two and a half, three stories tall at the highest point, new construction, fire resistive construction, so it was changing. And things were coming into the city. Again, were they rate-ables, were they given tax breaks? I think that was probably the case, but I'm not so sure of that. And since I've left from what I hear the city's making a big turn on enticing people to come in and new construction.

Jackson (interviewed 2016): There were gangs when I was young, but not like it is now, some people don't have any conscience and they're just murdering people for little or no reason at times. It was happening, but not as often. The city could get better, but I think it's going to take a lot of work because it's been this way for so long now. It's going to take people dedicated and willing to pick up the ball from people who start it because it's not something that I think one generation can solve. I just want to give back. That was my goal since I came on.

Alexander II (interviewed 2016): I think the city's on its way up. If someone says the renaissance city I say yes. I say yes. Give it another decade and you'll really see; you'll really see that renaissance. You can see the building blocks coming now. In another decade it'll be a full blossom, in full bloom. You'll really be able to see it.

J. Centanni (interviewed 2016): I know there's a lot of crime reported, but I think the city is coming up. The area I'm always in, Bloomfield Avenue, I never had any problems. I've been there for a long time. Going Down Neck and even here on Ninth Street & Fourteenth Avenue the people are always welcoming. They like the firemen. We get along good with them. We do a lot of events and occupy the blocks and stuff. I think it's doing well here. I think it's coming up.

Lee (interviewed 2016): Well, it has improved in some areas as far as development in the downtown area. And you have pockets of areas in the city that really have improved.

G. Pierre (interviewed 2016): The city's still a city. We're a big city out here. The violence is there. The poverty is there, but you can have a good time at NJ PAC. Downtown is beautiful right now. You have the Devils down there. The Prudential Center's down there now. It's the good and the bad, but I think that being a home grown, you know the dangers out there. I'm alright. Outside walking a block from here, I'll be alright in Newark.

I would definitely say the city improved. Especially from when I was young, when I was coming back from my college years, I would definitely say the city improved. The gangs are still there. There are certain places that if I had an option to run out to this particular club or stay at home, I guess it's just not worth it considering my career and what's at stake now. So, the dangers that exist in the city are still real, still present. It depends on what type of lifestyle you want to live. I spend a lot of time in the gym. You'll catch me running in the park before you'll catch me running in a club. Do I believe the city improved a lot? Yes. Where I live in the city now, I really love. I love the fact that you see cops walking the beat. You actually see cops walking the streets now. And that just makes me feel better. I'm a firefighter. If I see a cop walk up and down the block, that's old school. That's how you clean up the city. The city definitely improved considering the powers and the dangers that are out there. I would say that some of the risks and dangers of the city are real and are still prevalent, but I would definitely say I feel a lot safer today. Walking the city if I had to, I feel a lot safer today in Newark with my family than I would maybe ten years ago.

Pierson (interviewed 2016): It's still pretty dangerous. I worked that Tropicana route delivering to the *bodegas* in the city for about fifteen years. That was a little bit different because you're not going to these corner stores on a fire truck with five guys on it. You're just going to deliver. You get a good feel of what's going on because I was all over the city. Here it doesn't feel that much changed. The stolen car thing has gone by the wayside. You don't see that a lot anymore. And that's a good thing, but not a ton has changed. There are a lot fewer abandoned buildings. The fire work is slower.

There's a lot of progress downtown and I think it's finally starting to take a little bit of a foothold. So, for instance I would have never thought that a Home Depot would flourish in the Central Ward. It's been here and it's been pretty successful for at least seven, eight years now. That supermarket right down the street from Six Engine is a gold mine. The movie theater finally seems like it's going to stick around, up on Bergen Street. But then you have the minor league baseball team that was a total failure. And who knows how the PAC center is going. It's ironic that the things up in the Central Ward are doing well and the ones downtown, they're lagging behind. So, you see now they have a Whole Foods going in. I drove down Halsey Street today and it's a totally different street. And as long as there's police protection. They got their new office building. They're going to have a customer base. They're going to have people coming in from out of town. I do hear of people moving in. You've heard about it for a long time. It doesn't seem to change the overall picture that much. Maybe it's just a slow process.

Rosario (interviewed 2016): They started fixing a lot of places up. The projects were starting to come down. Projects were a big problem back then. Seventh Ave projects, I was born there. When I left from high school, all the projects were a big mess. They were still up, running, Prince Street, Seventh Avenue and all that. By the time I got back from the service, they started knocking them down.

I've seen the city get better in most places and some places haven't changed. You still have the West where it's still tough living over there. A lot of abandoned houses, a lot of burnt-out houses, a lot of crime, a lot of shootings, a lot of gangs. When we were growing up, we didn't have gangs the way they have them now. Now it's deadly. Before, you got into a fight, you got into an argument. Guys fought it out with hands. Now you have to watch out you don't get shot if you raise your voice at somebody. That's the big difference now.

Witte (interviewed 2016): There's been change, but there's still a lot of work to be done. There are still a lot of problems underneath. That's politics. There's no way around that. You get the politics out, maybe things can happen faster, quicker. In fact, I used to tell the guys, "It goes up into the clouds and it gets up there with the directors and there's nothing you can do about that."

The projects are gone. New buildings have sprinklers in the common areas. In fact, we had to shut off a couple of them that were in cold spots and froze. They require sprinklers in the buildings in the common areas, it's become more prevalent. It's cheaper with the plastic pipes and it works. 99%

of the fires are put out by one or two heads. That's huge and on top of putting out the fire, it also notifies us. It does two things. It puts out the fire and tells the fire department to come.

Gaddy (interviewed 2016): The city is kind of going down, but it's also rising up from the bottom. What I mean is downtown Newark, you can see the growth. You see that they're building new things. They're kind of pushing it up towards us where we are right now, Avon Avenue. But the urban communities are broken down. The homes more than likely are going to catch fire here. People are not going to care about their property more than likely here. You've got massive killings, car-jackings, things of that nature. You've got kids that don't have programs, so they're more susceptible to gangs and drugs. You've got broken foundations of fathers and mothers; you've got grandmothers. So as far as the environment, as far as the community, you might have a few great apples that might get through the cracks, but the majority of them are lost. Because they have no sense of understanding about what's going on. They only see small marginal things that are at their grasp and they think that's life. The only way they'll be able to go further is actually taking the time out and realizing what's going on around them and understanding what can they do to better their situation. But they're not able to get into that because of the environment that they're around. You get influenced into being in a gang or you're either doing drugs or you're selling drugs. It's either death or jail. That's kind of what's going on. There's a lot of shootings, robbery, drugs, so the city is not going up as you want it to go up. As far as the buildings being built, as far as you see business coming back, that's coming up. But the community, the people are still the same or even worse.

Corales (interviewed 2016): From the time I was young until the time I came on the job the city changed. There are a lot of new structures up now. You've got the Prudential Center, NJ PAC. It looks like it's on a nice come up. You've got the soccer field. It's not Newark, but it's Harrison. You get a lot of out of towners coming down. In the Ironbound section there are so many restaurants. You see so many different people, which is good, a lot of people traffic. The city's growing. It's headed in the right direction. Since I've been on the job, you can see when you're in uniform, you see that respect they have for firefighters. They're always saying thank you to me. They don't know I'm a probationary firefighter. They don't know I only started.

Earp (interviewed 2016): As far as me seeing the transformation of the city, when I was young, I saw a lot of vacant lots, a lot of abandoned structures. As I was growing up, I saw the transformation. There were a lot of new houses being put up. They were making buildings for people to have places to live or better places to live. And just make the city look better. That's like some of the transformation that I've seen personally. I think the city is going in the right direction as far as making it better and developing jobs downtown with the stadium and all the new structures that they have. I think it's making the city look better. It's offering jobs so that when people move to the city and the people that live in the city can continue to thrive and do better. That's one of the big changes that I saw.

Johnson (interviewed 2016): They have to get control of the drug wars and the constant shooting back and forth. It affects everybody, with the drug wars because people set other people's houses on fire. This is conflict back and forth. And there are incidents where there was burning for profit and it started to change again. It's changed a lot.

Bartelloni (interviewed 2019): I would say it is changing and today, maybe it looks like some parts are starting to turn around. You know the businesses and everything. Money's coming into the city. Some of those neighborhoods haven't really changed yet. Hopefully they will, but that's going to take time.

Carr (interviewed 2021): If you drive through Newark now, you see the landscape had changed drastically. Just the Prince Street area alone you have new building and new construction that's over there. You have the areas that burnt down like over by Ridgewood Avenue that were just all lit up. You have all new light weight construction that's over there now. The city has changed drastically. You know we have so many charter schools in Newark now. It's just different. I think that Sharpe James put a lot of things in motion for Newark to be where we are now. I think that some people have done well with the baton and ran. They have put their own stakes improving the life style and the culture of the City of Newark. I hope that they continue to do so.

They put up the PAC center. They put up the Pru Center, but the neighborhoods are touch and go. Some of the neighborhoods I feel that they concentrated on, you can see what I call a phase where a certain area of Newark is being improved on and then they add onto that and then they moved their way up and so forth and so on. If you look at Newark, you started seeing banks popping up downtown Newark. You saw Starbucks pop up. Then you start seeing the luxury condominium apartments popping up. Then of course you got the stadium and we have hotels on Broad Street. We have a Courtyard. We have Indigo. We have another hotel, FRP which is over there and the Robert Treat now I think is a Weston or something like that. Then we have other hotels down by Penn Station, so they've really done a lot to improve, to try to bring some kind of income and economic growth into the City of Newark. We have Panasonic that has an office down there now. They've done a lot of things to improve on the economic social structure as far as I'm concerned in Newark. They've done a great job. They can always improve. I just hope that whatever they do they do something to make sure that we have some type of way for kids to have bikes. To play basketball, baseball, soccer, whatever they want. Like we have the JFK Center and we have a few other rec centers in Newark. They just need to keep those programs going. To make sure, you know they do something for the youth of Newark.

DeLeon (interviewed 2021): At the time Sharpe James said Newark was a renaissance city it wasn't. But I thought it was for a little bit. This guy's going to build the tallest building, the Newark Nets were coming, and some businesses were coming in, so I was kind of on board with that for a little while. I was thinking, "Okay maybe he is doing something." But they have to start with that downtown and hopefully it will just filter out. If you go today, you'll see Springfield Avenue where you had all those fires. There's a Shoprite there now, Home Depot, new townhouses, so there is a lot of improvement, but there's still a lot to do that needs to be done.

You know I see the Prudential Center come in, but then I look at Jersey City and I look at their water front, what used to be and I look at part of Harrison and what used to be old houses. They're all gone. They moved a lot faster than we did. Somehow, I don't know what happened. I'm going to say politics was involved, that we didn't come along.

I remember they were going to build townhomes on Jersey Street next week and we're still waiting for the townhomes. They were going to knock everything down around Orange Street and build dorms. They were going to put a mall next to the train station where the old Westinghouse used to be. And they found out they had PCBs. They couldn't build on it so it was a superfund site for a little while. And I believe today they're still testing it.

There's a lot of history there. Now you talk about the riots, there's a big improvement.

I run my dad's business that he left and I go there every week still. I was there yesterday. Over there hasn't changed. Still problems. Still people hanging out. Cops are chasing people away. They don't know better. If something happens along the line where there's a lot of one parent households or the parents leave the kid alone, gone all day, don't even know or care what they're doing.

In the end, I don't think a lot has changed, honestly. Driving to Five Truck, kids at two in the morning, "Hey where's your parents? What are you doing out here?" I would get the middle finger or they would shape their hand like a gun and point it towards me. Like basically, get lost. None of your business. Don't worry about it. And I was very honestly, like wow these kids have got it tough. For them to do something like that, doesn't show a lot of improvement. You go to the West Ward, you go down Avon Avenue, Madison Avenue, South Thirteenth Street, all that, bad. I think today it's still that tough. It's like a mishmash I believe. Some parts of the city are okay, some parts are not. I like that they've got programs out there now for the kids.

Interviewees

Alexander I, Captain Donald, 2 September, 2016, transcript. (appointed 1987)

Alexander II, Firefighter Donald, 23 July, 2016, transcript. (appointed 2016)

Alfano, Firefighter George, 19 December, 2005, transcript. (appointed 1953)

Alfano, Captain Kevin, 9 August, 2016, transcript. (appointed 2006)

Alvarez, Captain Orlando, 26 July, 16 August, 2016, transcript. (appointed 1989)

Arce, Battalion Chief Orlando, 9 October, 2016, transcript. (appointed 1984)

Baldino, Captain Barney, letter to the author 20 September, 2002. (appointed 1951)

Banta, Captain Robert, 6 July, 2000, transcript. (appointed 1974)

Bartelloni, Battalion Chief Paul, 9 July, 2019, transcript. (appointed 1993)

Bellina, Deputy Director of OEM Frank, 17 August, 2016, transcript. (appointed 1981)

Bellina, Firefighter Norman, 5 September, 2020, transcript. (appointed 1986)

Bellina, Firefighter Michael, 18 August, 2016, transcript. (appointed 2008)

Belzger, Firefighter William, 4 October, 2004, transcript. (appointed 1959)

Bisogna, Captain Joseph, 25 July, 2001, transcript. (appointed 1974)

Butler, Captain James, 3 September 1993, transcript. (appointed 1963)

Benderoth, Captain John, 15 November, 2005, transcript. (appointed 1967)

Bitter, Deputy Chief Richard, 27 December, 2002, transcript. (appointed 1959)

Brown, Firefighter Anthony, 14 July, 1991, transcript. (appointed 1979)

Brownlee, Battalion Chief Walter, 4 September, 2019, transcript. (appointed 1973)

Burkhardt, Captain Kevin, 9 February, 2004, transcript. (appointed 1973)

Butler, Captain James, 3 September, 1993, transcript. (appointed 1963)

Cahill, Firefighter Joseph, 25 June, 1991, transcript. (appointed 1963)

Calvetti, Battalion Chief Francis, 8 July, 2005, transcript. (appointed 1966)

Camasta, Captain Joseph, 23 July, 1991, transcript. (appointed 1974)

Cardillo, Firefighter Felix, 5 October, 2008, transcript. (appointed 1959)

Carr, Captain Delwin, 30 April, 2021, transcript. (appointed 2000)

Carragher, Deputy Chief William, 1 November, 1994, transcript. (appointed 1960)

Carter, Battalion Chief Harry, 12 June, 1991, transcript. (appointed 1973)

Castelluccio, Deputy Chief Anthony, 23 August, 2016, transcript. (appointed 1993)

Centanni, Fire Chief John, 9 November, 2016, transcript. (appointed 1986)

Centanni, Firefighter Gerard, 31 October, 2016, transcript. (appointed 2013)

Centanni, Firefighter John, 31 October, 2016, transcript. (appointed 2014)

Charpentier, Firefighter Frederick, 22 August, 1993, transcript. (appointed 1959)

Coale, Captain Michael, 12 October, 2005, transcript. (appointed 1973)

Cody, Battalion Chief James, 18 October, 1999, transcript. (appointed 1964)

Connell, Battalion Chief Anthony, 26 February, 1999, transcript. (appointed 1974)

Conover, Firefighter William, 24 April, 2005, transcript. (appointed 1948)

Conville, Captain Francis, 20 November, 2009, transcript. (appointed 1940)

Corales, Firefighter Joel, 8 August, 2016, transcript. (appointed 2016)

Cordasco, Battalion Chief Matthew, 20 June, 2016, transcript. (appointed 1989)

Cosby, Firefighter Boisy, 17 June, 2003, transcript. (appointed 1963)

Cosby, Fire Prevention Specialist Joseph, 22 August, 1991, transcript. (appointed 1969)

Cruz, Firefighter Mellisa, 24 July, 2016, transcript. (appointed 2016)

Dainty, Battalion Chief Cliff, 6 September, 2016, 21 June, 2019, transcript. (appointed 1970)

Dalton, Captain Francis, 13 October, 2008, transcript. (appointed 1963)

Daly, Captain Phillip, 4 December, 2008, transcript. (appointed 1978)

Daniels, Battalion Chief Christopher, 22 July, 2016, transcript. (appointed 1989)

Daudelin, Captain George, 24 February, 2000, transcript. (appointed 1970)

DeCuester, Battalion Chief Steven, 22 May, 2019, transcript. (appointed 1984)

DeLeon, Battalion Chief Albert, 20 February, 2021, transcript. (appointed 1988)

Denvir, Captain John, 13 September, 1993, transcript. (appointed 1959)

Deutch, Firefighter Charles, 14 November, 1993, transcript. (appointed 1953)

Doherty, Captain John, 18 April, 2006, transcript. (appointed 1949)

Doherty, Captain Patrick, 18 September, 20 September, 2000, transcript. (appointed 1970)

Duerr, Chief of Apparatus Carl, 24 February, 2008, transcript. (appointed 1958)

Dugan, Captain Kevin, 23 July, 2016, transcript. (appointed 2006)

Dunn, Deputy Chief Edward, 14 August, 1991, transcript. (appointed 1959)

Earp, Firefighter Marky, 1 August, 2016, transcript. (appointed 2016)

Elward, Firefighter James, 9 July, 2005, transcript. (appointed 1962)

Farrell, Captain Daniel, 30 July, 3 August, 2016, transcript. (appointed 1996)

Figuereq, Captain Julio, 22 August, 2016, transcript. (appointed 2006)

Finucan, Deputy Chief James, 7 August, 1991, transcript. (appointed 1969)

Fortunato, Firefighter Michael, 20 August, 2016, transcript. (appointed 2014)

Freda, Deputy Chief Alfred, 12, 25, 26 July, 1991, transcript. (appointed 1959)

Fredette, Firefighter Reggie, 3 November, 1993, transcript. (appointed 1942)

Freeman, Captain Richard, 20 August, 1991, transcript. (appointed 1956)

Freese, Captain Miguel, 11 August, 2016, transcript. (appointed 1998)

Gaddy, Firefighter Saadiq, 7, 19 August, 2016, transcript. (appointed 2006)

Gail, Deputy Chief Richard, 16 July, 2019, transcript. (appointed 1993)

Garay, Firefighter Veronica, 16 August, 2016, transcript. (appointed 2014)

Garrity, Battalion Chief Joseph, 1 May, 1992, transcript. (appointed 1964)

Gaynor, Battalion Chief Robert, 22 October, 1999, transcript. (appointed 1965)

Gesualdo, Captain Albert, 21 July, 2003, transcript. (appointed 1978)

Gibson, Captain Richard, 22 April, 2005, transcript. (appointed 1953)

Giordano, Director David, 25 September, 10 October, 2020, transcript. (appointed 1984)

Goetchius, Captain Donald, 12 February, 1999, transcript. (appointed 1986)

Greene, Captain David, 29 July, 2019, transcript. (appointed 1988)

Grehl, Deputy Chief Frederick, 7 August, 1993, transcript. (appointed 1948)

Grehl, Captain Thomas, 29 May, 2002, transcript. (appointed 1971)

Griffith, Chief Operator Robert, 31 July, 1991, transcript. (appointed 1953)

Griffith, Captain Edward, 29 September, 14 October, 2016, transcript. (appointed 1983)

Griggs, Deputy Chief John, 23 April, 2005, transcript. (appointed 1956)

Griggs, Captain John, 28 September, 2016, transcript. (appointed 1988)

Haran, Captain Edward, 5 February, 2001, transcript. (appointed 1961)

Harris, Captain William, 13 December, 1999, transcript. (appointed 1961)

Highsmith, Firefighter Gerald, 2 June, 1994, transcript. (appointed 1963)

Highsmith, Captain Gregory, 8 August, 2016, transcript. (appointed 2000)

Hopkins, Captain Mark, 23 October, 2019, transcript. (appointed 1978)

Jackson, Fire Chief Rufus, 6 August, 2016, transcript. (appointed 1995)

Jenkins, Captain Thomas, 14 November, 2019, transcript. (appointed 2002)

Johnson, Captain Otis, 21 July, 14 August, 2016, transcript. (appointed 1984)

Kelly, Captain Michael, 26 April, 15 September, 2005, transcript. (appointed 1971)

Killeen, Battalion Chief Kevin, 28 September, 2009, 12 March, 2019, transcript. (appointed 1974)

Kinnear, Deputy Chief David, 28 September, 1992, transcript. (appointed 1947)

Knight, Firefighter Gerald, 19 June, 1991, transcript. (appointed 1964)

Kormash, Deputy Chief Michael, 24 October, 2016, transcript. (appointed 1979)

Kupko, Battalion Chief James, 25 August, 2 September, 2016, transcript. (appointed 2002)

Langenbach, Deputy Chief James, 24 October, 2002, transcript. (appointed 1973)

Langevin, Firefighter Robert, 23 February, 1999, transcript. (appointed 1974)

LaPenta, Battalion Chief Steven, 30 September, 2016, transcript. (appointed 1989)

Lawless, Battalion Chief Michael, 1 March, 1999, transcript. (appointed 1966)

Lee, Battalion Chief Sylvester, 5 October, 2016, transcript. (appointed 1986)

Luxton, Captain Charles, 14 January, 1999, 1 August, 2018, transcript. (appointed 1973)

Marcell, Firefighter Andrew, 23 September, 1998, transcript. (appointed 1959)

Marcell, Deputy Chief Kenneth, 22 October, 2019, transcript. (appointed 1970)

Maresca, Battalion Chief Albert, 17 August, 2016, transcript. (appointed 1987)

Maresca, Firefighter Brett, 25 August, 2016, transcript. (appointed 2012)

Masters, Firefighter Anthony, 24 March, 2004, transcript. (appointed 1947)

Masters, Captain Alan, 20 August, 2016, transcript. (appointed 1986)

Masterson, Captain Andrew, 6 April, 2005, transcript. (appointed 1949)

McCormack, Deputy Chief James, 14 June, 1991, transcript. (appointed 1949)

McDonnell, Captain Thomas, 30 March, 1999, transcript. (appointed 1970)

McGee, Captain Raymond, 22 October, 2000, transcript. (appointed 1956)

McGovern, Battalion Chief Thomas, 8 June, 2001, transcript. (appointed 1968)

McGrory, Deputy Chief Alexander, 31 August, 1991, transcript. (appointed 1957)

Medina, Captain Julio, 10 August, 2016, transcript. (appointed 2006)

Meier, Captain Donald, 9 August, 2016, transcript. (appointed 1996)

Melodick, Firefighter William, 1 June, 2001, transcript. (appointed 1970)

Mickels, Captain David, 18 September, 2020, transcript. (appointed 2002)

Miller, Battalion Chief Joseph, 16 August, 1991, transcript. (appointed 1959)

Miller, Battalion Chief Kenneth, 19 October, 2005, transcript. (appointed 1969)

Mitchell, Captain Michael, 20 October, 2004, transcript. (appointed 1978)

Montalvo, Firefighter Raymond, 5 August, 2016, transcript. (appointed 1996)

Morgan, Captain Bruce, 16 May, 2001, transcript. (appointed 1973)

Nasta, Deputy Chief Michael, 17 June, 2019, transcript. (appointed 1984)

Ostertag, Captain Steve, 29 July, 2016, transcript. (appointed 1994)

Partridge, Battalion Chief Peter, 26 July, 9 November, 2019, transcript. (appointed 1974)

Perdon, Captain George, 9 June, 2003, transcript. (appointed 1974)

Perez, Captain Joseph, 23 August, 2002, transcript. (appointed 1965)

Petrone, Firefighter Michael, 23 July, 2016, transcript. (appointed 1991)

Pianka, Firefighter George, 15 June, 2001, transcript. (appointed 1970)

Pierre, Captain Yves, 15 July, 2016, transcript. (appointed 2013)

Pierre, Firefighter Gregory, 14 August, 2016, transcript. (appointed 1995)

Pierson, Captain James, 28 August, 2016, transcript. (appointed 1991)

Pignato, Captain Nicholas, 30 May, 2000, transcript. (appointed 1974)

Prachar, Firefighter Andrew, 15 December, 2005, transcript. (appointed 1959)

Prachar, Captain Daniel, 12 August, 1991, transcript. (appointed 1968)

Prachar, Captain John, 10 July, 20 September, 2005, transcript. (appointed 1978)

Ramos, Firefighter Juan, 12 August, 2016, transcript. (appointed 1994)

Rawa, Firefighter Adam, 7 August, 2016, transcript. (appointed 2013)

Redden, Fire Chief Joseph, 16 September, 2002, transcript. (appointed 1947)

Reiss, Deputy Chief Thomas, 24 July, 2020, transcript. (appointed 1979)

Ricca, Battalion Chief Ronald, 1 June, 2000, transcript. (appointed 1974)

Richardson, Battalion Chief Scott, 2 August, 2016, transcript. (appointed 1994)

Roberson, Firefighter Luther, 22 August, 2016, transcript. (appointed 1996)

Rodrigues, Battalion Chief Deblin, 21 August, 2016, transcript. (appointed 1996)

Romano, Captain Peter, 28 September, 2008, transcript. (appointed 1972)

Rosamilia, Battalion Chief Gerard, 21 August, 2020, transcript. (appointed 1973)

Rosario, Captain Angel, 5 August, 2016, transcript. (appointed 2002)

Rotunda, Firefighter Gerald, 3 May, 2000, transcript. (appointed 1970)

Ryan, Battalion Chief John, 6 July, 2005, transcript. (appointed 1948)

Ryan, Battalion Chief Joseph P., 28 September, 1999, transcript. (appointed 1973)

Saccone, Battalion Chief Thomas, 27 November, 2000, transcript. (appointed 1969)

Sandella, Captain John, 6 August, 2020, transcript. (appointed 1978)

Schoemer, Firefighter Richard, 1 July, 2005, transcript. (appointed 1959)

Schofield, Firefighter William, 27 March, 2015, transcript. (appointed 1963)

Smith, Firefighter James, 30 June, 1995, transcript. (appointed 1959)

Snyder, Captain William, 1 August, 2016, transcript. (appointed 1993)

Sorace, Captain Michael, 18 August, 2016, transcript. (appointed 1986)

Sperli, Battalion Chief Joseph, 10 September, 2010, 21 August, 2016, transcript. (appointed 1989)

Stoffers, Battalion Chief Carl, 2 September, 1998, transcript. (appointed 1956)

Stoffers, Firefighter Raymond, 8 July, 1997, transcript. (appointed 1973)

Straile, Battalion Chief Joseph, 31 July, 2018, transcript. (appointed 1974)

Tarantino, Captain Anthony, 27 June, 18 July, 2019, transcript. (appointed 1989)

Vesey, Firefighter Edward, 15 June, 1999, transcript. (appointed 1948)

Vetrini, Captain Joseph, 14 September, 1993, 25 April, 2005, transcript. (appointed 1946)

Wall, Deputy Chief Edward, 13 September, 2000, transcript. (appointed 1954)

Wapples, Battalion Chief Arnum, 5 August, 1991, transcript. (appointed 1982)

Wargo, Captain Andrew, 26 June, 1991, transcript. (appointed 1964)

Weber, Battalion Chief William, 29 October, 2008, transcript. (appointed 1969)

Weidele, Battalion Chief William, 20 July, 2016, transcript. (appointed 1984)

West, Firefighter Charles, 12 July, 2019, transcript. (appointed 1989)

Willis, Firefighter James, 9 July, 2019, transcript. (appointed 1996)

Witte, Deputy Chief Michael, 13 August, 2016, transcript. (appointed 1978)

Zieser, Deputy Chief Richard, 25 July, 2016, transcript. (appointed 1978)

www.ingramcontent.com/pod-product-compliance
Lightning Source LLC
Chambersburg PA
CBHW031947090426
42739CB00006B/112